MW01070134

BATTLE ON, BATTLE OVER

How Every Man and Woman Can Find Permanent and Total Victory in Sexual Purity

Brenda & Fred Stoeker

with Mike Yorkey

Battle On, Battle Over: How Every Man and Woman Can Find Permanent and Total Victory in Sexual Purity
by **Brenda & Fred Stoeker with Mike Yorkey**

For bulk purchases of *Battle On, Battle Over,* please visit FredStoeker.com.

Copyright © 2023 by Brenda & Fred Stoeker

Published by The Core Media Group, Inc., www.thecoremediagroup.com.

Cover & Interior Design: Nadia Guy
Cover image provided by VM/iStock Getty Images.

ISBN 978-1-950465-77-4

Scriptures marked NIV are taken from *The Holy Bible, New International Version®, NIV®,* Copyright © 1973, 1978, 1984, 2011 by Biblica, Inc.® Used by permission. All rights reserved worldwide.

Scriptures marked NLT are taken from the HOLY BIBLE, NEW LIVING TRANSLATION (NLT): Scriptures taken from the HOLY BIBLE, NEW LIVING TRANSLATION, Copyright© 1996, 2004, 2007 by Tyndale House Foundation. Used by permission of Tyndale House Publishers, Inc., Carol Stream, Illinois 60188. All rights reserved. Used by permission.

Scriptures marked ESV are taken from the HOLY BIBLE, ENGLISH STANDARD VERSION (ESV): Scriptures taken from THE HOLY BIBLE, ENGLISH STANDARD VERSION ® Copyright© 2001 by Crossway, a publishing ministry of Good News Publishers. Used by permission.

Scriptures marked AMP are taken from the AMPLIFIED BIBLE (AMP): Scripture taken from the AMPLIFIED® BIBLE, Copyright © 1954, 1958, 1962, 1964, 1965, 1987 by the Lockman Foundation Used by Permission. (www.Lockman.org)

Scriptures marked NKJV are taken from the NEW KING JAMES VERSION (NKJV): Scripture taken from the NEW KING JAMES VERSION®. Copyright© 1982 by Thomas Nelson, Inc. Used by permission. All rights reserved.

Printed in the United States of America.

Table of Contents

A Note to the Reader
from Brenda and Fred Stoeker

Throughout the pages of *Battle On, Battle Over*, we will share frank and intimate details of our marriage and the lives of others. We intend to shine a light on these circumstances so you can learn about God's plan for sexual integrity.

Please know that most of the names and descriptions of individuals have been changed to respect their privacy. But the conversations we share are true and accurate.

The purpose of *Battle On, Battle Over* is to help you overcome sexual sin and avoid the struggles and suffering that we went through in the early years of our marriage. We know what it's like to go through the pain and the fire, but we also know what it's like to experience victory.

And that's what we want for you—a battle that's over!

Toward that end, we would like to offer you a free workbook that you can download by going to www.BattleOnBattleOver.com. The *Battle On, Battle Over Workbook* is an excellent resource that will help you go through the principles we teach in this book as an individual, as a couple reading and working together to heal your relationship, or as part of a men's or women's small group study.

In addition, we have created twelve video introductions for each week of this workbook that can also be downloaded for free at BattleOnBattleOver.com to help small group leaders kick off each study with a word from us.

Introduction
by Fred Stoeker

Do you yearn for freedom from sexual sin? Sexual immorality is a brutal master, enslaving many a soul. Sadly, most never truly engage in a battle of liberation.

Suppose you're one of those men or women hungry for sexual freedom. If that's the case, it wouldn't surprise me if there are two discouraging questions swirling in your heart and mind, stirring up doubt, checking your advance, and suspending any possible progress. They are:

1. Is sexual freedom even possible?
2. Why even engage in this battle? When I look around me, purity seems as rare in churchgoers as it is for everyone else.

Well, that's true. But that doesn't mean purity is impossible. Your battle with sexual sin *can* be over. But not within the context of those two troubling, faith-crunching questions churned up by the cultural lies about human sexuality established all around you and, quite probably, *in* you. If you believe these lies, your battle will likely never be over. Here are some of the biggest falsehoods and excuses we often say to ourselves:

- This battle for purity will rage on endlessly until I take my final breath.
- Not everyone can walk in sexual purity. Only some are given the grace to do so.
- 98 percent of men admit they struggle with their sexual purity, and the other 2 percent are lying.
- The Covid-19 pandemic really messed me up. With all the social isolation, I had to get release somewhere.
- Porn isn't so bad, as long it's "ethically produced" and only used to release sexual pressure.
- God would never have made us sexual beings only to ask us to abstain from sex outside of marriage. We must be missing something.

Likely you've believed one or all of these fallacies—or at least thought about them. It's likely also that they've restrained you from engaging in the battle with an attitude of optimism, hope, and faith. You cannot wage a war for purity in a climate of lies and justifications that cause doubts to pile up ceaselessly and bind your heart and feet. So don't accept these lies surrounding you. Don't focus on the failures of those surrounding you or the difficult times we're living in.

Instead, find the truth and fixate on that. Establish it in your heart and mind. If you launch from a position of truth, your battle can soon be over.

But you might ask, *Where do I find truth?*

Gratefully, you have a loving older brother in the faith named Simon Peter, who unquestionably knew truth from lies. As he neared the end of his life, he diligently set apart time to write a deeply personal letter to you, his beloved Christian sibling, to refute these very lies and to make sure you could recall the truth after he was gone, just as any good older brother would do:

> So I will always remind you of these things, even though you know them and are firmly established in the truth you now have. I think it is right to refresh your memory as long as I live in the tent of this body, because I know that I will soon put it aside, as our Lord Jesus Christ has made clear to me. And I will make every effort to see that after my departure you will always be able to remember these things. (2 Peter 1:12–15, NIV)

Peter kicked off his letter to you with a reminder that your faith is every bit as precious as his own. This wasn't just a buttery warm greeting for you to skim over to get to the meat of the letter. Peter was opening with an unshakable, established truth:

> Simon Peter, a servant and apostle of Jesus Christ, to those who through the righteousness of our God and Savior Jesus Christ have received a faith as precious as ours: Grace and peace be yours in abundance through the knowledge of God and of Jesus our Lord. (2 Peter 1:1–2, NIV)

Peter was one of the original twelve apostles, an eyewitness to Christ's entire ministry. He was taught directly by Jesus Himself for three solid years, face to face, day by day, moment by moment. Peter absolutely knew what Jesus knew about your faith—it is as precious as the faith of any of the apostles. That truth about your faith is foundational to your destiny as a sexually pure man, so Peter wanted you to know that truth as conclusively as he knew it and to accept this following priceless truth just as unconditionally:

Introduction

His divine power has given us everything we need for a godly life through our knowledge of him who called us by his own glory and goodness. Through these he has given us his very great and precious promises, so that through them you may participate in the divine nature, having escaped the corruption in the world caused by evil desires. (2 Peter 1:3–4, NIV)

That's established truth. Your battle may be on, but it can also be over. You can be free of sexual sin, despite the lies proclaimed throughout the milling, teeming throngs of failing men surrounding you. Your faith is equal in worth to the faith of Peter, and this faith, which was delivered freely to you with the Lord's divine power, has given you everything you need to escape your own illicit sexual desires.

You. Can. Be. Free.

Now, if that is true (and it is), what is your responsibility in establishing this victory for keeps? Thankfully, your diligent and loving older brother didn't leave you hanging, as Simon Peter immediately continued his thoughts by reminding you that you too must be diligent, in this case by adding some things to your precious faith so that you might confirm it and mature it:

[Since you have the Lord's divine power], make every effort to add to your faith goodness; and to goodness, knowledge; and to knowledge, self-control; and to self-control, perseverance; and to perseverance, godliness; and to godliness, mutual affection; and to mutual affection, love. For if you possess these qualities in increasing measure, they will keep you from being ineffective and unproductive in your knowledge of our Lord Jesus Christ. But whoever does not have them is nearsighted and blind, forgetting that they have been cleansed from their past sins. (2 Peter 1:5–9, NIV; words inside brackets added for clarity)

If you haven't added knowledge, self-control, and perseverance to your precious faith, your eyes have likely been closed to the truth, and it's unlikely you're participating in the divine nature and escaping the corruption in the world caused by your sexual desires.

But such blindness changes nothing, as the truth remains clear as day. It doesn't matter if your friends or your teammates or your favorite podcasters are saying something different. You have a faith as precious as that of Simon Peter, and you have Christ's divine power that, when coupled with a deep knowledge of Jesus Christ and His precious promises, should end your battle. If your battle is still raging on, then you're lacking one thing—you haven't added knowledge, self-control, and perseverance to your faith.

I can help you to do just that. As part of that process, I'll spotlight a major vulnerability in your sexuality that sets you up to fall into sexual sin, one that's prominent in both men and women. I didn't discuss this weakness in my first book, *Every Man's Battle*, where I focused entirely upon the flaws in the male eyes and the mind. That's why I've written *Battle On, Battle Over*—to spotlight this *second* major vulnerability in our human sexuality and to add even more knowledge to your faith. Happily, whether male or female, you can permanently shut down your sexual sin with a disciplined, maturing faith like Peter spoke of in his letter to you.

Near the beginning of that letter, Peter declared that he was making every effort in *his* life to remind you of the truth so that you could always remember it, even after he was gone, even if lies were swirling around you. Near the end of that same letter, Peter exhorted you to make every effort in *your* life to be found spotless, blameless, and at peace with the Lord (see 2 Peter 3:14). He also implored you to make every effort to add knowledge, self-control, and perseverance to your faith (see 2 Peter 1:5–9) so that you might escape the corruption of this world.

Your destiny rests on these truths, not upon the cultural lies bandied about your church, your work, or your exercise club. You are *not* a slave to depravity or to the sexual urges that have mastered you in the past (see 2 Peter 2:19). Your destiny is to walk in the divine nature, well above the sexual fray. It is your destiny to walk in the truth that your brother Peter worked so hard to help you remember.

Since Peter made every effort in his letter to you to remind you that you must be diligent in maturing your precious faith so that you can be free from this battle, and since I'm making every effort in this book to give you the rest of the knowledge you need to establish self-control and perseverance in your life, will *you* now make every effort to apply this knowledge and to be found spotless, blameless, and at peace with your Lord in your sexuality?

I hope so. Freedom is glorious, and freedom is yours to establish.

And remember, it's not just me that's making this declaration. Peter said it, unequivocally, in his letter to you. And so it only seems right to close this introduction with the very same words that Simon Peter used to close that letter to you:

> Therefore, dear friends, since you have been forewarned, be on your guard so that you may not be carried away by the error of the lawless and fall from your secure position. But grow in the grace and knowledge of our Lord and Savior Jesus Christ. To him be glory both now and forever! Amen. (2 Peter 3:17–18, NIV)

PART I
The Stealth Trap in
Our Sexuality

1
Where Was Victory?

From Fred

It was midnight.

I sat down heavily in my office chair and leaned forward over my desk, cupping my forehead in my cool, moist palms, still damp from washing away the evidence of one more failure a moment earlier. Desperation and frustration oozed from every pore as I slapped my right hand to the desktop and cried out, "Why can't I kill this thing?"

My racing mind stalled for a moment as my words echoed back lamely in my mind. Silence settled in again as I struggled with the utter confusion of it all. Clenching my teeth, I groaned deeply, my soul writhing in pain.

I hate this masturbation! I'm such a lousy Christian, such a loser! What is wrong with me?

Yet the practice refused to go away, no matter how much I despised it.

I leaned back against my chair with a frustrated sigh. Out of nowhere, my wife, Brenda, popped into my thoughts. She was nestled softly in a cloud of sheets and comforters a few blocks to the west, where I'd tucked her into our bed with a warm kiss before heading off to my office to catch up on some work. A small smile curled over my lips as I thought about the passion and fun we'd shared the night before in the midst of that soft bedding, musing, *I'm so lucky! She enjoys sex as much as I do and rarely says no.*

Another jarring surge of emotions crashed back over my heart, harshly sweeping my smile away. *Then why do you masturbate when you're not with her?* I jeered scornfully.

I had no answer. But the urge wouldn't let up.

I'd spent an endless number of agonizing, twisting nights at my office over the past number of months, pummeling myself over the losses that mounted despite my broad, dramatic early victories in this fight known as "every man's battle." I'd done everything God said to do, like guarding my eyes from all the sensual junk around me and starving my mind of lust. The losses should have stopped, but they hadn't.

I couldn't make sense of what I was dealing with as I sat alone in my office, utterly confused one more time. You see, I'd always believed that once I'd stopped gorging my sex drive through my eyes and my lust-crazed mind, I'd finally own my sexuality once and for all. Total victory would be mine.

And I *had* stopped. My eyes and mind *were* under control. So where was my unequivocal and permanent victory?

I should own my sexuality by now! I should not be masturbating anymore! What more must I do?

I had already accomplished so much on the battlefield, but that might have been expected. After all, my lust-filled thought life *had* been a target-rich environment, given my visual habits. My eyes had been relentless sensual heat-seekers, roaming freely over every curvy form or flank in view. I'm talking about full-bosomed young women in figure-hugging tops and skintight yoga pants that leave nothing to the imagination. Tanned beach babes in thong-like bikinis tracing the sandy edges of Georgia's coastal waters each summer. Silky soloists at church with the long, leggy slits up their skirts. The sensual sights always kept my sex drive humming at a high idle, only momentarily pacified whenever I pleasured myself.

At one time, masturbation was as regular as shaving in my life, as much a part of my daily routine as popping multivitamins with my orange juice and peanut-butter toast. There was no real respite, even on Sunday mornings, because shapely models in push-up bras beckoned my eyes while I perused the *Des Moines Register's* lingerie ads in the department store inserts. Weekday mornings were just as bad during my morning commute since I could easily spot lithe, trim female joggers in their sleek black bodysuits running along the shoulder. On road trips, I watched exercise shows in my hotel room, where "hard body" female hosts always seemed to work on their inner thighs for the camera.

That's how life was during those awful days. I *wanted* to change, *knew* I should change, but my eyes were so far out of control that there was no way to kill my masturbation habit. Sure, I was attending church, reading my Bible, and checking all the boxes that labeled me a Christian, but this was the one area of my life that I couldn't tame.

I certainly understood that the apostle John told us that God's grace was always there to forgive us when we fall, but he also told us that it was ridiculously senseless to settle for that as a way of life. If we say we are Christ's, we should walk in the same manner He walked (see 1 John 2:1–6). I didn't want to ladle grace over things every time I blew it. I wanted to stop sinning in the first place. I wanted to live up to the Lord's standards for me as a man.

But I didn't know what to do. Thankfully, the Holy Spirit *always* knows what to do, and He took me through a life-changing moment while I was driving along a key four-lane thoroughfare on the edges of my hometown of Des Moines, Iowa.

It all started when I saw her jogging on the side of the road, coming my way on the left. My eyes zeroed in on her bouncing breasts, and I took it all in lustily. If you read my first book, *Every Man's Battle*, perhaps you'll recall how I described what happened next:

> I remember the moment—the exact spot on Merle Hay Road—when it all broke loose. I'd failed God with my eyes for the thirty-millionth time. My heart churned in guilt, pain, and sorrow. For months, even years, I felt like such a loser. Lousy Christian. Like a pervert, even. Driving down Merle Hay Road, I suddenly gripped the wheel, and through clenched teeth, I yelled out: "That's it! I'm through with this! I'm making a covenant with my eyes. I don't care what it takes, and I don't care if I die trying. It stops here. It stops here!"
> …I can't describe how much I meant it. Floods of frustration from years of failure poured from my heart. I'd just had it! I wasn't fully convinced I could trust myself even then, but I'd finally and truly engaged the battle. Through my covenant with my eyes, all my mental and spiritual resources were now leveled upon a single target: my impurity.

Once a man truly engages this battle for sexual purity for the first time, as I did on Merle Hay Road that day, he releases the Holy Spirit to work freely on the matter. Man, does He ever get focused! Within hours, He reminded me of a forgotten fact I'd learned about pornography and a male's eyes back in my Human Sexuality class at Stanford University, where I earned my undergraduate degree. In that sex-ed class, I learned that guys draw gratification through their eyes from the sensuality around them. This sensuality becomes a lusty fuel line that guns their sexual engines endlessly. I said it this way in *Every Man's Battle:*

> For males, impurity of the eyes is sexual foreplay. That's right. Just like stroking an inner thigh or rubbing a breast. Because foreplay is any sexual action that naturally takes us down the road to intercourse. Foreplay ignites passions, rocketing us by stages until we go all the way.

No wonder my masturbation was out of control, and no wonder the Lord immediately pressed me to do something to control my eyes! The Holy Spirit was fiercely urgent on this score and clearly viewed my eyes as the deadliest vulnerability in my sexuality. Because the Lord had created my eyes, He already knew what I was only just learning—that my eyes were not defective, perverse, or broken. They were simply made to work this way. My eyes would continue to do precisely what they were designed to do until I defended this vulnerability by teaching them to bounce away from all the sensual scenes around me.

The truth regarding this *first* vulnerability in a man's sexuality (the eyes and the mind) provided the basis for my teaching in *Every Man's Battle*, and I'm reviewing it here because that truth is still consistent for all of us guys. You either train your eyes to behave, or you keep falling into sexual sin. Since there is no middle ground, it's vital to ask yourself this question: Which side are *you* standing on?

I knew *exactly* where I stood at the time. I was someone who'd lost too many battles—until I chose to flip sides on Merle Hay Road that day. Mobilizing my entire soul, I built a "defense system" that started with commanding my eyes to quickly glance away from the alluring curves whenever a beautiful female form was in my viewfinder. "Bounce the eyes" became my new mantra.

Let me be honest: I didn't experience immediate and total success in one moment. Quite frankly, my eyes's habits were too strong to control initially. I continued to latch onto sexualized images around me. There were many times during those first two weeks after my Merle Hay Road moment when my eyes would not fall in line and bounce away from getting a good look at the curvy women around me. During that fortnight, I chalked up failure after failure.

I didn't give up, though. I fought fiercely, knowing God was with me every step of the way because He promised He would always be there for me, just like He's always there for you. During the third and fourth weeks, I resisted the urge to look on multiple occasions—I said no! That was real, tangible progress. Hope dawned as I began winning about as often as I failed. Playing .500 ball in this battle may not seem that special to you, but to me at the time, given my past, this was an unbelievably encouraging change of events.

Things greatly improved in weeks five and six. My eyes were consistently bouncing away from the sensual. By the end of six weeks, I can honestly say I'd sustained an incredible victory. My formerly undisciplined eyes were firmly under control.

With that, I was certain my battle for purity was over. Without those sexy images in my brain to light my sexual fuses, my issues with masturbation receded like a low tide. Everything was going exactly the way I expected it to go. After all, I'd clamped off that lusty fuel line running through my eyes and calmed my engines considerably, and my habit was now under control in many important ways.

For instance, I stopped masturbating every Sunday morning because I was no longer lusting over the lingerie models in the newspaper ad inserts. I stopped masturbating in my hotel rooms on the road because I was no longer watching the sensual exercise shows before I checked out.

What a difference in my life!

If you haven't yet fortified your defenses around your eyes, you are fighting a losing battle. Don't ignore this vast visual nature in your sexuality. Any triumph in your battle for purity must start with you securing this vulnerability in your eyes. If you need help doing that, pick up a copy of the revised and updated twentieth-anniversary edition of *Every Man's Battle* for detailed instructions.

A Message to Women

I'm glad you are reading *Battle On, Battle Over* for two reasons. First, guys need the women in their lives to understand how men are wired sexually so that they understand why masturbation often plays a significant role in their sexuality. After reading this book, many of you will want to help your husband or boyfriend win their battle for purity. You'll need to be familiar with this content to build useful strategies together, and you'll both find Brenda's chapters later in the book to be very helpful for managing your relationship as a couple.

Second, research shows that porn and masturbation have become huge issues for women. For that reason, I've asked my wife, Brenda, to contribute a strong female perspective on the woman's battle for purity beginning in Chapter 3 of *Battle On, Battle Over.*

Guys, you need to read what she has to say there as well.

I knew that the lust of the eyes drives much of the masturbation in men. But evidently, not all of it. That's what had me stumped.

After all, my eyes were now tightly shielded and secure. And since the Lord had urgently pressed me to set up a defense perimeter around my eyes when I engaged the battle on Merle Hay Road, I naturally assumed that once I got my eyes and mind under control, my battle would be over and I would be free.

But that assumption looked significantly flawed on this particular night months later as I sat berating myself in my office at midnight, broken and alone, after having just masturbated once again. While I'd obviously had some clear successes in my battle for sexual purity, my late-night office hours had proven time and again that I hadn't yet slipped the last dagger into the heart of my masturbation habit.

I still didn't own my sexuality. On nights like this, I still couldn't say no, even though my eyes were under control. Granted, masturbation was no longer a regular part of my daily life, but the practice remained far too routine during these late-night stints at my office.

What's going on here?

My heart was battered and bewildered. *I thought I'd be free by now! I did exactly what God said I should do.*

I'd built a defense quickly and defended that visual vulnerability with all my heart, like no one else I knew at the time. What was I missing? *Am I just a rotten Christian? Maybe I am a pervert after all!*

Sound familiar? I wouldn't be surprised to hear that you've brutally pounded yourself with your own harsh words, but I want you to understand something very clearly, my friend. His divine power has given you everything you need to win this battle for good. It is your birthright to participate in His divine nature, live above your earthly, natural habits, and escape your sexual sin permanently (see 2 Peter 1:3–4).

You're not losing this battle because you're a rotten pervert. You're either losing because you haven't yet consistently applied the knowledge that you have, or you simply don't yet understand your vulnerabilities and how you need to defend yourself in this battle. That is where I was. I really wasn't a rotten person. In fact, I already had everything I needed inside of me to win this battle, just like you do. I was simply missing a critical piece of the puzzle.

But what was this missing piece?

It certainly wasn't sexual deprivation. I had no sexual hunger in my life. Brenda kept my sexual appetites sated, satisfied, and replete.

Was there a crack in my defenses? It wasn't a lust thing mentally, that's for sure. I relentlessly starved my mind and ruthlessly took every lustful thought captive.

There were no chinks in my eye armor, either. I bounced my eyes away from every bit of sensuality in my life, and the scene of my late-night defeats—my office—was clean of all visual temptation. There was no secret stash of *Playboy* magazines in the back of my file cabinets.

Still, I kept tripping up, and I was frustrated. The following thought began racing through my mind regularly: *If I'm not sexually deprived and if my mind and my eyes aren't triggering this masturbation in my office, what exactly is precipitating this mess anyway?*

As my late-night losses piled higher despite the exhaustive defenses I'd constructed around that first vulnerability (my eyes and my mind), I began wondering if there might just be a *second* vulnerability in my sexuality that I didn't know about yet, one that I hadn't yet defended as I had already done with the first. Was there some other common crack in a guy's sexual defenses out there that I wasn't yet aware of? Was there a second sexual fuel line that could gun a guy's engines this way?

I wasn't sure, but it had me by the throat, whatever it was. As I grappled with that question over the following weeks, I took a prolonged look at my life's circumstances to see if I could figure out what that second vulnerability might be.

One circumstance jumped out at me. At the time, I was in full-commission sales. No salary. No regular paycheck. For those who've never lived in that world, let me describe it in the frankest of terms: If you don't sell something, your kids don't eat.

That's pressure.

Since my career was young and my customer base was tiny, enormous financial pressure rested heavily across my shoulders. That pressure was the sole reason I worked late so often. I had to be out in the field during the daytime, pitching to prospects and potential buyers. That meant writing up proposals and sales plans at some other time of the day. Since the early evening was reserved for my wife and kids, the late-night slot became my go-to time to fill out the necessary paperwork and devise sales strategies.

I pondered these things, and the Lord revealed a distinct connection between this financial pressure and my masturbation. I realized that I masturbated on the nights when the fear and the financial pressure were at their greatest. On those evenings, I felt like I almost *had* to do it, as if I were practically being forced by gunpoint to lose control.

I looked closely at these themes of churning financial pressure playing across my heart, and it became sickeningly manifest to me that I didn't trust God when it came to my business and my finances. I also noticed that I couldn't trust *myself* either, which was a second critical discovery I made as I studied my life. I simply wasn't sure I had what it took to make it in the world of men.

When it comes to searching out your identity as a man, receiving a real man's blessing and stamp of approval is everything. You need a father or influential man in your life to put an arm around your shoulder and tell you that you belong, that you fit in the world of men, that you have what it takes.

But I was the only guy left in the house after Dad slammed the front door on his way out to be with his mistresses. Sure, after the divorce was final, Mom told me endlessly that I was becoming a fine young man during my high school years, and my two sisters said plenty of girls thought I was one handsome hunk of burliness. I heard the whispers of girls in my classes when they called me "foxy" and "cute."

But, alas, women don't count in this equation. Men become men in the company of men, not in the company of women. You'll *never* find your manhood by chasing girls, and if you're searching for it there, you're wasting your time, spinning away on your gerbil wheel, going nowhere. Only another man can declare that you belong in the brotherhood: *You fit in, boy. Come on up and stand with us, shoulder to shoulder.* And if the man saying this is your father, it's a hundred times better.

The trouble is, my dad never made that declaration to me. As time played out through the years, he never would. Fathers are crucial in bestowing manhood to their sons, but most botch the job miserably, and we sons pay dearly for it.

We try to keep these fears and this self-doubt hidden, of course. I'm sure that I seemed just fine to everyone else out there at the time. But to me, I was still no more than a little boy posing as a man, inadequate to complete the tasks at hand. No matter how steeply I grew the arc of my young sales career, I was terrified that sooner or later, everyone would realize that I was exactly what my dad regularly and publicly told me while I was growing up, which was this: "You're a dumbshit!"[1]

When I added the fact that my father, a National AAU wrestling champion, never forgave me for dropping wrestling to play football, it became clear to me—as I knew it was to him—that I'd never cut it as a man.

Sure, I could *pose* as a man with the best of them, just like you can. But for years, I never really felt like I measured up. Since I'm convinced that many of us men live this way, this too might accurately be called every man's battle—the fight to finally feel that genuine sense of manhood and find a sure and settled place in the world of men.

For reasons I'll delve into later in this book, this lack of affirmation of my manhood was a primary driver of my masturbation, along with intense financial pressure. I simply didn't feel what real men feel. Deep down, I had no calm assurance that I had what it takes to make it in this world of men. I had no specific knowledge that I could come through in the clutch with a paycheck every two weeks. I was alone. An outcast from the world of men. An imposter on a man's stage.

---

1. While I don't use profanity like this, I feel it's important to quote my father accurately for context.

While I'd come through for my teammates plenty of times on the gridiron back in my playing days, this was different, and I knew it. I'd had no success yet on *this* field of play, and there was no one around coaching me up or telling me I had what it takes as a man. The anxiety and self-doubt were often staggering.

Can anyone count on me? Probably not. Even I can't count on myself!

Because of earlier experimentation with masturbation as a teen, I instinctively knew that an orgasm was like a pressure valve releasing a calming balm of peace and a desperately needed sense of control and manhood to my soul, if only for a moment. And so, on many nights, my out-of-control insecurity and fear would get so high that every strand of my being screamed for release. I couldn't say no.

Yet once I tied my wispy sense of manhood and my crushing financial pressure to my masturbation habits, my head finally began to clear up on the matter. Remember, I'd started this self-inspection regarding my late-night sexual sin at my office with one driving question: *Was there some other common crack in a guy's sexual defenses out there that I wasn't aware of yet?*

Well, there was, and by now I was fully enlightened. There *is* a second vulnerability in a man's sexuality (and in a woman's sexuality, for that matter). I'd finally connected enough dots in my life for a huge and life-changing revelation to blast through my brain: *My late-night masturbation habit isn't a sexual issue at all! It's a financial trust issue! It's an identity issue, a manhood issue!*

This revolutionized my approach to purity. For the first time, I understood that not all sexual sin is sexual at its root. Unequivocally, this is the most important truth I ever picked up on purity's battlefield. Note it well, my friend.

Now initially, this revelation tied my brain into knots. I'd argue with myself, saying, *But I'm masturbating! It has to be sexual, doesn't it?*

But it wasn't. Sure, I *was* masturbating, and I *was* using my sexual apparatus to deal with the financial pressure and to cope with the father wounds that had shamed me and warped my sense of manhood. But the underlying issues were *not* sexual at all.

Once I'd wrapped my mind around all this, my confusion over my late-night masturbation evaporated. I wasn't a rotten, perverted Christian after all. I was simply an ill-equipped Christian man who hadn't understood the drivers of my late-night masturbation in my office. I didn't know that there was a second "stealth vulnerability" that needed defending, just like my eyes. As soon as I *did* understand this, I devised defenses for this second vulnerability, swinging an axe to the roots and cutting off my sexual sin for good. In other words:

Battle on. Battle over.

After realizing that my masturbation was really a financial trust issue, I stopped taking those pressures and fears into my own hands with a bottle of lotion and a towel. Instead, I took my fears to the Lord in prayer and asked Him to release the financial pressure that I was feeling. Once I understood that this habit was also a manhood issue from the deep wounds inflicted by my *earthly* father, I moved into a tighter, more intimate relationship with my *heavenly* Father through one-on-one worship. He healed those wounds and assured me that I *did* indeed have what it takes to make it in the world of men as *His* son.

Soon enough, my masturbation habit disappeared. The pressing need for that pressure valve vanished because I started releasing the stress and tension in the proper way with the Lord.

And so, my original suspicions were spot-on. There *was* a second vulnerability in male sexuality, a second front in every man's battle for purity. Even though I established victory on the first front by disciplining my eyes and my mind, the battle raged on until I *also* triumphed on that second front. Gratefully, there are only two fronts in this battle, and I've got them both covered now. That's why today, for all practical purposes, my battle is over.

Fred, how can you say that so confidently?

Answer: Because I haven't masturbated in over thirty years.

Let me repeat that: I haven't masturbated in more than three decades. Nor have I channel-surfed the TV or gone to the web to look for something racy or raunchy in over thirty years. That's freedom.

I'm not saying I can't fall again into sexual sin. I can. What I'm saying is that I *haven't* fallen again, and I don't intend to in the future. I've got my defenses up, and I'm keeping them up. You could say that I now own my sexuality. You can own yours too.

Perhaps you've read *Every Man's Battle* and built defenses around your eyes, but you're still struggling, still tripping up too regularly. That doesn't make you a pervert or a loser. It simply means that there's a second vulnerability you need to defend, and you didn't know about it. You haven't yet learned that not all sexual sin is sexual at its root, or that you must learn to work through your stress and your wounds with the Lord instead of with your sexuality.

Remember what I said in the introduction to this book. You have a faith as precious as that of Simon Peter, and you have Christ's grace and divine power that should end your battle. If your battle is still raging, then you're lacking one thing—you haven't added knowledge and perseverance to your faith. In short, you simply haven't learned to control your body yet, which you are unquestionably called to do (see 1 Thessalonians 4:3–5).

But you will. Through reading *Battle On, Battle Over*, you will connect your *own* dots, and once you do, your battle can be over for good, just like mine has been for over thirty years. After all, it's your destiny as God's child to be free of sexual sin, and that's the absolute truth.

<hr />

Even after sharing my story, I realize that you may still be a bit fuzzy about how stress, fear, and lack of trust can trigger sexual sin. You may be thinking, *How does that even work inside us? It sounds nonsensical and even bizarre to me.*

I understand. That's why I like to call this second vulnerability our "stealth vulnerability." On the surface, there *is* a lack of obvious connection between our stress, our wounds, and our sexuality. That's precisely why very few of us actively defend this vulnerability, but it's there, and it's the very stealthy reason why we often struggle to find complete victory and purity in our lives.

To help you understand this "stealth connection" even more clearly, let me share Logan's story of how porn and masturbation put his marriage in jeopardy.

As you'll see, Logan had been doubting his manhood too.

2

Logan's Story

Buried in thought and jarred by the sound of my ringtone, I snatched my smartphone from its holster, plainly irritated by the disruption. I didn't recognize the phone number, but I swiped the screen with my thumb anyway and laid the device to my ear.

"Hello, this is Fred," I said far more cheerily than I felt at the moment.

"Hey, brother, this is Logan! You got a minute?"

My mood brightened instantly.

"Logan! Sure do, man! I always have time for you."

I meant it too. While I hadn't known Logan that long, he was a former high school wrestler who still walked with the confident air of a guy who knew he could take down any man in the room and flip him on his back at will. My dad, also a top wrestler, always walked like that. To me, Logan was downright cool, a man's man by any measure.

He was also a God's man through and through. While we've never attended the same church, I'd met Logan many times at citywide Christian events. I'd learned from mutual friends that he was raised outside of Christ, but once he met the Lord, he embraced Him like a little child clinging to a palm tree in a hurricane. With an engaging wife, Paige, and their beautiful girls, his family painted an inspirational picture of love, commitment, and laughter whenever I was around them.

"Thanks, Fred, that means a lot to me," Logan responded. "I was just wondering if we could get together at Starbucks sometime over the next few days. I've got an issue I'd like to talk over with you, and I think you can help me."

I was shocked, nearly speechless. With studied ease, I managed to reply, "I'd love to help. What's a good time for you?"

My mind raced while I listened to Logan throw out a couple of dates and times. I was stunned to my toes by his request. Sure, meeting a friend at Starbucks sounds innocuous enough for most guys, but never for me. Ever since *Every Man's Battle* was released, it's always been the same. Whenever a guy asks me to meet him at a coffeehouse to discuss an "issue," it's never about getting a handle on his budget or helping his son with his throwing mechanics. He invariably wants to talk about his sexual sin. And that's why Logan's invitation astounded me.

You see, his best friend once told me that Logan had dumped his teenage porn habits long ago and had entirely owned his sexuality ever since. What could have happened to bewitch this ardent lover of Christ back into his pornographic pit?

We settled into our seats at Starbucks the following Monday afternoon. As Logan finished his first long draught on his latte, he set down his cup and began in earnest. "Fred, this is hard for me because I respect you so much. I know you live out your life exactly the way you write about it in your books because of how your children carry themselves as men and women of God. I look up to you because you've been so successful with your purity. Sadly, your success is now forcing me to share my failures. I need help, and I think you can help me, so here goes. Over the past few months, I've stepped back into pornography and masturbation again. It's so frustrating, Fred! I don't even know why I'm doing this!"

Notice his manner here? He was indeed a man's man. I appreciated his direct approach and how he didn't hold back.

"Before we even start, Logan, I want you to understand something that's unequivocally true from the Word of God," I began. "As a Christian husband, it's your birthright to live a sexually pure life. Purity is normal for each of us in marriage—or should be. In essence, it's our default position as sons of God. If you aren't living purely today, it simply means that there's an undiscovered reason why you're missing the mark these days. You and I will discover that reason together, and let me assure you, it's always there. It could be in your heart, it could be in your mindset, or it could be in your relationships, even if it doesn't seem obvious to you right now. Still, it's always there. I just need to ask you a few questions to help us find that reason. Will that be okay with you?"

"Sure, fire away!" Logan seemed encouraged.

My thoughts logically run to the same starting point with every guy I counsel. *Perhaps his eyes aren't completely under control.*

"Logan, how exactly do porn and masturbation play out in your life? When does it happen for you?"

"Almost always at night," he responded. "Sometimes my wife falls asleep in bed while we're watching a show. I start flipping through the channels, and perhaps a sensual show or commercial comes on. That gets my mind going in a certain direction, and one thing leads to another until I get up, slip into my home office, and begin looking at porn on my computer.

"But honestly, it rarely starts with the television. Most of the time, it happens when I'm working late in my office after the family has gone to bed, and I'm literally just minding my own business. I'm not even thinking about it, and yet these days, I somehow end up sliding into porn on the computer anyway.

"Whenever that happens, it's just so devastating to me! I thought I was over looking at porn years ago. I completely crucified it, yet now it's storming back into my life like some awful zombie. Only this time, I can't seem to kill it."

Judging from my past counseling experience, it was pretty clear to me that poorly disciplined eyes were not at the root of his current problem. After all, he'd had them disciplined tightly for years, and that kind of discipline doesn't just evaporate for no apparent reason. There had to be something else at the root, and we still had to find it.

"I'm angry with myself," Logan continued, "because I love God and He's saved me from so much. Yet here I am, pulling this junk back into my life!"

There's a possible clue, I thought. "Logan, tell me more about your relationship with the Lord. How much time are you spending alone with Him these days?"

Logan shrugged. "It's not that bad, considering the porn and everything else. I still love going to church, and my worship is going great. Even though I'm not spending as much time alone with Him, it isn't like I've completely disconnected either. Sometimes I feel too guilty to approach Him, which usually happens when I'm angry with myself over my sin."

I'd obviously hit another dead end. While Logan's relationship with the Lord had weakened some, I reckoned that this was more of a symptom of his porn use than its cause. Moving on to investigate another possible culprit, I probed into his marriage a little bit.

"How are you and Paige doing with your sexual connection? Have you seen any changes lately?"

"None at all. Our relationship has always been excellent that way. She initiates things as often as I do, and if I want more sex, all I have to do is ask. Honestly, she's just that type of woman. There isn't a lack of sexual intimacy here. In fact, that's one of the reasons I'm so confused. Given our good sexual relationship, it seems unbelievable that I've fallen back into porn and masturbation in this way.

"Think about it, Fred! My office is right in my home, just down the hall from the master bedroom. If I'm working late at night, all I have to do is take a few steps down the hall, slip between the sheets with Paige, and have all the sex I want at a moment's notice. And yet I don't do that! Instead, I turn to cyberspace and masturbate. It makes no sense and makes me flat-out sick of myself, yet I keep doing the same thing over and over instead of turning to Paige. What kind of sick weirdo must I be?"

Tears pooled in his eyes, then flowed like streams from a dark valley of gut-wrenching angst. It was pure torture watching this brother in Christ suffering such torment and misery, but I was also encouraged. Our last interchange clearly established that his sexual sin was not sexual at its root. I sensed that we were about to locate that root issue currently driving his porn-and-masturbation habit. I may have hit a series of dead ends so far, but I was coming up to one of my favorite questions.

"Logan, tell me something. How's your business doing?"

My friend stared at me in disbelief. He would later tell me that he almost stood up and punched me in the nose when I asked him that question, shocked and dumbfounded by my apparent lack of concern for his pain. He had just spent a full twenty minutes pouring his guts out and crying all over our table at Starbucks, and my response seemed to duck and dodge the whole messy topic with a casual change of subject. How coldhearted I must have appeared to him!

But as you already know from my own story and experience, I wasn't changing the subject at all. I was actually right on top of it, like a fiercely focused hawk diving after a field mouse.

"Fred, I have no idea why you're asking this question, but I'll be straight with you. My business is collapsing right now, and what's happening is scaring me to death."

Bingo, I thought.

"You see, business isn't panning out the way I expected," he continued. "It's been very slow. I should have known that starting a contracting business in November was a huge mistake."

If you've ever lived in the upper Midwest, you'll understand why launching a construction business after Halloween isn't the best idea. We have this thing called "winter." Since it's usually too cold in Iowa to pour and cure cement properly in the winter months, housing starts are few, which means contractors and carpenters are often limited to doing "inside work" until the weather warms up. What's more, Logan was relatively new to our area, so he didn't have the name recognition, reputation, or contacts to drum up enough indoor remodeling projects to keep his business afloat during his first winter. No wonder things were slow.

Still, Logan had an ace in the hole—a gigantic pickup truck that matched his colossal work ethic. When Iowa's icy temperatures slowed down the construction industry, there was one specific brisk winter business option for those willing to do the work—plowing snow-filled driveways and parking lots. He'd already borrowed a good chunk of money and purchased a huge plow blade for the front end of his truck. Logan planned to hustle up some business and spend the long, cold Midwestern nights plowing snowdrifts off driveways and parking lots around town to feed his family while the building business was slow.

He had a great plan. He really did. Logan would ride the waves of wintry storms until construction picked up in the spring. What he hadn't planned on was the perfect storm of *no* storms. It stopped snowing in early November. Completely. All winter long.

Iowa's deep summertime drought had extended into winter—a phenomenon I'd never seen in the five decades I'd called Iowa home. When Logan and I sat down in Starbucks, it was late March, and the dry winter winds had blown through Logan's savings account. Deep financial terrors hounded him mercilessly, chewing him apart.

"Fred, there's no work at all. No building, no remodeling, no plowing. At this moment, I have no more than two or three weeks' worth of savings in the bank, and after that, I've got no way to feed my family. When I moved my family here from the East Coast, I sensed God was telling me to go ahead and start my business. Now I'm not so sure. I like being self-employed, but I guess that's over. I've got to work for somebody else and leave this business thing alone. I'm crushed and so scared. What if I can't find a decent-paying job? Then what do I do? The stress of all this is overwhelming."

Finally! The root of his sexual sin! I bore in with the all-important question.

"Logan, tell me: How are you feeling as a man right now?"

"I don't feel like a man at all. I feel worthless, like I've let my family down. I must find some way to feed these kids, and Paige wants to get pregnant again, but I can't even afford the ones we have! Yesterday I had to call my mother-in-law to borrow money to buy groceries. That about killed me."

"I'll bet," I commiserated.

"I've been living through some of the most embarrassing times I've ever gone through in my life, Fred, and I can barely look at myself in the mirror," Logan continued. "It's unbelievable. Everything is out of control. I can't support my family, and I'm worried that I won't be able to feed my kids. I feel like a complete loser."

It was time to let Logan in on the truth.

"You know what, my friend? I don't think you have a sexual sin issue at all. I think you have a financial trust issue."

He stared at me blankly, as though I'd just dropped a coconut on his head from twenty feet and now he was counting stars. I figured I needed to explain myself.

"Yes, I know it's an odd thought at first," I said, "but it will make perfect sense once I explain some things about male sexuality and how guys share intimacy with women. Once you understand that, there's a good chance you'll stay sexually pure for the rest of your life."

I began by explaining a critical difference between men and women in the way they naturally draw intimacy from one another. By nature, men get their intimacy tanks filled primarily from what they do just prior to and during sexual intercourse. As men, sex is our "native language" for communicating our intimacy with a woman.

While we can and should learn other languages over time, sex is the language we naturally long to use when we yearn to share the heartfelt intimacy we feel for our wives.

Women are quite different. When it comes to expressing and experiencing intimacy with a man, they are multilingual by nature. They easily fill their needs for intimacy by talking, sharing, hugging, touching—even by heading out with their husbands to a strip mall for an ice-cream cone.

Now, there's no doubt that I like two scoops of butter pecan ice cream as much as the next guy. Probably a *lot* more than the next guy. And there's no doubt I've grown in my ability to draw intimacy from such moments together and have made a conscious effort to do so.

But the truth is, when I'm around Brenda and her lovely eyes are sparkling, her lovely smile is flashing, and my heart is stirred to connect with her soul, a scoop of Häagen-Dazs just won't cut it. Sharing an ice-cream cone is not my mother tongue when it comes to communicating intimacy, and I have no intention of stopping there if I have some say in the matter. We men long to express our hearts in our innate language of physical love.

This native language, however, can also create real trouble for us guys, and it creates a key vulnerability in us toward sexual sin. To understand why, you must consider two things. First, remember that nearly all of the body's most powerful chemicals are involved in a wash of blissful contentment that floods the brain's pleasure centers during an orgasm. Nothing in life feels better. Second, remember that when we use our natural language for communicating intimacy with a woman, it always includes an orgasm.

Now, if orgasm is the natural end of every act of intercourse, it follows that an orgasm is also always part of the passing and receiving of genuine intimacy with our real, in-the-flesh wives. In other words, orgasm and the passage of genuine intimacy always happen simultaneously for us when enjoying sex with our soulmates. Naturally, then, the physical feelings of an orgasm are subconsciously indivisible from the warm emotions of genuine intimacy in us. None of this is problematic within the tender confines of the marriage bed.

But what if an orgasm happens outside the marriage bed, without an in-the-flesh soulmate? Well, complications arise very quickly. Soon, we're ensnared by the second vulnerability in our sexuality, which I've come to call *the stealth trap*. It's the place where nonsexual roots can take over our sexuality. I lived unwittingly in this trap for years.

It happens like this. Once we discover that we don't need a real woman to get that sense of intimacy with another human soul, the trap is set. We can masturbate with a fake woman—a video, a picture, a memory, or a sex doll— and the orgasm that follows feels inseparably like genuine intimacy to us. In other words, the pleasure chemicals released in the body during masturbation can quickly become a seductively powerful false substitute for the genuine intimacy that we naturally experience with our wives in the marriage bed.

They feel the same, which is the stealth trap's sly and irresistible bait. Think about it. Let's say you're lonely. Deeply wounded. Stressed to the max financially. Intimacy's false substitute can be an extremely potent draw.

After all, every husband knows how an orgasm feels physically. But have you ever stopped to think about how an orgasm feels to you emotionally? Let me lay it out for you, and I think you'll find these feelings familiar, even if you haven't thought about them before:

- First, an orgasm produces a solid *sense of control* in a guy at the point of release, almost a sense of conquering.
- Second, an orgasm produces a robust *sense of manhood*. Though the sensation is fleeting, men feel dominant, strong, and manly at the point of release.
- Third, because it's our natural language for experiencing intimacy with a woman, men feel a moving *sense of intimate connection* with another human being at that moment, even though the experience is over in a flash and even if that "human" is just a pixilated female image on a computer screen or smartphone.

Now consider the man teetering under heavy stress, emotional wounds, or despair. Do you see how an orgasm could become an extremely potent draw to him? Read Logan's words again:

> I don't feel like a man, not at all. I feel worthless, like I've let my family down . . . I've been living through some of the most embarrassing times I've ever gone through in my life, and I can barely look at myself in the mirror. It's unbelievable. Everything is out of control . . . I feel like a complete loser.

If anyone was teetering, it was Logan. He had lost control of his life. He seriously doubted his manhood and his ability to come through in the clutch for his kids. Disconnection was seeping into his relationships, and he was terrified that Paige would discover what he already knew he was—a complete loser.

An orgasm offers a man the perfect antidote to this kind of emotional pain. The Big O reestablishes a sense of control at that point of release, fleeting though it may be. A climax assuages self-doubts, delivering that deep sense of manhood at the moment of orgasmic release and a genuine sense of intimate connection to another human. Is it any wonder that porn and masturbation were suddenly yanking Logan down into the pit again, even though he'd shaken the original habits a decade ago? His emotional pain was unbearable, and orgasms became the soothing, numbing balm to pour over his pain.

While Logan hadn't consciously yearned for porn for years, his subconscious brain had never forgotten what masturbation could do for him and his pleasure centers when the going got tough. This explains why he was led naturally and *subconsciously* back to the trough for his medication when things began falling apart.

But I also want you to notice something else that is especially important here. Never once did Logan consciously make the connection between his masturbation and his painful emotions until we met at Starbucks. Most guys never do make that connection on their own. Again, that's why I call this our "stealth" vulnerability because we naturally think sexual sin is *always* sexual at its root. We're using our sexual apparatus in the process, after all.

But the fact is, a masturbation habit is often more of an emotional issue or a wound issue than a sexual one. Sure, self-stimulation sometimes fills sexual deficits for us, especially when our spouse isn't as interested in sex as God asks them to be (see 1 Corinthians 7:2–5). But in marriage, masturbation more often fills emotional holes, especially the gaping, painful ones like father wounds and financial stresses. It becomes our medicating drug of choice. In some ways, masturbation is better than drugs or alcohol because an orgasm does more than get us high; it genuinely delivers real intimacy, if only for a moment.

Look, marriage does not preclude stress, despair, loneliness, discouragement, and disconnection from our lives, does it? It only stands to reason, then, that our inner doubts and hidden wounds can still leave us gasping for true intimacy and an authentic sense of manhood even after our wedding day, leaving the door wide open for us to grasp at that fleeting "false intimacy" with our own hands and lotions rather than seeking genuine intimacy with our God and with our wives. Eventually, masturbation becomes an addiction that dominates our lives, both emotionally *and* physically, because of the chemistry involved.

So when it comes to the second major vulnerability in our sexuality as men, our pain, wounds, and self-doubt will be at the root of it all, not our lust.

After sharing with Logan how our sexuality can morph easily into a delivery system for pain-killing medication, I backed it up with the story of my own confusion spawned by my late-night masturbation in my office all those years earlier—the same story I shared with you in Chapter 1. The parallels, of course, were remarkable. I'm sure you've already noticed that too.

"I'm telling you, Logan, my sexual sin back then was not sexual. Like you, I had a financial trust issue, and my sense of manhood was in shambles. I didn't think I had what it took to make it in the world of men, and I was desperately trying to prove my worth on my own, without God's help."

Logan was listening with rapt attention, motioning me to continue.

"Now that you've heard my story and learned how a guy's sexuality works, let's go back over everything you've told me today and see if we can make some connections for you. First, you said to me that everything is out of control and that nothing is working. What can bring back a sense of control for a guy, if only for a minute?"

Logan didn't hesitate. "An orgasm."

"Absolutely! You also said you don't feel like a man these days, that you feel worthless, like a failure and a loser. What can medicate that pain and restore a sense of manhood?"

"Masturbation."

"Right again," I replied.

"Fred, it's starting to make sense to me."

"I thought it might. You see, that burst of false intimacy from porn and orgasm is the quickest way for a hurting, disconnected guy to feel connected again, to feel intimacy again, to feel in control again, even though it's fleeting. Think about it. Because of your financial collapse, your soul was constantly screaming for an emotional pressure release, and your brain knew full well where to find that relief because of your past porn habits as a teen.

"That's how you've ended up here in porn's grip again. You're no sexual deviant. It seems confusing to you because it looks *exactly* like a sexual sin issue, but it's not sexual at its root this time, so you can't deal with it the same way you did as a teen."

"Then what do I do?" he asked.

"You've got to target the proper root, which should be easy now that I've made these connections. When I was in this situation, I decided not to focus on stopping my masturbation at all. Instead, I focused on my trust issues and on my identity in Christ as a man. Remember, the masturbation was merely a symptom anyway, so I figured that the masturbation part would take care of itself if I got to the real roots, and it did. Since it worked so well for me, I can only suggest that you forget about the masturbation too. Instead, do what I did. Focus on dealing with your inner fears and your lack of trust in God."

"How do I do that?"

"First, immediately turn your finances over to the Lord in prayer and do that over and over whenever you feel the pressure building and your fears pushing things out of control for you. In other words, you must switch pressure valves. Refuse to release the pressure by taking matters into your own hands with cyberporn and a jar of Vaseline. Instead, use prayer as your pressure valve. When I did that, everything changed quickly. Memorize His biblical promises of financial protection and review them again and again—and trust Him on that. In other words, rest in Him when the pressure's high, not in cyberspace.

"Second, and most important, spend more time singing and worshiping the Lord in private, one on one, just you and Him sharing intimacy. You need to increase your connection with Him. Remember, disconnection in your relationship with God will always feed a masturbation habit, but a deeper, intimate connection with Him will starve it."

Logan exhaled a sigh of relief. He now had a roadmap.

"Fred, I'll start on both of these right away."

About six weeks later, Logan and I met together again at Starbucks. I immediately asked him how things were going with the porn and masturbation.

He relaxed and laughed. "You know, Fred, our first talk was bizarre at times. I know I looked like a deer in the headlights when you told me I had a trust issue—and not a sexual sin issue."

"Well, let's just say I've seen that look before," I chuckled.

Logan set down his latte. "When I was a teen and struggling with porn, I met with a handful of counselors. They all said the same thing: 'Logan, every guy has a porn issue. Relax. You'll get over it one day.' None of them hinted even once that porn and masturbation might not always be sexual."

I held up my hand, nodding. "It can get confusing, Logan, even for a professional counselor. After all, men have two vulnerabilities toward sexual sin in our makeup, but only one of them is easy to spot. Sometimes, of course, it's an obvious addictive eye problem driving a sumo-sized sex drive in a guy. Every counselor gets that, so that is what they focus on. But again, most guys don't even know that there's a second 'stealth vulnerability' hounding us, including counselors."

Logan nodded. "Well, I sure understand it now. When you told me last time that I didn't have a sexual sin issue, it changed everything in my battle. Before then, I just saw myself as an out-of-control scumbag getting his jollies with porn. Once I realized that the financial pressures were driving me to porn sites, I simply decided to pass on the porn and deal with the stress issues in my life like a man and trust God to provide for us. I exchanged targets, just like you said."

"How'd that work out for you?"

"Fantastic! As I began to meditate on what you taught me, I looked back and realized that trust had *always* been a huge problem for me. Here's why. I'm a man. My business was too important to my identity to leave it in anyone else's hands, not even God's. I've always been desperate to handle business things on my own because I also have an issue with my dad, which complicates things."

"What does your father have to do with it?"

"Well, I haven't told you much about my father, but he has a Midas touch in business. He's a legend around my hometown, and I always felt an inner drive to be like him, almost a desperation to prove myself to him. He's made it clear that I've been nothing but a disappointment to him, and it kills me inside. Because of that, I never handed my business over to the Lord because it meant too much to me to succeed. I *had* to show my dad that I had what it takes, and I was pretty sure God wouldn't care as much about that as I did. But after talking to you and thinking this over, I decided that I couldn't go on like this anymore. I had to quit worrying about what my dad thought. I had to lean into God more instead."

"So what did 'leaning into God' look like for you?"

"Well, first, it meant getting a part-time job pounding nails with a guy at church. That was humbling for me. I'm an entrepreneur, so taking on a side carpentry job felt like defeat. But at that moment, my family needed me to take one for the team, to humble myself, even though it was gonna kill me emotionally. But the truth is, I needed to take that job because humbling myself was necessary to win my battle for purity. The financial pressure was huge, and it was tripping me up sexually. The pressure on me dropped instantly the moment I started pounding nails.

"Second, I decided to pray more and make more personal time with the Lord, to connect with Him intimately in worship. I just couldn't do it for a few days because of my schedule, but I tried to spend at least thirty minutes a day with Him like this, especially when finances were especially tight or on days when work stress was heavy. I forced myself to spend more time with the Lord because I felt different whenever I spent time with Him. The pressure wasn't there any longer, whether I had a negative ten dollars in my account or a positive thousand. Everything is now in God's hands. That's all that matters, and trust in Him has become very real to me."

"What happened to the porn after you made these changes?"

"Well, it wasn't like a switch flicked off and I instantly stopped looking at porn, but within a few weeks, I noticed I wasn't going online and looking at porn sites any longer. The victory just kind of happened. The best part was figuring out what this meant for my purity in the future.

"Fred, now that I know how the stress and the temptations are connected, I don't fear them anymore. When the temptations come, I say to myself, *Hey, this is not a porn issue; it's a trust issue*, or *Hey, this is just a work-stress issue*. I can now deal with the temptations immediately and recognize them exactly for what they are."

"That's amazing to hear, my friend."

Before we move on, let's review and hammer home a few points drawn from the parallels between Logan's story and what I shared about myself in Chapter 1. First and foremost, not all sexual sin is sexual at its root. This truth is an absolute game changer in the battle for purity.

Second, these nonsexual drivers are nearly always linked to your view of your manhood, especially when wounds from your father warp that view. The truth is, if you want the battle for purity to be over, everything rests upon your answers to these questions that haunt every guy:

Am I really a man?

Am I powerful?

Have I got what it takes . . . when it counts?

These familiar, raw questions come from author John Eldredge in his book *Wild at Heart*, in which he also poignantly asks, "How come when men look into their hearts, they don't find something dangerous and valiant, but instead find anger, lust, and fear?"

When you look back into my story and Logan's account, you'll find that we both naturally and effortlessly turned to our sexuality to sort through our doubts about our manhood. The enemy didn't need to assault either one of us directly with a barrage of pornographic bombshells; that came later. He simply softened us up by stirring up doubts about our manhood exactly when life was pouring serious stress into our wounded places.

Soon we were waltzing our way into the depths of masturbation and its medicating balm, all on our own. Then, because of the stealthy nature of this vulnerability, confusion reigned supreme, and we began calling ourselves names like "sleazeball" and "loser" while doubting our connection with God. The whipping whirlpool of self-doubts and stress swirled deeper into the same twisting angst that Eldredge himself had experienced:

> This is every man's deepest fear: to be exposed, to be found out, to be discovered as an imposter, to not really be a man . . . One thing a man *does* know is that he knows he is made to come through. Yet he wonders . . . Can I? Will I? When the going gets rough, will he pull it off?

I know that place well. In fact, too well. These were the questions I asked myself:

Will I be exposed?

When it matters most for my wife and kids, will I come through with a sale and put food on the table?

Am I a real man or an imposter, just posing in the world of men?

For many of us, such anxious questions shape the nonsexual roots that drive our sexual sin. Find the wounds in your manhood, and there you'll find the lack of trust and the emotional disconnection that feed your porn and masturbation.

Tragically, few men make these connections, so they remain trapped in their sexual sin for years. But not anymore, at least not for you. Hopefully, you'll now be able to spot them in your own life because of these two stories I've shared.

Now that you understand how this stealth vulnerability works, you'll see that the surest defense you can build around this susceptibility is to link your sexuality to an authentic sense of manhood and an honest, interpersonal intimacy with God as His beloved child, and with your wife as her beloved husband. If you're willing to dig into this a little more deeply, I'll help you toss out that false orgasmic balm and replace it with a genuine balm of intimacy that will heal these wounds for good. We'll teach you how to do that later in this book.

But before we do that, let me introduce you to my wife, Brenda, who, in the next chapter, explains how an identical "stealth vulnerability" in women exposes our wives and daughters to the same kinds of sexual traps that we experience as men.

By nature, the fairer sex does not experience the first sexual vulnerability of the eyes anywhere near the same degree as we guys do, so I never address that issue with them. But this second stealth vulnerability exists throughout human sexuality, leaving all of us susceptible to the same obscured snare, whether male or female.

Let's face it. The percentage of women hooked on sexual sin is rising exponentially today. Clearly, gals aren't making the conscious connections between their sin and their wounds and emotions any better than we guys have been doing it. This means we must address this issue with the women head-on so that they can learn to spot these same stealth connections in their own lives, just like we must do as men.

Male or female, you will appreciate what Brenda has to say.

3

Women and the Stealth Trap

From Brenda

Fred and I are targeting *Battle On, Battle Over* primarily toward married men and the wives who love them—wives who want to help their husbands win their battle for purity. I'm deeply concerned, however, that women are just as susceptible to this stealth trap as men. I say that because our younger generations now include the first tsunami wave of women heavily consuming porn and masturbating regularly to medicate their wounds and stresses, struggling against the same addictive chains as our men.

My husband and I first discovered the breadth of this development when he spoke at a Bible school in Canada some fifteen years ago. In an attempt to ascertain the state of the student body before Fred's arrival, college leaders conducted a survey of the entire student body. We were told that 100 percent of the young men enrolled at this Bible school said they were looking at porn at least once a week. While this number definitely arched my eyebrows—really, every single guy?—it certainly didn't shock me, given what I knew about male sexuality and how their roving eyes are so attracted to female nudity.

It was the second finding that floored me. The survey stated that *87 percent* of the female students were also looking at porn at least once a week. Now *that* was a startling statistic I couldn't comprehend at all. You must understand that women are simply not visual like men. I remember when *Playgirl* magazine went belly-up for lack of interest from women. Most women I know—myself included—wouldn't find it the least bit interesting to look at centerfolds of naked men posing in the buff.

Upon reflection, Fred and I came to understand why so many more women are looking at porn today than they did in the past. Look, women are still nowhere near as visually stimulated by sexuality as men are. They continue to be far more attracted by the depth of their relationships with men than by the chiseled shape of a guy's body or a glossy picture of a naked stranger. Nothing has changed overnight in the basic hardwiring of women.

What *has* changed is the pornographers' way of luring us women. Once they realized that we are more relational in our sexual makeup than visual, they stopped trying to attract us through raw, static nude photos. Instead, they turned to film and began weaving plot lines of romance and relationship— heavily contrived, though they are—into certain movies like the *Fifty Shades of Grey* franchise and hard-core online videos to better market them to us. The simple adjustment of adding the romantic storytelling did the trick. Suddenly, porn had a barbed hook into our female sexuality.

And just as suddenly, female sexual addiction was not uncommon anymore, nor was heavy emotional dependence upon regular masturbation. If that's your situation currently, I want you to please take a deep breath, relax, dump the shame, and turn your heart toward God on this matter.

In Fred's previous chapters, you've read about the relationship between a guy's orgasm and a release of feel-good chemicals in the pleasure centers of the brain and why emotional wounds can drive men to use their sexuality as a "source of drugs" to chemically "medicate" their pain. In my mind, Fred made a life-changing connection for the guys reading this book: Sexual sin is often nonsexual at its root, and the act of masturbation has a lot more to do with loneliness, disconnection, wounds, and pain than it has to do with lust.

Making that connection is vital for you as a woman too. Orgasm releases pleasure chemicals in your brain as well. Once you understand that, you can change your approach to loneliness and painful emotional wounds and find freedom in God, just like Fred did, instead of using masturbation to cope with your pain.

Let's talk about this chemistry for a moment. The chemical impact of an orgasm inside your body is *extremely* powerful and creates a significant physical and emotional dependency. One of the silliest things you can do is to laugh it off and underestimate the addictive consequences delivered by self-stimulation.

There's been a tremendous revolution in our understanding of the human brain over the last twenty years, especially regarding its underlying structure. Your brain is nowhere near as static and inflexible as once believed by scientists. Instead, the brain is so "plastic" and malleable that your personal behaviors and actions, including porn use and masturbation, can mold and shape your brain's underlying wiring—its neural pathways—and trap you more deeply into sin the longer you're involved. Clearly, your "neuroplastic brain" (and your ability to change your neural pathways through your actions and choices) will impact purity's battlefield immensely.

With each session of porn and each orgasm, the pleasure-giving neurotransmitter dopamine surges through your brain and lights up your pleasure centers. But dopamine also stimulates neuroplastic change. Simply, the same surge of dopamine that thrilled you in the short term also strengthens and consolidates the synaptic relays involved in your porn use and masturbation for the long term. Newly enlarged and strengthened, the synaptic connections associated with your actions will actively drive you toward future episodes with porn and masturbation.

You see, dopamine efficiently lays down memories in your brain. The next time you're in the same place at the same time of day and sensing the same loneliness and disconnection (remember Fred's story about his office at night), your brain will remember where to turn to get "medicated" again and will actively urge you to do so. In short, your brain learns exactly how to press hard to get what it wants—another hit of soothing medication.

Based upon your conscious daily decisions regarding porn and your sexual relations with yourself, you can either bolster your synapses and rewire your neural pathways toward deeper addiction (through "behavioral repetition"), or you can let the pathways languish through lack of use, weakening your addiction. Clearly, masturbation isn't just another warm and innocent form of entertainment as others love to parrot around.

I know that right about now some of you are thinking, *Isn't a plan of no masturbation inherently flawed because it's repressive and unrealistic?*

This plan isn't flawed at all. More likely, your understanding of human sexuality is flawed, probably because of how sex is discussed in our schools and how our sexuality is depicted in movies, TV shows, and music.

In fact, the entire concept of "repressiveness" is flawed from the outset. There is no such thing. You are not "repressed" if, for example, you're single and aren't currently expressing your sexuality. You aren't somehow damaging your psyche, your well-being, or even your long-term sexual capabilities. You are simply choosing not to use or enjoy your sexuality at the current time. It is nothing more than that, and nothing less. That's the truth. Choosing not to use your sexuality is *quite* realistic, especially when it comes to masturbation.

Consider looking at the topic in another way. Modern science reveals that the effects of masturbation and orgasm on the brain's pleasure centers are chemically *nearly identical* to heroin addiction. Now, imagine a heroin addict approaching you and complaining, "My rehab plan is inherently flawed because it's repressive. After all, I'm getting no heroin at all during rehab!"

I don't know how you would respond to this addict, but I'd call her crazy. We need to cut off her supply of heroin to get at the deeper heart issues driving her addiction. We wouldn't call that repressive. We would call that a necessary course of action and a wise understanding of what's going on chemically inside the addict's brain.

Cutting off masturbation (or extramarital sexual play, which can also be addictive) is necessary for you too. It's simply a necessary course of action. You can't get to the nonsexual root issues beneath the addiction until you stop medicating your wounds, pain, and stresses with the orgasmic pleasure chemicals. Since your sexuality has become a numbing, emotional crutch, you need to put your sexuality into a different, healthier place in your life and relationships.

While you've probably never heard anyone in the popular culture say this before, it's actually healthy to restrain your sexuality because it's the *only* way that you're going to get in touch with yourself and the pain that's driving your dependency.

This is also the only way you'll learn how to *own your sexuality* rather than having it own you, as it does now. Right now you're addicted, and you can't stop. Instead, you need to turn to God with your wounds and build a fresh, intimate connection with Him through prayer and worship like Fred did and Logan as well. You must turn to others and build intimate, nonsexual connections with them.

Frankly, you need to build a nonsexual connection with *yourself*, without masturbation.

Whether or not you can imagine doing so at this moment, the bottom line is simple: You can *easily* live without porn and masturbation indefinitely, and you can *happily* live without porn and masturbation indefinitely.

Now, because of our experience teaching on these topics, we know some readers will hastily jump to unwarranted conclusions about our overall position on masturbation, so let me be clear. Masturbation has its place in the marriage bed. Mutual masturbation between a husband and wife is certainly not wrong, and it's a perfectly suitable way for married couples to pleasure each other. Furthermore, some women have a difficult time learning how to have an orgasm. If you're in a clinical setting and a counselor has recommended masturbation as a beneficial means for learning how to experience more pleasure in your sexual relationship with your husband, feel free to follow their instructions (within the context of the marriage bed as a couple, of course).

Having said that, it would help you immensely to get far less concerned about the repression of your sexuality and get far more concerned about the repression of your *spirituality*, which is the direct effect of your masturbation. If you eliminate masturbation from your life, Fred and I have more than twenty years' worth of emails confirming that you'll soon declare the same universal testimony that the others did, which is this: *Since I've quit doing that stuff, I feel closer to God than I've ever felt before!*

In other words, shut off the porn and the sex with yourself, and you'll instantly stop inhibiting your intimacy with God. Consider what Tanya had to say on this topic in her email to Fred:

I just finished reading *Every Young Man's Battle* a couple of weeks ago, and I'm so thankful for the thoughtful and relevant advice and wisdom you shared. I purchased the book a couple of years ago because I was curious about what guys think about certain sexual issues. I flipped to the middle, read a couple of pages, and shut the book, figuring I had the gist of it.

A few weeks ago, my boyfriend noticed my copy of *Every Young Man's Battle* on my bookshelf and commented that it was weird that I would have this book since I'm a girl. I simply said I was curious about guys, but his comment sparked an interest to start reading it again. When I pulled it off the shelf, though, my expectations were low since my mom had forced over a dozen books about sexual purity under my nose over the years, and I found those disappointing.

This time, though, I looked through the Table of Contents and noticed a whole section on masturbation. I was shocked by that, but I was determined to learn whatever I could. You see, I'd been battling masturbation myself. This time, when I started reading from the beginning, I was instantly drawn in and didn't want to put the book down.

There was a point in my life when I was a slave to this habit for five straight years, and I didn't even know the name of it when I started. I only turned to masturbation because my dad was abusive, and masturbating would temporarily relieve my pain. The problem is this: the emotional pain always came back worse.

Recently, I started masturbating again. I wanted to stop because I valued our friendship deeply, but in my heart, I had no idea how it was possible to stop. When I told my boyfriend, he was crushed. Being raised in a strict Christian home, he was completely repulsed by the idea. He made me promise to never do it again, saying that our relationship would have consequences if I continued.

You can't imagine how thrilled I was to find your book and to employ its helpful strategies in battling this temptation. You were so encouraging, and you didn't increase my shame at all. Because of my dad's abuse, I had been plagued by shame my entire life, but your book showed me a better way.

The past few years (before my masturbation started over again), I had an amazing relationship with Jesus. I went to church simply because I loved Him, and I found my heart completely on fire for Him, mostly because of the struggles that went down with my dad. Being part of a good church brought me closer to God as He worked on my heart.

Once the most painful parts of my emotional recovery were behind me, though, I found myself slipping back into the same old habits I'd had before I met Christ. Your book gave me hope that I could break these habits for good. I know I'm not made to live as a slave to sin (and a slave to masturbation) but rather as a friend of Jesus. Thank you so much for delivering these truths to me when I knew there was something more but I wasn't quite sure how to find it or even exactly what I was missing.

I've changed the music I listen to, and I'm careful about what I watch on television and the films in movie theaters in order to block inappropriate sexual thoughts. It's been just a couple of weeks since I started doing this, but already I can feel the changes. Because of these changes, I'm now remembering to pray during the day, and what a difference *that's* making.

Jesus has started to become more than just an "add-on" into my life again, and that's because your book has truly been inspirational to me. *Every Young Man's Battle* was well worth the time it took to read it.

Maybe you have a story similar to Tanya's. If you have father wounds or emotional pain and you're using masturbation to numb it down, then you should take these steps:

- Read *Every Young Man's Battle* as Tanya did and learn about the physical and sensual drivers of the habit.
- Finish reading the book you're holding in your hands. You must learn how your life's stress, wounds, and loneliness can drive this habit.

Finding deeper intimacy with Christ is the key to breaking the power of sexual sin in your life. Fred and I will help you find that intimacy with Him later in this book, but you must first choose to seek Him with all of your heart. If you're to eliminate your dependence upon this medicating, false intimacy you've found through pornographic videos or mommy-porn books, it's time to replace it with the genuine intimacy that truly heals your wounded heart, an intimacy that's only found in Him. Do you know the Lord this intimately? Once you do find that intimacy, your freedom will be at hand.

Christian author John Piper once said, "You can find God as beautiful, all satisfying, and the highest treasure of your life. There are more treasures at His right hand, more eternal joys in His presence than you could have in ten thousand sexual trysts. The question is, do you know that? Because if you know that, sin will lose its dominion in your life."

You'll *know* these eternal joys only by experiencing them one on one with Jesus. That's why you need to turn from your sexual sin and turn your heart and eyes upon the Lord.

But perhaps you have another question: *The Bible doesn't talk about masturbation directly. If self-stimulation hurts us so much spiritually, why didn't God condemn the practice more clearly?*

That's a great question, but it isn't very helpful because no one knows the answer. Like you, I've heard people say, "Hey, since masturbation isn't expressly named in the Bible, it must be okay for us to do it. It must not matter to Him either way."

That is a ridiculously simplistic and very risky assumption. It obviously matters to Him whether you are stimulating yourself sexually! He made you. He understands perfectly the chemical and emotional impacts of the practice far better than you do.

I'm sure the Lord had good reasons for not addressing masturbation directly in the Word, and one day He'll explain it to us. But when you get right down to it, that doesn't matter as much as you might think it does because the Bible does indeed discuss masturbation *indirectly*.

In 1 Corinthians, God commands us to test all our conduct by whether or not it manifests His characteristics and brings Him glory. While the Bible may not address masturbation by name, the apostle Paul uses 1 Corinthians to lay out four very clear criteria by which we can judge this behavior (or any other unnamed behavior) in the Word:

1. Is it beneficial and helpful? (1 Corinthians 6:12)
2. Is it enslaving? (1 Corinthians 6:12)
3. Does it edify and build you up? (1 Corinthians 10:23)
4. Does it hinder the spiritual growth of a brother or sister in Christ? (1 Corinthians 8:13)

Now apply these four criteria to your masturbation habit, and God's take on masturbation will be apparent to you, just as if He'd addressed the matter directly.

Masturbation isn't beneficial to us spiritually or it wouldn't be consistently inhibiting our intimacy with God. As I mentioned earlier, we have received thousands of emails from readers over the years, and it's universal across the board—for both sexes—that when people eliminate masturbation from their lives, their testimony becomes something like this: *I feel closer to God than I ever have before.*

That's a beautiful testimony that God wants for you and your sons and daughters.

Masturbation isn't beneficial or helpful to our romantic relationships over time because the practice changes our sexual focus. In the Bible, the Lord only talks about sex within the context of two people—it's something to share in tandem with a soulmate in the marriage bed, a woman with her man. Scientific studies confirm that porn and masturbation twist our sexual focus inward while erasing our more normal and natural concern for our partner's pleasure and a mutual connection. Our personal, sexual intensity in the experience becomes more important to us than our shared intimacy. This is not beneficial to any married couple and certainly brings no glory to God.

Modern science asserts that the addictive nature of orgasmic pleasure chemicals is clearly enslaving. The more we do it, the stronger the neural pathways involved in the addiction will become. Furthermore, since we depend upon the false intimacy of these medications to deal with our wounds and afflictions instead of turning to God for genuine healing and intimacy, our wounds persist, our emotions wobble unsteadily, and our spiritual life remains immature. Masturbation, therefore, does not edify us or build us up in the Lord either.

The truth is clear. You don't need this medication. You need to edify yourself and build yourself up. As we stated in the introduction, you have a faith as precious as that of Simon Peter, and you have Christ's divine power so that you may participate in the divine nature and escape all sexual corruption. Your only responsibility in this is to be diligent in adding knowledge, self-control, and perseverance to your faith so that you might confirm it and mature it.

What's the alternative? I think back on Fred struggling so hard in his office late at night to feed and clothe us and yet falling into sin because of his wounds and stress. How miserable and how pitiful for him!

Then I think about who he is now, an intercession leader in our church for over twenty-five years. He's confirmed and matured his faith and edified our entire family in the process. Today, it's hard to even imagine him turning to a "drug" like masturbation instead of turning to the Lord, no matter what his level of pain is.

What if he had continued in his dependencies instead of diligently doing as Peter commanded? His fully developed Christian manhood would have been severely stunted. Would that have been edifying for Fred? Would his masturbation have helped *my* spiritual growth through the years while simultaneously stunting his own spiritual growth through this practice? Would his masturbation have helped the spiritual growth of our children?

The answer to all three questions is no. The habit would have hindered all of us spiritually, without question. Masturbation is not beneficial or helpful, nor does it edify. Instead, the practice enslaves and hinders spiritual growth. By God's indirectly declared standards, masturbation misses the mark completely for us as Christian sons and daughters.

God does not mince words when it comes to sexual self-control:

> It is God's will that you should be sanctified: that you should avoid sexual immorality; that each of you should learn to control your own body in a way that is holy and honorable, not in passionate lust like the pagans, who do not know God. (1 Thessalonians 4:3–5, NIV)

Masturbation makes it unlikely that you'll ever learn to control your body over time, which is clearly God's will for you. The curve of your spiritual growth will flatten out if you don't learn to control your own body.

Let me close this chapter with this thought. Great testimonies come at a great cost. Do you really want to teach your children that it's okay to give in and masturbate whenever the going gets tough? Or are you willing to do the more costly thing, which is to spend the necessary time teaching them how to control their bodies and avoid sexual immorality so that they can gain a great testimony like Fred?

Don't say to them, "Go ahead and masturbate, kiddo, because the Bible doesn't expressly forbid it." Instead, set a mark more fully representative of the Bible's teaching. Say something like this: "You have been given all grace through Christ's death and resurrection. Yes, you'll be forgiven for every misstep as you learn to control your body. But it also means that because God's new life and power are living inside you, grace also gives you the power to become more than that."

Help your sons and daughters to become something more. After all, it's possible to grow to adulthood and never masturbate. All four of our children have done so. We taught them early how to control their bodies and worship God intimately, one on one. Through personal worship, they developed genuine intimacy with Him that strengthened them in this fight.

I don't share this testimony to make anyone feel guilty. Guilt is irrelevant, I can assure you. I only share these thoughts to let you know what is possible. I want the Holy Spirit to ride into your life upon our testimony, convincing you that if God can do that with the Stoekers, He can do that with you and your family. That's the point of a good testimony—it stirs faith in your heart. God wants to do what He's done in our family in you and your family.

So set a new mark for yourself. It isn't the least bit beneficial for us to do anything less than that. Instead, be edified and regenerated by a deeper reliance upon God rather than a deeper reliance upon masturbation's numbing medication.

4

Misgivings About Our Manhood

This is every man's deepest fear: to be exposed, to be found out, to
be discovered as an imposter, to not really be a man . . . One thing
a man does know is that he knows he is made to come through. Yet
he wonders . . . Can I? Will I? When the going gets rough, when
it really matters, will he pull it off?
—John Eldredge, *Wild at Heart*

From Fred

Now that you've seen how loneliness and disconnection can snare women in the same old familiar trap as it does us guys, let me pull your attention back to my closing thoughts in Chapter 2, excerpted below and with italics added for emphasis.

It's imperative that you recognize how our fatherless culture inaccurately ties male sexuality to manhood.[1] Once you grasp how universally we buy into this lie—this false, contrived link between male sexuality and a man's identity—you'll see how any misgivings about your manhood can easily set this stealth trap against you:

When you look back into my story and into Logan's story, you'll find that

---

[1]. While you female readers don't struggle with manhood *per se*, you'll surely recognize parallels connecting your wounds, identity, and sexuality, so stick with me.

we both naturally and effortlessly turned to our sexuality to sort through *our doubts about our manhood.* The enemy didn't need to assault either one of us directly with a barrage of pornographic bombshells; that came later. He simply softened us up *by stirring up doubts about our manhood* exactly when life was pouring serious stress into our wounded places.

Soon we were waltzing our way into the depths of masturbation and its medicating balm all on our own...[these doubts] shape the *nonsexual* roots that drive our sexual sin. *Find the wounds in your manhood* and there you'll find the lack of trust and the emotional disconnection that feed your porn and masturbation. Tragically, few men make these connections, so they remain trapped for years...

Your doubts about your manhood will sink your sexual purity, and you'll rarely know what submerged it. I've lived it, my friend, and I've had a lot of company. This pattern is endemic in our world as men.

It needn't be this way. As a Christian man, your destiny is freedom. As a Christian husband, it's your spiritual birthright to live a sexually pure life, in the sense that, at salvation, you were given everything you need to walk in purity (see 2 Peter 1:3–4). You already have what it takes.

Then why are so few of us walking in victory, Fred? Why does practically every guy I know believe that the opposite is true—that his battle will never be over until he takes his last breath?

Answer: Because most guys have serious misgivings about their manhood. As I said, it's endemic. When you look at how our culture approaches manhood and male sexuality, it's easy to see why so many guys have the wrong view of their destiny and their ability to live sexually pure lives.

In his classic book *Wild at Heart,* John Eldredge suggests that men don't know how to *be* men, and they never learned how to fight for their own hearts *as* men, as Eldredge attests:

Most men have never been initiated into manhood. They have never had anyone show them how to do it, and especially, how to fight for their heart. The failure of so many fathers, the emasculating culture, and the passive church have left men without direction...

First and foremost, we still need to know what we never heard, or heard so badly, from our fathers. We need to know who we are and if we have what it takes...Where do we go to find an answer...to The Question?...

You see, a man's core question does not go away. He may try for years to shove it out of his awareness and just "get on with life." But it does not go away. It is a hunger so essential to our souls that it will compel us to find a resolution. In truth, it drives everything we do.

Let me bring this a bit closer to home. Think back to my earnest doubts about my manhood while buried under suffocating financial stress during those late nights in my lonely office. I didn't know who I was, and I sincerely doubted that I had what it took to make it in the world of men. That core question pounded away at my heart, echoing mercilessly in my soul.

Will I somehow sell something to put food on the table?

Can I pull it off for my family when it matters most?

Then, as a Christ-follower, I endured a *second* set of haunting questions slinking through the darker corners of my consciousness, where no one else can go:

Can I come through under pressure, like a man, all on my own—just God and me?

Or must I limp along on my orgasmic crutch, medicating my way in shame?

Such queries reverberate endlessly through a man's shaken soul in bleak and hollow tones. This isn't how it was meant to be for men.

A father is supposed to initiate his son into manhood early on, teaching him how to come through when the going gets rough. He coaches him up so that his son knows how to fight for his heart when life dishes out rugged setbacks. The initiated son knows his place as a warrior, and he knows how to come through when it really matters on life's battlefield. When he proves he has what it takes on the tangled field of play, he emphatically establishes his manhood in the clutch, just like his father did before him. He earns the right to stand shoulder to shoulder with other men in this world. His doubts are gone forevermore.

Masculinity is an essence that every boy naturally craves, just as he longs for food and water. I certainly did, consciously and with all my heart. I ached to know whether I belonged in the world of men, standing shoulder to shoulder with the others.

The trouble was that I was never initiated into manhood by my father. I wasn't taught how to fight for my heart in the heat of battle or how to come through in the clutch. The core questions lurking in my soul—*Do I have what it takes? Will I come through when it matters?*—had no answers, at least from my dad.

At a time when I needed Dad to be there for me, he chose to leave our home to chase tail in Mistressland. But his absence wasn't the real issue. I couldn't have trusted him for answers even if he *were* around.

After all, my respect for him was in shambles. Even as a young teen, I was savvy enough to wonder openly, *How can I trust Dad to know the first thing about genuine manhood? He values sex with a bunch of different women over a relationship with me and my sisters. What could he teach me about manhood?*

So much for my initiation.

Fathers are meant to be critically involved in a son's developing manhood, but like many of us coming of age in this fatherless American culture, I was forced to go elsewhere for my answers. Predictably, I turned to the same place for initiation that most of us do—to my sexuality and our culture's fast and loose sensuality—hoping to somehow cobble together my own jerry-built, makeshift initiation into manhood.

That spawned a serious problem for my sexual integrity, as expected when a father flops miserably in his role. A father's failure to initiate his son into manhood nearly always ends in impaired sexual integrity in that son.

My friend Patrick Middleton, a gifted sexual addictions counselor, explains why this is inevitable: "I deal with a lot of men, and it never fails that the men with deeper sexual issues also have uninvolved or missing fathers. Their sexual issues are directly and severely impacted by their dad's failures as a father to connect with them. That's because there's a point in the development of a boy into a man—say from eleven to thirteen—when the boy needs to move into a deeper relationship with his dad."

But because of widespread ignorance, disengagement, or divorce, most dads never provide that much-needed relationship with their sons. "I know this sounds a bit weird," Patrick told me, "but I've never found a better way to say it: Dad has to be close enough to his son to call the 'heart of a man' out of the boy."

I was intrigued by the concept. I wondered, *How does a father call the heart of a man out of the boy?*

To me, a key connection was drawn when Patrick mentioned the ages of eleven to thirteen. As I meditated on his words later, my mind flashed back to Psych 101 at Stanford University and something I learned from the work of brilliant Swiss psychologist Jean Piaget. He discovered that the human brain changes dramatically around that time, enabling young teens to think abstractly for the first time about God, life, rules, and relationships. It's at this time of early adolescence that new questions arise for young teens, questions like:

Is God real?
Is He my God too?
Why is life so hard?

Of course, the ability to reflect on one's thoughts is simply a rite of passage and a normal sign of growing maturity. If the father is around, a boy can vocalize his reflections to his dad and the initiation process can begin in earnest.

Granted, a son's abstract introspections aren't *always* voiced out loud like this to a father because they sometimes include sexual themes:

Why do I always get erections when I stare at Megan in math class?
What's this masturbation thing all the guys are talking about in the locker room?
What's up with wet dreams anyway?

Such questions are of utmost importance to every young man, and getting proper answers is key to his developing manhood. But your son won't bring them up to you if you haven't already opened the door wide on the topic of sexuality and created a safe place for him to come to you for answers.

Suppose you haven't connected with him. In that case, you may also lose the opportunity to make a connection with him in many other important areas, including critical issues related to his developing manhood. That's where even more important questions arise:

Where's my place in this world?

In life, what works and what doesn't?

How do I become a real man to be reckoned with among those around me?

What is worth applying my strength to? Pouring my life into?

Engaging our sons during these early years of introspection is how we "call the 'heart of a man' out of the boy." These questions pour from the very core of their young male hearts. This is where we can catch and release those hearts in a genuinely masculine direction and align their conscious understanding of masculinity with God's original design for men, including how to fight the big battle for sexual purity and how sexual purity is crucial in defending the beauties in our lives—our wives or our girlfriends, our sisters in Christ.

So what happens when a father isn't there during those times of growth and introspection? What happens when he isn't close enough to his son during those early teen years to call the heart of a man out of a boy?

Here's what happens: the boy must turn elsewhere for that initiation into manhood and for answers to his deepest questions about life. The problem is, it's in this "turning elsewhere" that sexual integrity is shattered and the seeds of a sexual drug dependency are sown in a young man.

I'll let Patrick Middleton fill you in on the usual pattern: "If the father fails to call out the heart of a man, the next window of opportunity for a young man to try to feel like a man is through his emerging sexuality. So if Dad isn't there early in adolescence to help answer questions about manhood, the boy will use his sexuality as an arena to answer his questions about being a man."

As I said earlier, because of widespread ignorance, disengagement, or divorce, most dads never provide that much-needed relationship with their sons. And because of that, most of us are forced to seek our manhood through our sexuality instead. Incredibly, we truly believe that we'll find our manhood there—with the willing assistance of our half-dressed girlfriends.

Our entire culture has been duped into thinking this way. For instance, you could randomly pull a hundred young guys off any city street and expect the same answer to the following question: What's a guy's ticket into manhood?

Odds are, every last one of them would respond, "Going to bed with a girl."

But the sad thing is, every last one of them would be wrong. Going to bed with a girl gets you nowhere when it comes to genuine manhood. It's a false finish line, a big, fat dead end.

I'm aware that this might appear to be a dramatic, even jaw-dropping statement to make, especially given the way our culture, through music and movies, links the exploration of your sexuality (going to bed with a girl) with developing manhood (he became a man that day).

Still, the truth is the truth. Premarital sex, porn, and masturbation *impede* your development as a man, stunting your growth at the core. Sexual exploration is *not* your ticket into manhood. Instead, it's your ticket *away* from manhood. Over time, it's devastating to your leadership in the home and in your local church.

But, Fred, this doesn't make sense to me. How can saying no to sex enhance a guy's manhood?

The reason it doesn't make sense to you is because you live in a bogus cultural world that claims that having sex with a girl delivers manhood. Rejecting this worldview requires a paradigm shift: Sex *can't* deliver manhood, and God's call to control your sexuality is *not* unfair. In fact, a robust campaign for purity on your part could be the most glorious and wondrous adventure of your lifetime and help you cultivate the central core of your masculinity.

To understand how every man's battle works as God's developmental gift to you and your manhood, you must first understand what lies at your created core as a man. Remember what Middleton said about how the "heart of a man" must be called out of the boy by his father in his early teens.

What exactly is the makeup of the heart that a father is to call out of him? The best description I've found comes again from author John Eldredge in *Wild at Heart* (with italics added for emphasis):

> There are three desires I find written so deeply into my heart that I know now I can no longer disregard them without losing my soul. They are at the core of who I am and who I yearn to be.
>
> I gaze into boyhood, I search the pages of literature, I listen carefully to many, many men, and I am convinced these desires are universal, a clue to masculinity itself. They may be misplaced, forgotten, or misdirected, *but in the heart of every man is a desperate desire for a battle to fight, an adventure to live, and a beauty to rescue.*

That's the heart of a man—a desperate desire for a battle to fight, an adventure to live, and a beauty to rescue—that must be called out of the boy.

After reading this passage from *Wild at Heart*, I was stopped in my tracks. Such simple words, and yet so infinite in scope. I instantly recognized those same desperate desires lying at the center of my own soul, and I believe those same three passions exist at the core of every boy, yearning to be called out by his father.

I called the "heart of a man" out of each of my boys, and the results were remarkable. When a father succeeds in initiating his son into manhood, the young man will know how to live life straight up, by God's design and for His purposes, and he'll have little fear of men or their alternative views. He'll know how to fight for his heart through personal, one-on-one worship and obedience to God's ways, trusting the Lord to teach him how to come through as a man when it matters most, both spiritually and physically.

He'll also have a *big battle to fight* in his crusade for sexual purity, and he will come through in a big way, against all odds. He'll ride out on a *great adventure* with a wondrous woman at his side and build a countercultural home on the Kingdom's frontier, one filled with joy and laughter in the face of a demonic world filled with darkness, distraction, dissonance, and dysfunction. He won't turn to the left or right as he *defends and rescues his beauty* at every turn because rescue lies at the core of his being and the center of his responsibilities to God. That's what real men do.

And you know what? It's been rolling out for my sons precisely this way. They never needed to "turn elsewhere" into their emerging sexuality to get their answers, as I was forced to do. They never doubted their manhood in the troubling ways I sincerely doubted mine. They never required orgasmic medication. They *always* knew how to fight for their hearts as men from the beginning, while it took me many jagged and painful years to learn how to do the same.

Without a doubt, Jasen and Michael belong in the world of men, standing shoulder to shoulder right next to me. They've fought the big battles and lived great adventures in both the spiritual and physical realms, and they've always come through when it has mattered most. They've always known that they belong at my side because I've told them again and again, more often than anything else I've ever told them.

My dad never told me that I belonged in the world of men, ever. I sure wish that he had.

You'll learn more about how Jasen and Michael's initiation process worked in my home later in *Battle On, Battle Over*, but for now, let's explore how things play out for the boy whose father *fails* at this initiation process.

If the father never calls out the heart of a man, the next window of opportunity for a guy to try to feel like a man is through his emerging sexuality. I was forced to clamber through that second window of opportunity, which means I can share how things roll out for guys like me.

First, when you flop through that window, you know nothing about your manhood *or* your sexuality. On the other side are your "teachers"—the young teens from the locker rooms and classrooms of life. They're just as ignorant as you are yet quick as vipers to declare "brilliant truths" like "Are you telling me you don't masturbate yet? You'd better get with the program or you're going to explode down there!"

Feigning calm, you gratefully set up a three-days-a-week regimen of masturbation—maybe daily—to avert the impending blast warned of by these "experts" around you. As you faithfully implement your regimen, the addictive nature of masturbation asserts itself in your brain and body.

Continuing the story, the pressures of life push in from all directions as you pass through middle school, high school, and then college. Cliques form, but sometimes friends drop you from their activities altogether, or you feel like a third wheel when you hang out with them. When that sort of rejection occurs, you masturbate to ease the disappointment or emotionally deal with the situation.

Medication soon becomes your way of life. From time to time, stress piles on following a bad week of basketball practice, and you're afraid you might lose your starting spot, so you turn to a relaxing, orgasmic jolt that reaffirms your manhood. Perhaps your girlfriend toys with your emotions, hissing one moment she wants to break up and purring the next that she wants you to hold her close.

Or perhaps it's finals week in your first semester in college, and your life explodes from the pressure to make grades. There's no time to sleep, no time to rest, and everything seems on the brink. Orgasm brings a sense of control back into your chaotic life, and that sense of release is something you feel that you desperately need. Masturbation is your show of force, the proof that you're a man to be reckoned with. For an instant, you feel like a man, and that's all that counts.

While your emerging sexuality makes you *feel* like a man momentarily from time to time, all you're really learning is how to *medicate* your life instead of how to *live out* your life with masculine purpose and according to God's purposes. This is how searching out your manhood through your emerging sexuality leads to a dependency upon orgasmic drugs instead of genuine manhood.

Your dependencies are set in place by the time you're into your twenties, and masturbation becomes your reliable refuge when life goes haywire. I was reminded of this when I discussed the "stealth trap" with a professional baseball pitcher bouncing around the minor leagues. I asked him if he understood the connection between high stress and his sexuality.

"Absolutely," he replied. "As you were talking about it, my mind raced back to those many nights when I'd get shelled with three home runs and a flood of hits. After the last out, I'd shower and head to my hotel room, broken in spirit. I'd toss and turn in bed, moaning, 'I'm no good! What am I doing here playing ball anyway?'

"I didn't feel like a man at all, so I'd masturbate to reestablish my manhood and reassert some control over my life. While I didn't make the connection between the stress and my sexuality back then, I sure can understand the stealth trap now."

I used my sexuality the same way during my early twenties, also without making that connection. That's why I carried the same habits into marriage and carried the same deep doubts about my manhood right into fatherhood and into my struggling career in sales. When masturbation became my go-to play in life's stresses, my manhood was stunted.

Mature men don't turn to self-medication in the big battles of life. They depend upon God and battle from their knees. When the storms come rolling in over their great adventures and battlefields, they set their jaws and stand with God to defend themselves, their girlfriends, their wives, and their families. They turn away from orgasmic drugs and place their trust in God. They make a stand—like men.

I was an immature man. I *tried* sorting out my manhood in the arena of my sexuality by paging through porn magazines and letting my eyes roam over curvaceous women, but that approach worked out miserably for me, as it always does. The reason was elementary: there was no big battle to fight and win in the sexual arena. There was no great adventure to live and no rescue to mount.

Our masculinity simply can't be established in the sexual company of women, no matter what our culture tells us. It will only languish in its development while a stubborn, awkward orgasmic drug dependency is sown in its place.

I didn't know any of this stuff in high school. I bought into the whole scam, just like the rest of the guys in the locker room. From everything I'd seen and heard, I was positive that going to bed with a girl was my ticket into manhood. Turns out I couldn't have been more wrong in my beliefs, and my masculinity languished in the wake of that counterfeit ride. Here's what happened:

Late in my senior year, my divorced father was away from his "bachelor pad" for the weekend, but I had the spare key. As I unlocked the door that evening and gently welcomed my cuddly girlfriend inside, I thought I stood at the threshold of manhood. But did I?

As I mentioned earlier, John Eldredge described what lies at the core of our manhood, yearning to be awakened. God places in the heart of every man a desperate desire for a battle to fight, an adventure to live, and a beauty to rescue. These three desires form the crucible through which our manhood is refined, so let's use them as a filter to sift through my momentous evening and discover whether or not my ticket into manhood—losing my virginity—was a genuine one or a counterfeit.

Were any of these three desires awakened in the guest bedroom of my dad's bachelor pad that night? Did my girlfriend's willingness "call the heart of a man" out of this boy? Let's look at these questions together.

There was certainly no big battle to fight that evening. There was nothing to challenge me as a man or stoke the fires of my male heart. Okay, so I vigorously fought down my guilt and insecurity long enough for us to send our sexual engines screaming past the red line and vaporize our moral brakes in the passion and heat of the moment. But once there, we slid together as easy as pie. No battle, no challenge. Nothing there to develop my masculine heart.

There was certainly no great adventure to live out that night either. Diving recklessly between a set of silky sheets delivered nothing of the sort. Sure, I experienced wonderful new feelings, but even those thrills soon waned. Our relationship was quickly reduced to sneaking out as often as possible to look for a place to be alone and have sex. There was no adventure of any consequence in that, let me tell you. We soon tired of each other, and I moved on to the next girl.

But here's the thing. My commitment to sports and a D-1 athletic scholarship dwindled during those months. My vision and dreams for my future faded, and the great adventures that I *had* been living languished in neglect. It turned out that sex *wasn't* my ticket into manhood. As I look back now, doing the deed seemed to make me less of a man and cost me dearly. The only heart called out of me that first evening was a selfish and lazy one.

I fared no better with Eldredge's third mark of manhood. I wasn't protecting the beauty in my life that night in bed. Instead, I formed a sexual bond with my girlfriend that would eventually inflict great pain and grief on her when we parted ways, leaving her far worse off for having known me. That wasn't manly at all, by any definition.

Had anything but sperm been called out of me that evening? I'd have to say no. When the sun broke over the horizon the next dawn, the truth was as clear as it had ever been: I was no more a man that morning than I'd been the day before. That shouldn't surprise anyone because all of it was just so goofy on its face from the outset.

I had bought into what the popular culture promised: that if I magically waved my fleshly penile wand over and inside my starry-eyed virginal princess, I would make her a woman, and I'd become a man.

Umm . . . that didn't happen. Sex didn't make me a man that evening, and it won't make you a man either. There's nothing in premarital sexual intercourse that can stoke Eldredge's three passions at the core of your male heart.

What's more, nothing in your emerging sexuality can deliver anything more to you than an emotional dependency upon the chemistry behind porn and orgasm. When I look back on my years between puberty and the wedding altar, it's clear how naturally that dependency unfolded. Perhaps you'll recognize similar parallels in your past.

It's through the steady stream of life's zigs and zags and jumps and lumps that masturbation becomes your go-to defense when the chips are down. You discover that masturbation delivers a soothing, false sense of intimacy and manhood, and those rushing orgasmic highs become your drug of choice to medicate your pain, your doubts, and your fears—often before you even understand what's happening. That's what ties the chemistry of lust and orgasm to the *nonsexual* aspects of life. That's what creates the stealth trap, where the roots of your sexual sin become nonsexual, and that's why your go-to play follows you right into marriage.

None of this is conscious. When I felt a tug toward porn and a desire for masturbation, I always just passed it off as a harmless way to relieve the physical pressure of my overheated sex drive. But masturbation's orgasm is *not* just a harmless release of sexual pressure. Over time, these orgasms create an emotional and drug dependency that stunts a man's developing manhood. The urge to masturbate often has little to do with the release of *sexual* pressure and has everything to do with the release of *nonsexual* pressure since it's meant to medicate your pain, stress, and wounds.

This became clear to me when I was finally married. Since I had a wonderful and regular sex life with Brenda, I didn't even have any build-up of sexual pressure, but get this: I still ran to masturbation any time life's pressures got too high.

Sexual pressure, my eye! The real culprit was that I still had questions about my manhood and whether I had what it took to stand and succeed in the world of men. I was medicating my emotional pain from life's pressures in my young marriage, just as I had been doing with my emotional pain and life's stresses since puberty.

You'll never find answers in porn, masturbation, and orgasm. You'll find them only in the battle to become a man of purity and a man of destiny, a man of His kingdom.

John Eldredge said in *Wild at Heart*, "God made the masculine heart, set it within every man, and thereby offers him the invitation: *Come, and live out what I meant you to be!*"

I believe God is calling you to engage the battle and live out what He has always meant you to be. Doesn't that call grip your male heart? I believe it should.

When I finally chose to get up and live out what I was meant to be in that battle, I found out that I *did* have what it takes, to my surprise. I *could* come through when it mattered most.

And you know what? I never saw every man's battle as a fight *only* for sexual purity. I always literally saw it as a fight for my manhood. And check this out: I found my manhood in that fight.

Think about what I'm saying here. When the going gets tough, and you sit down in front of your computer screen with a bottle of lotion—like I used to do in my office late at night—that's not living out what He meant you to be. God meant for you to step to His side and grow as a man as you fight the big battles and live the great adventures with Him, not to grab yourself down there for a bit of medication and relief. This big battle for sexual purity is intended to develop you as a ferocious warrior and a real man in God's kingdom.

Real men train diligently to stand their ground in the grace and power of God in times of stress, in complete dependence upon Him. Real men turn to God for strength when their wounds are bleeding. Real men turn to God in prayer. Real men turn to face their enemies head-on, in God.

Real men don't turn to chemical relief. They know when they're chasing porn and masturbation that they're no longer fighting big battles or living great adventures. They're merely training their hands for masturbation and their fingers for cyberporn's keyboard, stunting their growth as men.

I dumped the medication and began living a great adventure called sexual purity. Satan learned who I was during that battle—he learned that I am Christ's man. As a result, I don't fear the devil anymore. I learned how stress and sexual temptations were connected, which allowed me to deal with them immediately for exactly what they were.

Can you admit your orgasmic drug dependency? Can you see how it stops you short of the mark of manhood? Until your sexuality is put into its proper place in your life, your hopes for manhood will remain swirling in a death spiral. Instead of becoming more of a man, you'll become more and more like a little boy, unable to grow up and grow out of your fascination with sex and porn.

In exchange, you'll lose the ability to lead and be your wife's hero. As a husband, you'll be so caught up in lustful deeds that you can't become an effective leader. Your home—and your wife's heart—will be filled with frustration, fear, and insecurity.

But it doesn't have to be that way. Your manhood can be refined in this battle, and your heart can be proven so that your beautiful damsel can learn to count on you to defend her in all the ways it matters most.

We can exhibit how that looks in marriage by sharing an excerpt from a book we wrote called *Every Heart Restored*. These paragraphs will teach you how a woman feels when she knows that her husband's battle is over, leaving her confident that he will *always* come through for her in the clutch. Here's Brenda in her own words:

> Fred loves me for me and is very satisfied with who I am and what I've become. Knowing that I'm married to a man who keeps his eyes to himself gives me incredible security. Even after four babies and nearly forty years of aging together, I live unthreatened by any woman around me.
>
> When my husband prays, I'm confident that nothing hinders his connection with God. If I knew of dark hidden areas, I'd have no faith that his prayers would even rise to the ceiling, but I've seen how a pure man's prayer packs a spiritual punch.
>
> My confidence in Fred's spiritual protection is unbounded. Christianity is not a game to him, and image means nothing. He'd rather *be* a Christian than seem like one. I never wonder if there are open cracks in our spiritual defenses where the enemy can slip through into our lives.
>
> Fred has every right to make the decisions for our family because it's God's plan, but even if it weren't, he's earned that right through his actions. He's proven in battle that his commitment to the Lord and his love for his family are the highest priorities in his life, and we simply rest in his strength.
>
> This normal, godly pattern leaves everyone flourishing, and this wouldn't be possible if blatant sexual sin were clogging things up. I know who he is, and I know where he will not go in the secret places of life.

You can make your wife feel the same way about you.

Perhaps you're still hacking your way through adult life with adolescent-like behavior and a stunted manhood, where orgasmic relief has become a welcome and regular crutch in your wounded life. If so, things don't have to stay that way for you.

Your battle can be over. God's grace makes all things possible. You can toss your crutch away, just like I did. To do so, you'll have to make some changes in how you approach stress and how you tend to your wounds.

In the next chapter, I'll start teaching you how to do that, beginning with constructing a soul in accordance with the new life God has put within you.

5

Pushing Past the Threshold

Many of us prefer to stay at the threshold of the Christian life,
instead of going on to construct a soul in accordance with the new
life God has put within us. We fail because we are ignorant of the way
God has made us, and we blame things on the devil that are actually
the result of our own undisciplined natures.
—Oswald Chambers, *My Utmost for His Highest,* May 20 devotional

I hate to break the news to you, but if you read the first four chapters closely, then you're no longer ignorant of the way you're made. You can no longer chalk up your actions and habits to the devil or some uncontrollable desire in you.

You've certainly seen how you're made by now. Your body is naturally set up to fall into addiction if you're careless with your eyes and mind (vulnerability #1), or you don't acknowledge how your stress and wounds can drive your sexual sin (vulnerability #2). This explains why your battle isn't over yet.

If you are to defend yourself from these two vulnerabilities in your sexuality, you must go beyond "the threshold of the Christian life" and "construct a soul in accordance with the new life God has put within us," to use Oswald's words. Will you do that?

I hope you've been doing some serious introspection as you've been reading, pondering questions like these:

- What unresolved stresses and wounds have been chasing you down through the years? Has there been a stealth connection between these and your sin habits?
- Did your father provide you a genuine ticket into manhood, or did

his disengagement force you down a counterfeit path? Have you been seeking your manhood through your sexuality?

If you *have* been musing over these questions as you've been reading along, you've discovered the stealth connection between your masturbation and your stress and wounds, perhaps for the first time. While it may surprise you to hear it, that discovery is all that some of you will need to put your battle to rest for good.

That's how it happened for me. You see, all I needed was to know that a second vulnerability existed. I already had everything else in place necessary for a quick victory. In the words of Oswald Chambers, I'd already pushed past the threshold of the Christian life to construct a soul in accordance with the new life. Or, said another way, I had already done the necessary spadework to establish a soul that could support a sexually pure life.

Let me explain. My sexual sin seemed confusing and intractable, lingering on and on. But despite that, I'd already been hard at work constructing my soul, pushing hard to apply God's principles to develop my business and my home, where Brenda and my kids were blossoming beautifully.

I'd successfully tackled my roving eye issues a few years before. I had just completed my fifth year in a row of reading the entire Bible in a year. I'd begun developing a vibrant worship connection and a profound personal intimacy with Christ and my heavenly Father each morning. I'd intentionally developed friendships and relationships at church that challenged me to greater heights. In short, my soul was ready to support a sexually pure life. All I needed was for the Spirit to reveal that my sexual sin was *nonsexual* at its core. I was ready to make a stand.

So, let me ask you this:

- What is the current state of your soul, not by the world's standards, but by the standard of God's Word? Have you pushed past the threshold?
- Have you been seeking God with all your heart, soul, mind, and strength?
- What evidence can you provide that you're seeking God like this, the kind of evidence I provided about myself in the previous paragraph?

Given the state of the Christian church today, it wouldn't surprise me if many of you haven't yet done the necessary spadework to establish a soul that can support a sexually pure life. If that's the case, then it's time for you to do the work necessary to construct a soul in accordance with the new life God has put within you.

I'm here to help. That's why I'm dedicating the next three chapters of *Battle On, Battle Over* to help you build the infrastructure you need to experience complete victory. It's time to step up and punch your ticket into full manhood and come through for your family. That's what real men do—fight to win and experience unconditional victory.

When I joined the Lord on the front lines, I wasn't a spectator, and you can't be either. I needed to attend to Chambers's two issues if I expected to win this battle for good. In other words, I had to:

1. Learn how I was made.
2. Go forward and cross that threshold into the Christian life by constructing a soul that lined up sexually with the new life that God had placed in me at the moment of salvation.

Now, that doesn't mean you are doing this on your own. Far from it. God's work and your work are never separate once He's living inside you. Never forget that.

Think about how one of the fruits of the Spirit is *self*-control. That fruit is undoubtedly *of the Spirit*, but the word "self" tells you something about your role too. I'm talking about a joint destiny, where God's work and your work are inseparable. God won the victory at Calvary to deliver grace into your life, but in a very real sense, His grace merely gives you the *freedom* to run with God. You must still *choose* to run in the spiritual maturity that He expects of a son. You must still choose to construct a godly soul.

Here is another way to look at it. Every Christian child—everyone "born again"—has his Father's DNA. That comes from God. But only the *mature* child has his Father's character. That comes from you yearning and learning to think and act like Him. This is what Christianity is all about, and I never would have developed His character had I not personally chosen to push past the threshold of the Christian life.

You needn't wait for some cloud of holiness to form around you before moving to engage in the battle. You'll be holy when you choose not to sin. Even though you're already free from the power of sexual immorality, you won't be free from the *habits* of sexual immorality until you choose to be—until you say, "That's enough! I'm choosing to live purely!"

So get after it. You have a job to do here, and Scripture couldn't be more straightforward about this. Consider these verses that highlight your responsibility in the fight for freedom, with my own emphasis in italics:

> In the same way, count yourselves dead to sin but alive to God in Christ Jesus. Therefore *do not let sin reign* in your mortal body so that you obey its evil desires. *Do not offer any part of yourself to sin* as an instrument of wickedness . . . (Romans 6:11–13a, NIV)

Who is the apostle Paul talking to in this passage? He's talking to *you*. Without question, it's your job to "do not let" and to "do not offer."

A few verses later, Paul writes this:

> Thank God! Once you were slaves of sin, but now you *wholeheartedly obey this teaching* we have given you. Now you are free from your slavery to sin, and you have become slaves to righteous living. (Romans 6:17–18, NLT)

You are the one who chooses to "wholeheartedly obey" out of your own integrity or not to do so. The choice is up to you:

> Just as you used to offer yourselves as slaves to impurity and to ever-increasing wickedness, *so now offer yourselves as slaves to righteousness* leading to holiness. (Romans 6:19b, NIV)

The apostle Paul is clearly exhorting you, personally, to offer up your body parts to God. The Lord provided you the freedom to make that choice through grace. You must still choose to offer them up though:

> Since everything will be destroyed in this way, what kind of people ought you to be? *You ought to live holy and godly lives* as you look forward to the day of God and speed its coming . . . So then, dear friends, since you are looking forward to this, *make every effort to be found spotless,* blameless and at peace with him. (2 Peter 3:11–12a, 14, NIV)

Spotlessness isn't only God's job. The apostle Peter charges *you* to make every effort. It's your duty and obligation. The apostle Paul backs up Peter's position in these next two verses:

> Therefore, since we have these promises, dear friends, *let us purify ourselves from everything that contaminates body and spirit,* perfecting holiness out of reverence for God. (2 Corinthians 7:1, NIV)

> The night is nearly over; the day is almost here. *So let us put aside the deeds of darkness* and put on the armor of light. (Romans 13:12, NIV)

I'll close with my favorite verse on this score:

> It is God's will that you should be sanctified: that *you should avoid sexual immorality;* that each of *you should learn to control your own body* in a way that is holy and honorable, not in passionate lust like the pagans, who do not know God . . . (1 Thessalonians 4:3–5, NIV)

It's certainly the Lord's will that you "avoid sexual immorality," right? But apparently, God's desire isn't enough here to get the job done. If it were, your battle would already be over. He'd have done it for you.

You are the one who must learn to control your body in an honorable way. It's plain that it must also be *your* will to avoid sexual immorality, or it won't get done. Will you choose to learn?

It's not like you aren't capable. After all, His divine power has already given you everything you need for godliness through your knowledge of Him and His very great and precious promises. Because of this, you may participate in the divine nature by *choosing* to escape the corruption in the world caused by your own evil desires (see 2 Peter 1:3–4). The Holy Spirit will continue to direct and empower you if you ask Him to do so.

Despite all that, you can *still* choose to allow the sinful nature to hold sway in your life, so which will it be? Paul says you must work to bring the sinful nature, and your flesh, to its knees:

> So then . . . continue to *work out your salvation* [that is, cultivate it, bring it to full effect, actively pursue spiritual maturity] with awe-inspired fear and trembling [using serious caution and critical self-evaluation to avoid anything that might offend God or discredit the name of Christ]. (Philippians 2:12, AMP)

Your responsibility is clear. It's time to run your race (see Hebrews 12:1) and come through for yourself and your family. It's time to build a godly soul that matches up with the new life inside you.

But, Fred, how do I build my soul? I'm not even sure I understand what my soul is!

That's a great question. Happily, we don't have to dive too deep into the weeds for an answer that serves our battlefield purposes.

So let's start here. You are made in God's image. Since He is a triune being (Father, Son, and Spirit), it shouldn't surprise you that you were created with three parts to your nature—spirit, soul, and body, as this Scripture explains:

> May God himself, the God of peace, sanctify you through and through. May your whole spirit, soul and body be kept blameless at the coming of our Lord Jesus Christ. (1 Thessalonians 5:23, NIV)

When it comes to the soul, all you need to understand, for our purposes, is how it works as the *interpretive interface* between your spirit and your body. You see, we humans are the only created beings that can function in both the spiritual and physical dimensions simultaneously. We are made for the two realms.

So, on the one hand, you live in a physical realm that groans beneath the curse of sin. On the other hand, your spirit lives and moves in the spiritual realm, praying, "thy kingdom come, thy will be done on earth as it is in heaven." You must take what you sense happening in the invisible realm and make it manifest *visibly* in you and your character here on earth. That's how you destroy the works of the enemy. That's your assignment. That's why you're here.

Your spirit cannot bring all of that directly to bear on the physical realm, so it needs your soul to be the interface between the two realms. The soul allows all the things you see and learn in the spirit realm to bear upon your character in your daily life and on earth.

The soul is the seat of self-consciousness and is comprised of three parts: your mind, your emotions, and your will. The soul's interface works something like this: your *spirit* receives from God, but what you receive in your spirit cannot be manifested directly on earth through your body because the two realms are separate. What you receive spiritually must come through the interface of your *mind* and your *emotions*. Then you must decide in your *will* to carry out this *spiritual* directive in your *body*, in the physical dimension.

Perhaps the following word picture will be a little more helpful to you, as it's always been for me. Think of your spiritual nature as your upper arm and think of your body as your lower arm, and then picture your soul as the elbow, which connects the upper and lower arms (body and spirit) as the interface.

The elbow (soul) determines how well your spirit and body work together. If the elbow is "broken" somehow, things won't go well, and your soul won't support a sexually pure life. Your broken elbow—that flawed soul—is what you must fix when you decide to move past the threshold of the Christian life and go on to construct a soul in accordance with the new life God has put within you.

Before salvation, of course, there was no upper arm—no spiritual nature. You were living it up in the world, and your spirit was dead. Your "elbow"— your mind, emotions, and will—only responded to your lower arm, where your bodily desires, like sex, food, and pleasure, live. Your soul was ruled and consumed by what your flesh wanted, and it naturally built patterns of thought and feelings to support those desires. That's all your soul knew, and that's all the input it received.

Then you got saved and believed that Jesus came onto this earth to die for your sins, that whoever believes in Him will not perish but have eternal life. Suddenly, there was life in your spirit, and there was a new higher realm—the upper arm—that your soul had to attend to as well.

Once you accept Christ as your Savior, as long as your soul keeps saying yes to the new life the Lord placed in you, sanctification continues. You move toward having the full mind of Christ with a mature character that matches your spiritual DNA as a Christ-follower. In your spirit, you're thinking, *Why would I ever want to say yes to the old life again? God has saved me from so much! Why would I say yes to my lower nature when my spirit is alive and equipped with every weapon necessary to win this battle?*

Well, here is your dilemma. While you are indeed born again with a living spirit, your soul hasn't yet given your spirit complete ascendency in your life. This is where you are supposed to be heading, but spiritual ascendency isn't automatic, and there's a good reason for that: your elbow is still listening to your lower arm.

While your *spirit* was saved instantly and cries relentlessly on behalf of God's truth, your *soul* is only saved through a process of renewing your emotions, your mind, and your will, a process that the apostle Paul calls "working out your salvation" and that Oswald Chambers calls "constructing a soul in accordance with the new life God has put within us."

You might also call it "healing your elbow."

Until you take responsibility and renew your soul, your spirit won't have complete ascendency in your life, your manhood won't fully develop, and you'll never have total victory over sexual sin. Without that renewal, your soul remains so used to taking orders from your body that you'll still find yourself saying no to the new life in you, even though that goes against your spiritual will and your mind's logic and is done despite your loving emotions toward God.

Too many of us stop at the false finish line of salvation and refuse to move on toward a manifest spiritual maturity. That's why your soul can remain a servant of your body and be ruled by your physical and emotional appetites. Instead of shrugging off its importance and mopping away the evidence of your immaturity with a loud appeal to salvation's "grace" and "forgiveness," a repentant appeal to Christ's power and a responsible move past the false finish line will move you toward obedience and maturity.

That's why I was masturbating and medicating the pain of my father wounds—I stopped at that false finish line and still believed that I didn't have what it takes to be a man. My body was used to dealing with the pain in this way, and I wasn't about to listen to my spirit's take on the issue. My mind and emotions hadn't yet been adequately renewed, so they impeded my ability to take on the big battles of my life like a man.

I was also masturbating and medicating due to my dire financial stress. My brain knew where to get the drug and yanked me in the direction of getting that balm. My mind and emotions hadn't yet fully been renewed, hampering my ability to fight this big battle and live out that great adventure of supporting my family like a man.

Perhaps your counterfeit ticket into manhood stopped you short at the threshold of the full Christian life, where your soul—your elbow—was broken, and you learned to turn to your lower arm for the medication of sexual sin instead of turning to the upper arm in prayer and dependence upon God. This stunted your growth into full manhood and full development of a mature Christian character.

You don't have to stay there. A well-constructed soul has a mind, will, and emotions that will no longer impede you in your big battles, disrupting your great adventures and flattening your ability to protect your beauty.

In the upcoming Part II, you'll be given practical steps to reshape the mind, the emotions, and the will as you embark on your great adventure—the battle for sexual purity.

PART II

Rebuilding Your Soul

6

The Emotions

Therefore, my dear friends, as you have always obeyed—not only
in my presence, but now much more in my absence—continue to
work out your salvation with fear and trembling, for it is God who
works in you to will and to act in order to fulfill his good purpose.
—Philippians 2:12–13, NIV

In your mind, I want you to picture the most muscled guy that you've
personally known. When I do this, I see my good buddy Chris, who built a
fabulous gym in his basement so he could work out any time he wanted with
everything he's got. He knows how to build out a body, and he loves his work
down there.

The apostle Paul valued physical training too, but he would have equipped
his basement for a different exercise. He preferred working out his soul:

> . . . rather, train yourself to be godly. For physical training is of some
> value, but godliness has value for all things, holding promise for both
> the present life and the life to come. (1 Timothy 4:7b–8, NIV)

Time for a pop quiz: Do you spend more time working out your body these
days or working out your salvation? Which do you cherish and appreciate more?

I don't know how you scored on that quiz, but I *do* know that if you've
been losing your battle for sexual purity, you'll need a robust build-out of your
soul to establish victory in your life. To make that happen, I want you to deal
with all three parts—your mind, your will, and your emotions—in this and the
following two chapters, starting with the emotions side.

I'm tackling the emotions first because I'm anxious to tell you about the most crucial action I ever took in my battle for purity—something that permanently changed the course of the war.

Now, I know that if you're a guy, you might prefer to ignore your emotions rather than wrestle with them, but you can't do that on this battlefield. If you do, you'll be mowed down like cannon fodder, and the reason should be crystal clear to you by now.

The entangling emotions of constant stress and deep-seated wounds are driving your chronic porn use and masturbation. This habitual sin naturally spawns painful feelings of isolation and shame. Over time, your desire to medicate all these draining emotions with the false intimacy of masturbation ramps up exponentially.

This spiral can only be broken by (1) healing your wounds and (2) eliminating your isolation and shame. I can help you, but I want to manage your expectations because I can only help you with the isolation and shame. I can't heal your wounds.

I couldn't even heal *my* wounds back in the day. Your wounds are God's responsibility, and He can help you through the work of the Holy Spirit and professional counselors He's called into the counseling ministry.

You *do* have a part to play here though. To heal, you must open your heart and emotions to the Holy Spirit *and* avail yourself of the help of professional counselors when needed. Men are often too prideful or blind to do this, but your wife or girlfriend will help you see where you need help if you'll listen. She's on your side.

I knew I needed Brenda's help back then. I simply didn't know what to do with the father wounds, financial stresses, and doubts about my manhood. Brenda didn't know that I was masturbating and medicating that pain behind the scenes. But to be honest, that practice was the least of my worries because my emotional mess wasn't just spilling over into the sexual arena and causing addiction. Rather, the emotional turmoil was boiling over into the visible places in my life, which Brenda spotted quickly.

For better or worse, a husband's wounds become his wife's wounds in marriage, and she can't miss the bruises and lacerations being laid across the relationship. Your wife will be no different because no one will know your wounds like she does. She likely knows your pain and your blind spots, and she probably understands the broader impacts they're having on the family better than you do. Make her your trusted friend and open your heart to her. Allow your wounds to be the vehicle to a deeper relationship with her. She's your helpmate and wants you to grow into all God meant you to be.

Brenda sure noticed my wounds because I'd been drowning her and our kids in my bad temper and disagreeable attitudes for quite some time. In my case, the buried pain was wrecking my home, causing us both to feel desperation, as you can see in this portion from *Every Man's Marriage:*

> When I reached age thirty-five, the lack of my father's acceptance suddenly rocked me deeply. This pain severely affected my relationship with my wife and kids, as I returned to my harsh ways [of treating them]. Brenda tried to explain away my behavior to the kids, but after a year, she became frustrated. One day she told me, "All right, then! Fine. Just tell us how long you plan to stay like this, so we can all prepare for it!" Then, she stormed out of the room.
>
> I sat there speechless for quite some time. How long was I going to stay like this? Ten years? Why ten? Why not five? If I could decide to change at the end of five years, why not after one? And if after one, why not . . . *today?*
>
> After her single stiletto question pointed into my heart, I knew it was time. Starting immediately, I found a counselor. Shortly after, I attended a Promise Keepers conference in Boulder, Colorado. That first night God spoke to me through the speaker and revealed an aspect of His love I'd never understood. Sitting that evening in the bleachers at the University of Colorado's Folsom Field, I felt the pain from my dad dispersing. I had acted decisively, and I was being healed.

If your wife hasn't asked you that same stiletto question, allow me the honor: *Dude, can you tell me how long you plan to stay like this so everyone can prepare for it? How long will you let your wounds from the past keep bruising your wife and kids? If you can change, why not do it in the present? Why not change today?*

Let's steady our eyes here and get straight to the bottom line: my wounds were never my fault. I bore no shame or responsibility for *being* wounded in my past.

At the same time, I knew I would bear great responsibility by *staying* wounded. People around me were counting on me. Real men don't allow decades-old pain to pound their wives and kids to smithereens. They admit they need help. They become transparent and deal with their emotions, even if they naturally hate such inner work. Real men come through when everything's on the line.

I came through for Brenda because I knew the stakes and did the one thing that most men are loathe to do: I booked an appointment with a local Christian counselor. His name was Gary Rosberg. Of all the family decisions I've ever made, this one easily lands in my top five.

Gary is brilliant, gifted, and strong. In the years since, he's become a trusted friend and a well-known Christian writer and speaker. At the time, though, he was just another counselor in the Des Moines area, and I was just another name slotted onto his daily docket.

Gary listened closely to my backstory and then applied logotherapy in our ongoing sessions, a technique based upon the seminal work of Viktor Frankl, the famed Nazi death camp survivor. This therapeutic approach crystallized the meaning of life and, even better, began shaping my identity in Christ. Gary also invited me to join that busload of guys heading west to a Promise Keepers event at the University of Colorado. It was at Folsom Field in Boulder where God met me and changed my life.

I owe Gary a lot. Like all counselors, Gary spent years of his life sacrificing and training to apply effective techniques to chaotic lives like mine, and I'm very grateful for his skills.

But, Fred, I went to a counselor once, and it was horrible.

Me too, but what of it? Some counselors are lousy despite their hard work and schooling, just like some auto mechanics don't know what they're doing despite years of training. Just move on and find another, as you would do with anything else. Counselors are no more perfect than you and I are, but their service to God is immeasurably valuable, and they deserve our deepest honor and respect. So if your wife has suggested you see a counselor, quit crossing your arms and pouting like an irascible toddler. Be bold. Step out and come through for her. Change your life.

In the end, perhaps the best thing Gary did for me was fundamentally alter my perception of my father and our relationship. You see, Dad was born the seventh of eight kids, and his dad ran out on his mom during the Great Depression. She was left to raise a large brood on her own with no job and little money. Overnight, Dad became fatherless and was scarred for life.

Upon hearing that story, Gary suggested that I'd been missing something.

"Fred, I don't believe that your father was *unwilling* to love you in the way you needed it. He was broken himself," he said. "I think he was *incapable* of loving you. He had no role model, and because of deep pain in his life, he couldn't figure out how to love you on his own either."

That thought had never occurred to me.

You see, I'd always assumed that my dad rejected me because I was somehow deficient and unworthy. I believed he chose not to love me because I wasn't worth it, which crushed me. But Gary's words were a revelation to me. In truth, Dad had chosen nothing. He was merely incapable of loving me.

Hearing Gary say this changed everything in my attitude. I could finally release the pain because I no longer held my dad accountable for the wounds that he inflicted on me or on our miserable relationship.

I can describe the impact of Gary's revelation in another way. Let's say I expect my son Michael to complete a twenty-foot pole vault, but he fails to arch gracefully over the bar. I can't get angry or hold him accountable for that flop. After all, Michael is six-foot-six and weighs three hundred pounds! He's incapable of such a leap. It would be illogical and absurd to be bitter over my dashed expectations of him and his vault.

In the same way, I naturally expected my father to love me because I was his son, but he failed—and for good reason. Yes, he botched things, but holding him accountable for the stripes he laid across my psyche would be ridiculous. Dad was broken. He was incapable of expressing a father's love. I could feel sorry for him, but I couldn't stay bitter.

This epiphany, along with my soul-changing experience at Promise Keepers, dissipated the power of these wounds. My bad temper and harsh attitudes disappeared with it.

Let's get back to where we began in this chapter. Just as I couldn't heal my own wounds by myself, I can't heal your wounds either. You were wounded, and that stinks. But you don't have to *stay* wounded. You can put yourself in the place of healing by admitting you need to change and by opening yourself up to God, your wife or girlfriend, and perhaps a counselor, just like I did. If you do, your cycle of sexual sin will break as those wounds heal.

Now, while I can't help much with your wounds, I *can* eliminate much of your isolation and shame if you take my suggestions. I *can* teach you to develop a deep, vibrant worship connection that brings a profound personal intimacy with Jesus Christ and your heavenly Father so that you'll never feel ashamed, lonely, or isolated again. This will dramatically tilt the battlefield in your favor.

Let me start by reviewing what I said about my battle for purity back in Chapter 1. When I got my eyes under control after about six weeks, I thought that ended my battle. It didn't. A portion of my sexual sin remained, and the reason became clear in time. Over the years, I had trained my brain to deal with financial stress and doubts about my manhood with the soothing orgasmic drug of masturbation without ever making the connection between the two.

Eventually, I did connect the dots between my emotional pain and my sexual sin. I saw that my "pull" toward sexual sin was not sexual at its root. It sure felt like I needed sexual release, but it was merely a need for drugs and medication.

No more drugs. Through prayer and submission to God's ways, I decided to face my stress and doubts like men of God do and turned to the Lord with my financial stress and doubts about my manhood.

The strategy worked. Very soon the battle was over. Not just 85 percent of the way or 95 percent of the way. It was over. All over.

I want your battle to be over too, but I never shared the most crucial part of my story in Chapter 1, so let me do that now. Before making that fateful connection between my emotions and my sexual sin, I made a seemingly unrelated move that eventually had more to do with my long-term victory than anything else I'd ever done.

Before I tell you about it, let's freeze-frame this moment: an author who has been free from sexual sin for over thirty years is about to tell you the most important action he ever took in his battle for purity. Obviously, you must give some serious weight to the words I'm about to share because I live on the other side of this war.

The crucial part of my story that I left unshared and that shifted the tide of my battle was my resolve to build a more vibrant one-on-one worship connection with Jesus Christ.

To explain how and why this happened, it's essential to understand how this rolled out in my life so that you can step up too. I'll start at the beginning when God initially stole my heart on a cool, dusky California evening at the midpoint of my twenty-third year. Far too many promiscuous days and nights had left me sick of myself and broken in my approach to nearly everything in life. One year out of Stanford University, I came bursting out of the blocks to chase Jesus Christ with all my heart. This was my prayer: *Lord, I'm ready to work with You if You're ready to work with me.*

We were a match made in heaven—Jesus had a lot to teach me, and I had a lot to learn. I sped joyously past the outer threshold of the Christian life and deep into its center. No sliding into a pew once a week on Sundays for me. Instead, I took on a focused daily study with some of the wisest Christian men of the day.

As an owner of a small business start-up, I was constantly running to meetings to scare up new business. As I was out and about, driving and waiting between appointments, I soaked up all the Christian teaching available to me at the time.

This happened back in the audiocassette days, so Audible books and Bibles hadn't been invented. YouTube didn't exist. There were no streaming podcasts or archived sermons.

But I *was* living in the golden age of Christian radio. Many of the greatest Christian teachers of the day were broadcasting biblical wisdom from dawn to dusk on Christian radio stations. In Des Moines, God penciled in some heavy hitters at the top of His lineup card, including Jon Courson, Charles Stanley, Chuck Swindoll, and Dr. James Dobson.

From my quiet corner of the dugout, I drank deeply of their wisdom and studied how the big leaguers played this game of life. The first three used their half-hour slots to broadcast portions of past sermons, while clean-up hitter James Dobson used his *Focus on the Family* broadcast to host insightful guests and authors, all exhorting me to excel as a husband and father. Of the four, Dr. Dobson became my wise and vocal father figure because I'd been essentially fatherless and had no example to emulate as I built my marriage and family.

The greatest single thing I ever learned in the dugout came from Chuck Swindoll however. It happened one morning during an unguarded moment at the end of his *Insight for Living* broadcast. His co-host teed up a simple question about Chuck's approach to prayer. My ears perked up because my prayer life had been in a slump. Still, little did I know that his next few words would usher in the most sweeping, boundless impact upon my soul that I would ever hear on the radio—or anywhere else, for that matter.

"I never, ever approach prayer without first singing to the Lord in worship," Chuck Swindoll began simply.

My brain was instantly scrambled. *What in the world? I thought worship only happens in church! He must be singing to God someplace else on his own, one on one.*

I'd never heard of such a thing and had no spiritual gridwork for this whatsoever. Then Chuck continued, "You see, I can't seem to find the throne room unless I first sing to Him."

All my paradigms of prayer lay ruptured on the ground.

What in the world does he mean by "finding the throne room"?

I hadn't the slightest clue. The only thing I knew for sure was that I'd never even *heard* of a throne room in relation to prayer. I was also fairly certain I'd never stepped into one.

I was at a complete loss, and my racing mind struggled to grasp what this one-on-one worship might look like in practice. Before Chuck could share any details, the clock had swung to the bottom of the hour, and the broadcast was summarily ended. I'd been left hanging, twisting in the breeze with my fragmented thoughts.

Even so, a deep peace settled over my heart. While the broadcast had ended too soon, I'd heard enough to know intuitively that worshiping God during my morning devotional time would remove my prayer life from life support. I also knew, unequivocally, that I didn't have to be a famous preacher broadcasting across two thousand radio stations to find my place in the throne room.

Chuck Swindoll is a great man, but he's only a man, I mused. I never doubted these two certainties for a nanosecond, probably due to the work of the Holy Spirit.

So, with an inspired heart, I plotted a new course for my prayer time as dawn broke over central Iowa the following day. There I stood in my basement with a boombox in one hand and a couple of audiocassette tapes in the other, planning to sing three or four love songs to Jesus before heading into prayer. Slipping a favorite tape into the slot, I pressed play and turned my face upward to sing. With my eyes closed and my palms facing up, I baby-stepped my way across the carpet from one end of the room to the other, worshiping the Lord out loud, searching for His heart.

Before long, though, I stopped in my tracks, dismayed. Things weren't good.

I felt *so* weird and thoroughly self-conscious, terrified that my kids would sneak down the stairs, giggling and snorting. "Look at Daddy sing! What is he *doing*?"

At the far end of the room, my eyes routinely popped open, spooked that a neighbor might spy me through the window and sputter, "What's that crazy loon up to *this* time?"

After a few more mornings of traipsing across the basement carpet, the most unnerving thoughts about me had become my own. Here I was, the former Athlete of the Year and class valedictorian, the ex-quarterback with the chiseled frame and linebacker's heart, crooning passionate love songs to the drop ceiling as I minced my way from one end of the basement to the other.

For the first ten days or so, I couldn't escape the sense that I'd become nothing but a farcical, romantic buffoon rather than the ripped, stable, feet-on-the-ground intellectual I'd always seen myself to be. What's more, I'd seen no trace of a throne room, so there was no spark of new life in my prayers.

But for some reason, I refused to quit. Like a mindless battering ram, I kept pounding away on those walls of self-consciousness, with these words incessantly echoing through my mind: *God likes it when Chuck Swindoll worships Him, so He must like it when I worship Him. It doesn't matter how it feels. I will keep doing what is right.*

These were mythic days for me and rugged in a curious sort of way. Even though nothing was working, I kept going. Typically, I would have changed course and tried something else since I had no clue how to find His throne room or whether this oddness would ever fade away. Since Chuck Swindoll never told me and the Holy Spirit wasn't talking, I pushed on.

With each passing day, I grew hungrier and hungrier to find that throne room, whatever that might mean. Soon, and without warning, that oddness faded sometime near the end of the second week. That was encouraging! Those dissonant, self-conscious feelings were now in remission, so I threw my entire heart, mind, soul, and strength into the process.

At the end of the fourth week, it happened.

It was as if the Lord Himself entered the room. Believe me, I was utterly overwhelmed by His presence. I sensed I was sitting on my heavenly Father's lap, like a beloved son. I *knew* I belonged there. I felt His calm affection as His love poured through me. I snuggled back into His chest in total peace and harmony. Soon it was over, ending just as quickly as it began.

But in another sense, it wasn't over and never would be again. Everything changed in my relationship with God that morning for keeps. Ever since that glorious day, I find that throne room connection whenever I sing love songs to the Lord out loud before prayer.

Now let me be clear. I don't sense that I'm in His lap and laying my head against His chest every time I go to prayer these days, and I don't think I've ever sensed Him enter my prayer room again in that same intense and manifest way. But I seem to have paved a permanent pathway into the throne room that has universally transformed my relationship with the Lord.

You can do this too. If you make the same effort, I believe your battle for purity will get much easier. However, there are some critical details that you must keep in mind as you begin to build this worship connection, or you may torpedo your efforts.

First, your song choices are crucial. You might guess that quieter songs are more effective because they naturally feel more intimate, and you would be right. But the most important criterion is that all your songs employ the second-person pronoun "you."

Many of the songs that we sing in church use third-person pronouns like "we" and "our" and "he" and "his." There is nothing wrong with these songs. Many of them sweep my soul away in joy and exhilaration, but the truth is, when we sing those songs, we aren't singing *to* God. We are singing *about* God and singing *to* each other.

In my morning worship, I'm there for only one thing: to tell my Lord that I love Him. I want to touch God's heart as He has touched mine. Only one kind of song will do—love songs that I can sing straight to Jesus from the deepest, most passionate corners of my heart. Songs that address Him directly, either by name or by the second-person pronoun "you." Songs that attest to His beauty and character with lyrics like, "You are altogether lovely," "You are everything I need," and "I am Yours, and You are mine."

If you expect to build an intimate connection with the Lord, singing second-person love songs is a must. It's been my experience, though, that some men have a tough time grasping the concept of second-person love songs and have trouble picking out "songs of pursuit and passion" for their worship times. If you're one of these guys, let me help you with a list of thirty songs I've used myself, followed by the artist. Once you listen to them, you'll get the hang of what I'm saying:

1. "My Heart, Your Home," Watermark
2. "Captivate Us," Watermark
3. "The Purest Place," Watermark
4. "Lord, You Have My Heart," Lenny LeBlanc
5. "Jesus, Draw Me Close," Lenny LeBlanc
6. "There Is None Like You," Lenny LeBlanc
7. "Draw Me Nearer," Meredith Andrews
8. "Spirit of the Living God," Meredith Andrews
9. "In Your Arms," Meredith Andrews
10. "Beautiful," Gateway Worship

11. "Pure," Gateway Worship
12. "When I Speak Your Name," Gateway Worship
13. "You Are for Me," Kari Jobe
14. "Sweep Me Away," Kari Jobe
15. "What Love Is This," Kari Jobe
16. "Magnificent," Matt Redman
17. "Majesty of the Most High," Matt Redman
18. "Unbroken Praise," Matt Redman
19. "Sweet Jesus," Selah and Jill Phillips
20. "Oh, Draw Me, Lord," Selah
21. "You Are My Hiding Place," Selah
22. "Ever So Gently," Brian Doerksen
23. "Eternity," Brian Doerksen
24. "Faithful God," Laura Story
25. "There Is Nothing," Laura Story
26. "You Satisfy My Soul," Laura Hackett Park
27. "Wonderful," Christy Nockels
28. "First Love," Chris Tomlin
29. "I Belong," Kathryn Scott and Integrity's Hosanna! Music
30. "Take What I Have," Peder Eide

As I finalized this list, I was reminded of a common mistake that men often make in building a deep, intimate connection with the Lord. To illustrate, I recently gave a similar list of songs to Justin, whose wife was divorcing him. I knew he needed the genuine intimacy that a daily worship connection with the Lord would bring into his life at a painful, lonely time.

A month later, I asked him how it was going with the songs. "I took them and made a playlist on my smartphone," he replied. "I listen to them a lot. They're nice."

Ugh. That is *not* what I told him to do. The idea was to sing these songs *to* the Lord as a way to worship Him, not be a bystander who listened to the songs.

Still, you would be surprised how often guys think that just listening to a worship playlist gives them an intimate connection with the Lord. I'm afraid it doesn't. Sure, it might boost your emotions as you go through your day, and it's certainly healthier for your soul than binging on hip-hop songs filled with vulgar language. But those results aren't your goal.

"Listening" and "worshiping" are entirely different things. Listening is passive. Worshiping requires your full engagement. You need to find that place where you've forgotten everything else in your life and you're totally immersed in the present moment with Christ, heart to heart. That's your goal.

This brings me to another critical truth I've learned in my basement: I can't really do one-on-one worship in silence and expect to find the throne room. I've found that I'm not fully engaged if I'm not singing out loud. Let me explain.

Like most of us, there are times when I go to bed late and get up early. Because I'm tired, I sometimes lie down on the floor to worship rather than pace the floor. There is nothing wrong with lying down, but if I let myself slip into a listening mode in my sleepy stupor, I can't reach the Lord's heart in the way I want to. The worshipful lyrics aren't enough because listening isn't worshiping. Worship requires expression, and that means singing out loud.

There's one last obstacle to getting it right in your worship place. Don't focus on how long it's taking to find the throne room and what it might mean about God's love for you. Yes, I pressed in every day for four weeks before the Lord responded. But four weeks is by no means a magic number.

For instance, when I shared this story with my pastor, he responded that he had once done the same thing when he was young, single, and lonely for connection. He told me it took six weeks for God to respond to him. I can assure you that dwelling on how long it's taking matters little, and it only plays with your head and your faith.

My daughter Laura had an even longer process. She had just been accepted for a dual-degree position in graduate school, and while she was beyond excited to be chasing her dream, she also knew that Raleigh, North Carolina, was a long way from Des Moines, Iowa. Everything she held dear would be a two-day drive away.

Once she settled into her apartment in Raleigh and took on her first year of veterinary medicine, the days could be long and lonely. I told Laura that in lonesome times like these, building a one-on-one worship time with the Lord and having a much deeper intimacy with Him would help her overcome the feeling of isolation. I told her my story and that of our pastor, and she was ready to go. She dug right in.

Laura wasn't too concerned when she passed the four-week mark without making that deeper connection with the Lord. She knew it had taken six weeks for our pastor to find it. She was a bit unsettled when she passed the six-week mark, though, but she figured there were natural variances to these things.

After eight weeks, Laura began to get really concerned. Phrases like "What's wrong with me?" and "Why isn't God listening?" peppered our conversations.

After ten weeks, tears of frustration began to flow freely and often. By twelve weeks, sheer panic had set in.

"I must mean nothing to Him! Am I even saved?" she cried out.

My heart hurt from hearing her share her pain, but what could I do? I couldn't respond for Him. I urged her to carry on.

At the fourteen-week mark, Laura was worshiping one more morning when her emotions cracked. She collapsed onto the carpet in the middle of her living room, wrenching and rolling in broken sobs.

"God, where are You? I need You so much!" She sobbed and sobbed and sobbed until suddenly she sensed the Lord say this clearly and distinctly: *Psalm 45.*

Laura grabbed her Bible and began reading verse one, but nothing clicked. She kept reading. When she reached verses 10 and 11, she lost it completely:

> Listen, O daughter,
> Consider and incline your ear;
> Forget your own people also, and your father's house;
> So the King will greatly desire your beauty;
> Because He *is* your Lord, worship Him.
> (Psalm 45:10–11, NKJV)

Look at that!

He addressed her directly as His daughter, and then He asked her to forget what she'd left behind in Des Moines and focus on Him. The Lord said He was enthralled with her beauty and longed for her continued worship.

It was a dreadfully long fourteen weeks, but Laura has never been the same, and her connection with her Lord was established for good.

Why did it take so long for my daughter? I don't know. One thing I *do* know is that it doesn't matter how long it takes.

Remember, the time it takes to find that intimate place with the Lord does not define your worth. Only Jesus defines your worth, and He says you're priceless. He wants intimacy together as much as you do. The best you can do is to soften your heart and turn toward the love of your life in relentless pursuit.

Forget about the time it's taking. Instead, pump up your daily consistency and fan the passionate desperation of your pursuit. In other words, worry only about the things you can control, down to the kind of songs you choose and the discipline to sing them out loud. That'll be enough.

So that's my story. Beginning one-on-one worship was the seemingly unrelated decision that eventually ended my purity battle.

Now let's turn our attention back to the isolation and shame caused by your sexual sin. Hopefully, you can see how I built up my soul through one-on-one worship, which became a rich source of interpersonal connection that eventually eliminated my sense of isolation and shame.

Don't fall for the flimsy excuses that the deceiver will whisper in your ear:

- *A man like you can't worship one on one. It's too gushy and emotional.*
- *Jesus may have met Fred like this, but He will never meet you this way.*
- *If it's so important to Jesus to have intimacy with you, why hasn't He made the first move?*

Sigh.

Dump the flimsy excuses. Risk doing Christianity right. Take the practical steps to abide in His love. Live in that place where you desire alone time with God. Consider how I framed this discussion in my book *Tactics*:

> The Bible calls the church the bride of Christ, comparing His passion for us to a husband's devotion for his wife. But when I try to come up with the language to explain the intimacy I feel during my personal worship times with the Lord, I cannot. The words that come closest are "romance," "fascination," and "intoxication."
>
> Nothing I've ever experienced beats the electricity of these moments with the Lord—the captivating touch, the deep passion, and the emotional tears you might expect in a love relationship, but without any of the sensuality or self-focus that's part of relationships with girls. It is all about Him and His overwhelming beauty. Your heart becomes one with His in those moments, and nothing else matters but Him.

Jesus wants this with you.

And in terms of your battle for purity, fervent intimacy with Christ is so vital in claiming long-term victory over sexual sin that it would be difficult to overstate it.

Distilled down, it's a simple equation. Porn use and masturbation are more of an intimacy issue than a sexual one, used to medicate pain and disconnection in your life. Abiding in Christ's love spawns a companionship that naturally eliminates the disconnection driving your sin, so seek His face and experience His love and tight friendship. In short, seek Him and you'll find Him. Build out intimacy with Him and abide in His love. As you do, you'll stand stronger against sin.

Sure, you must still bounce your eyes away from the sensuality around you. You must still take every lustful thought captive, just as the Lord commands. There simply is no substitute for these disciplines. You won't get free without them, so if you haven't established these good habits, I urge you to do so.

But I still say that one-on-one worship is the most powerful weapon on purity's battlefield. One-on-one worship locks down a genuine intimacy with

God that eliminates isolation and replaces your yearning for the false kind you can conjure up with masturbation.

Worshiping the Creator also eliminates your shame. At its root, shame is an identity issue. Shame is not about what you've done but about who you are and how you see yourself. Shame is a negative identity, a residual humiliation from your past, either at the hands of your dad or someone else. It's a belief that you are damaged goods and that you'll never fit into the world of men. In your mind, shame makes you small.

Satan's master plan is to use your shame to freshen your wounds and to keep them from healing. He wants you to believe God's condemning you, but He's not. The Lord loves you and has taken your shame and rejection away. Condemnation should have no part of your life, and it won't if you abide in His love.

Look, I don't know where your soul needs rebuilding. If you've had a clinical personality disorder diagnosis and need extra professional help, that's fine. Get professional help.

What I *do* know is that most guys could dump their shame quickly by moving in closer to their Father and by abiding in Christ's love each morning. But they aren't doing it, at least in what I've seen with many guys.

Let's say I asked my readers, "Does God desire your worship?"

One hundred percent would respond, "Absolutely, without a doubt."

Then let's say I followed by asking, "Are you worshiping the Lord every morning, just you and Him, one on one?"

Most would reply, "No, I'm not."

This is doing Christianity wrong. The Bible defines what's normal and true:

> When You said, "Seek My face,"
> My heart said to You, "Your face, LORD, I will seek."
> (Psalm 27:8, NKJV)

> Awake, my glory!
> Awake, lute and harp!
> I will awaken the dawn.
> (Psalm 57:8, NKJV)

This kind of normal living leads to a healthy identity and the death of shame. When you're in His presence, it's impossible to feel like damaged goods. He accepts you. You feel it every morning.

Once your identity is settled, condemnation and shame vanish. You can't deal with your shame without abiding in the love of God. One-on-one worship taught me that I'm His boy, and nothing can change that, not even my sin.

In time, God tuned my ear to His frequency, and I tuned out my dad. This was a precious gift to me. My earthly father disdained me as a dumbshit. My heavenly Father revels in my company and looks forward to meeting me every day.

As a boy and a young man, I was desperate for my dad's love and acceptance, but he couldn't give it. My dad also failed to initiate me into manhood. He didn't know how. But that's okay now. I've changed dads.

Gratefully, I had a second Father, a heavenly one, who *did* establish my manhood. In fact, He now counts on it and calls me deeper and higher because He knows how well I fit in the world of men.

This same second Father will establish your manhood too. As you get closer to Him each morning, you'll soon have the power to grasp how wide and long and high and deep the love of Christ is.

And when that happens, you'll experience a love that passes all understanding, a love that fills you to the brim with the fullness of God.

7

Rebuilding Your Will

As someone who's liked working out in the gym since my high school football days, I'm always amazed when guys stomp around and bellow like gorillas before settling in under a bar to attempt a personal best in the power squat. What happens during the lift is all about adrenaline and "psyching up" the will to succeed.

I've played the ape a few times in the weight room. Works occasionally. But I'm not here to teach you a grander way to grit your teeth or jut your jaw in the face of sexual temptation. You won't find rest from your enemies by ramping up that kind of "will." You must intensify your "willingness" instead, which is something else entirely. I'll clarify the difference between these two with a quick story.

I rarely counsel men who live at a distance geographically, which is why Trey recently traveled from central Nebraska to Des Moines to meet with me. Because of his long-term sexual sin, his wife was suffering severely.

We settled into our seats at Cosi Cucina, a favorite Italian restaurant of mine. Trey quickly opened the conversation.

"I've always struggled with containing my natural sexuality," he began. "It seems unfair for God to ask me to do that since He made me this way. It also seems unfair that my wife asks me to do that. After all, I am who I am."

If Trey had been struggling with a weak "will to win," all he would have needed from me was an intense, shrieking rant to get his head back into the game and gin up his passion for playing and conquering.

But Trey's use of the word "unfair" twice revealed a different story. Trey wasn't struggling with his will to win his purity battle. He was struggling with his "willingness" to accept the pain and loss that come with obedience. For him, the cost was too high.

I understood why: obedience and suffering travel together by definition. You can't obey without suffering personal loss. Perhaps you've never thought of it like this before, but if you want to win your purity battle, you'll have to submit your will beneath God's and give up your rights and freedom to choose as an individual. That hurts, and you may feel diminished to a degree, but that's how God set it up as His required maturing process in His kingdom. I call this pain and suffering, spawned by your obedience, *developmental suffering.*

Essentially, Trey struggled with his willingness to embrace the pain and suffering that come from obedience. He knew that submitting his will to his Father's will guaranteed a deep loss to him sexually. He was unwilling to accept that loss as right or fair.

The willingness to accept developmental suffering is not only central to any proper soul, but it's also a core element of genuine manhood. When you obey in the face of that pain, you grow and move from having God's DNA as His child to having God's full character.

The pain of submitting your will to the Father's will is critical to Christian growth and sanctification. It has been part of God's plan for His children since the dawn of time, even within the perfection of Eden. You can't grow into your potential as His child without building a complete willingness to embrace that pain because unless you do, you can't effectively resist temptation.

Wait a minute. Can you clarify that, Fred? How is my willingness to embrace pain tied to resisting temptation? I honestly don't see the connection between the two.

Perhaps you're over-mystifying or over-spiritualizing temptation. You may think of temptation as a full-frontal assault upon your spiritual gates by a horde of ax-wielding demons riding black chargers, but that picture is a vast over-exaggeration of the actual X's and O's in our enemy's temptation playbook.

The truth is relatively mundane. For the most part, temptation is simply an offer of a flight from pain, nothing more. I've found from experience that if you start to look at temptation in this manner, your battles with temptation will finally make more sense to you. Consider this simple draw play that Satan will run at your defenses hundreds of times until you prove you can stop it:

1. Satan spots pain in your life.
2. He offers you an inviting yet immoral shortcut around God's ways to escape it.

The pain relief is the lure. That's the draw, and that's all he needs. No demon hordes need apply.

Obedience and suffering are two sides of the same coin. If you've embraced the suffering side of obedience, the enemy has nothing enticing to offer you. There is no draw, so it's a broken play. But if you *are* aching for a shortcut, you'll be offered one, sure as day. The enemy will hang around your ear, hissing his whispered promises that he'll ease your suffering if you'll just step off God's path for a moment.

Temptation is that simple. Here's an example of something you might hear from the deceiver: *You don't have to put up with that pain and frustration, my friend! Face it—you're lonely, and that girl from marketing is lonely too, so a phone call is all it will take. She'll be right over tonight to spend time with you. Your pain and aching desire for physical intimacy will be satisfied. You know it can happen, so make it happen.*

A strong *will* alone won't stop this play. Satan never stops running his mouth, and he'll persuade you to take the obvious flight from pain most nights. But if you've built out your soul with a tenacious *willingness* to accept the pain of obedience as a normal part of your life, the negotiation is over before it starts. You don't need pain relief if you're okay with the pain.

End of temptation, end of story.

Perhaps you've never viewed temptation as "a flight from pain." I know I never did when I first engaged in the purity battle. But as the losses mounted, I couldn't miss it, and God revealed what was happening to me. Recall how things rolled out in my story in Chapter 1:

> After realizing that my masturbation was really a financial trust issue, I stopped taking those pressures and fears into my own hands with a bottle of lotion and a towel. Instead, I took my fears to the Lord in prayer and asked Him to release the financial pressure that I was feeling. Once I understood that this habit was also a manhood issue from the deep wounds inflicted by my *earthly* father, I moved into a tighter, more intimate relationship with my *heavenly* Father through one-on-one worship. He healed those wounds and assured me that I *did* indeed have what it takes to make it in the world of men as *His* son.
>
> Soon enough, my masturbation habit disappeared.

Once I'd recognized and embraced the pain in my life and began handling things God's way through prayer and submission, I was no longer kicking around my office at night looking for shortcuts and escape routes. Temptation held zero attraction to me.

What changed? Well, I took on a new attitude and purpose. My attitude was choosing to fight like real men do. My purpose was to hang in there with God until He healed me. If He never did, I was still good with the pain. There would be no more shortcuts. I was done with sin and medication.

I didn't notice it at the time and take no credit for it now, but through the Holy Spirit's guidance, I took on the same biblical approach to temptation that

Jesus modeled during His ministry years. The apostle Peter spoke about it in his first letter to the Church:

> Therefore, since Christ suffered in his body, arm yourselves also with the same attitude, because whoever suffers in the body is done with sin. As a result, they do not live the rest of their earthly lives for evil human desires, but rather for the will of God. (1 Peter 4:1–2, NIV)

Now consider the Amplified version for a moment:

> Therefore, since Christ suffered in the flesh [and died for us], arm yourselves [like warriors] with the same purpose [being willing to suffer for doing what is right and pleasing God], because whoever has suffered in the flesh [being like-minded with Christ] is done with [intentional] sin [having stopped pleasing the world], so that he can no longer spend the rest of his natural life living for human appetites *and* desires, but [lives] for the will *and* purpose of God. (1 Peter 4:1–2, AMP)

To win this battle, you must take on an attitude and willingness to embrace pain and refuse shortcuts. Settle it now by saying this out loud:

> *I am willing to suffer, whether it be rejection by the influencers around me, or by suffering loneliness and disconnection, or...*

You can fill in the blank.

Take on the mindset that you're willing to suffer and obey God, no matter how different you look from those around you or how strange it might appear at the time.

Jesus took that same approach toward sin and temptation, and what Peter was saying was that Jesus had a settled emotional and mental stance toward life that said, "You know what? I'm willing to feel pain, but I'm not willing to sin."

That attitude and willingness became an armor of defense that kept Him from temptation and shortcuts. In the original Greek, "arm yourself" means "put on as armor." In short, Jesus armored up. When the enemy offered enticing pain relief, the temptations bounced off. Satan had no pull on Him.

The fate of the world depended upon Jesus taking on that attitude and purpose. He was offered the same old flights from pain by the devil when He was hungry and thirsty after fasting forty days in the desert, but Jesus understood Satan's playbook and refused all shortcuts and pain relief:

> Again, the devil took him to a very high mountain and showed him all the kingdoms of the world and their glory. And he said to him, "All these I will give you, if you will fall down and worship me." Then Jesus said to him, "Be gone, Satan! For it is written, 'You shall worship the Lord your God and him only shall you serve.' " (Matthew 4:8–10, ESV)

Look at what the devil was offering Him as a shortcut: *Listen, if You just bow before me, I'll give You all the kingdoms of this world now. Then You won't have to go through all the pain.*

But Jesus stiffened His resolve because of His tight relationship with the Father. Once He took on that attitude, shortcuts no longer held any enticement for Jesus.

Consider the shortcut He could have taken on His way to Calvary. The night before His death, the Garden of Gethsemane was the last peaceful place He'd be on this earth. He could have stayed as long as He wanted at a single word:

> And behold, one of those who were with Jesus stretched out his hand and drew his sword and struck the servant of the high priest and cut off his ear. Then Jesus said to him, "Put your sword back into its place. For all who take the sword will perish by the sword. Do you think that I cannot appeal to my Father, and he will at once send me more than twelve legions of angels? But how then should the Scriptures be fulfilled, that it must be so?" (Matthew 26:51–54, ESV)

Look at that power! Twelve legions of angels—a legion is 6,000 angels, so we're talking 72,000 angels—could do some damage. But Jesus chose obedience and embraced the coming pain for the sake of His Father's will.

Take another peek through Gethsemane's cool air:

> And he withdrew from them about a stone's throw, and knelt down and prayed, saying, "Father, if you are willing, remove this cup from me. Nevertheless, not my will, but yours, be done." And there appeared to him an angel from heaven, strengthening him. And being in agony he prayed more earnestly; and his sweat became like great drops of blood falling down to the ground. (Luke 22:41–44, ESV)

Again, He embraced the agony instead of taking the shortcut that was as close as His next gasping breath.

Now let's go to the most offensive, mocking cries from around the cross:

> "He saved others; he cannot save himself. He is the King of Israel; let him come down now from the cross, and we will believe in him." (Matthew 27:42, ESV)

The final test of His spirit was being willing to stay on the cross and not spit back in their faces—and embrace the pain instead. He was obedient, even unto death on a cross (see Philippians 2:8). By doing so, He completed God's plan for man.

You can always take temporary relief from pain, as the offer is always open to you, but Jesus never did. Your willingness to suffer is the secret to overcoming temptation. Experience and embrace pain. Refuse shortcuts.

Take the long way home, God's way.

How do you strengthen your willingness? Certainly not by gritting your teeth and vowing to press on through sheer determination. You do it by choosing God's way over your way. You do it by obeying, come what may, and by embracing pain as a lifestyle.

Did you know that we can look to Scripture for guidance on practicing obedience and embracing pain? We sure can, and it's called fasting.

Fasting is all about setting your will beneath God's will. It's about dumping your personal desires (like eating food), embracing the pain involved, and rooting out attitudes that keep your will vulnerable to enemy exploitation.

When you fast, your will and desires align properly with His. That's why fasting works in the kingdom of God. Your willingness is strengthened in God, and you begin to cry out *His* desires as if they're *yours*.

Here's an example: *God, Your kingdom come. I want You more than I want food. Lord, I want Your will more than I want my ways. Humble my heart and make me tender.*

True confession: I didn't fast much during my battle because I didn't know much about fasting. I was a younger Christian back then with no Christian heritage or experience in my family line.

But my friend Luke Messerschmidt had both heritage and experience, and I want to share his story about the impact of fasting in a purity battle. He told me that as a twenty-something young man, he'd been fighting off intermittent battles with porn for some time, which impacted his relationship with the Lord. "Porn was everywhere, even in the break rooms at work. It was hard to avoid," Luke admitted.

He had two church friends with high hopes for Christian ministry, but they were struggling with porn too. One had a similar situation where pornographic magazines were spread all over the break room. The other had had a significant porn addiction in the past that kept pulling him in.

"We were tired of the porn," Luke confessed. "We decided to try meeting once a week and to be accountable to each other for our actions. We confessed, and we prayed. We confessed, and we prayed. We did better, and then we did worse. It seemed that the mechanics of accountability were not breaking the chains for us. Then one day, one of the guys blurted out, 'Hey, let's try fasting.' It was almost an afterthought."

"Really?" I said, quite intrigued. "What happened next?"

"The honest truth? Fasting quickly and powerfully changed the nature of things for all three of us," Luke replied simply.

"Were you surprised by that?"

"Nope," Luke replied. "I had a fair expectation that fasting would change everything. The funny thing is that the guy who suggested we try fasting didn't have much faith that it would work, and the third guy had practically no faith.

"But I come from a different place than most Christians. You see, my dad fasted all the time for spiritual reasons, so much so that I thought *everyone* fasted. I assumed that fasting was normal behavior for Christians."

"Having known your dad, I can see how you might think so, Luke," I responded.

"Over time, though, fasting dwindled out of my life, but I was very familiar with the power of fasting because of Dad. So when my friend suggested fasting, I could see how a fast focused specifically on overcoming porn could work."

"Man, Luke, this is so exciting to me," I exuded. "I did not have a Christian heritage like you had, but I want to build one for my family. So tell me: what was the plan for you three? Did you set up a fasting schedule so you could fast on the same days together?"

"No, we didn't set a schedule," Luke replied. "We decided that each of us would fast on the days of our choosing during the week, keeping things as flexible as possible for our work and families. As it played out, we each generally fasted twice a week. We drank only water on those days.

"It was incredible, Fred, even for me. The turnaround was dramatic. We went from confessing how many times we'd fallen to sharing, 'I didn't mess up this week at all.' Suddenly there was victory all over the place for each of us.

"Oh, and I almost forgot," Luke added. "Part of our commitment when we began fasting was that we would not be praying just for ourselves, but we were also praying for breakthroughs for each other."

"So cool," I replied. "How did you feel as you were fasting? Did it make you feel stronger? Did it break the chains spiritually somehow? I'd love to know more because I remember fasting a couple of days during my purity battle. Whenever I was tempted, I would say to myself, 'Rats, if I give in to this temptation, I will waste all this starving, and I'm just not going to do that. I'm going to stand strong here.' "

We chuckled together, and I could tell he'd experienced those same thoughts and emotions when he was fasting. Then I motored on.

"I literally felt this commitment inside, 'Hey, I'm done with this sin!'" I continued. "It seemed that once I stepped up and chose to ignore food for a time, I could also choose to ignore sexual sin, at least for a time. So I'm curious: what exactly did fasting do inside of you? Can you describe it at all?"

Luke's eyes quietly turned to a distant point in the room as he gathered his thoughts.

"For me, it removed the pull and tug for porn and masturbation," he said. "If there was a tug, it was a weak tug, like maybe the difference between a small panfish hitting your fishing line as opposed to a forty-five-inch northern pike crunching down and curling away hard. Perhaps that's not how it works for everybody, but there's a sense in my heart that it does. Fasting forced me to submit my will to God with one physical desire of my body—the craving for food—so I could gain victory over another physical desire of my body—looking at porn."

"Fascinating," I responded. "You're saying that building out a measure of control over your eating gave you a measure of control over your sexuality?"

"Yes, I think so. Perhaps that is how fasting works mechanically and why God tells us to fast regularly. It helps us crucify the flesh and keep it in its place."

I paused, reflecting on my thoughts for a moment. "How about this, Luke? Did you feel any sense that fasting was like a spiritual weapon? Did you feel like you had a bat in your hand and clubbed the enemy over the head with the weight of the fast? Or was the impact something happening only inside of you and your will?"

"One thing I'm certain of is that fasting is not just a one-directional thing that only impacts me internally," Luke answered. "What I love most about fasting is that it brings a deeper awareness of the spiritual realm to my mind. Not only does it diminish the strength of the physical pull of temptation, but it also heightens the awareness of the spiritual. I became more aware of the value of purity from a spiritual point of view, especially in comparison to porn. Fasting helps me value the things of the spirit.

"Let me explain it this way. These days, if I ever feel even the slightest pull toward sexual sin, I'll say, 'Let's throw a day of fasting at this.' Before long, my spirit is swooning, saying, 'Man, I can feel this wonderful communion with God! Why would I want to do anything sexually to ruin this?' "

I next turned our attention back to the consequences of fasting upon Luke and his friends as a group. "Okay, so you all fasted, and you all saw victory. What happened to you as a group over time?"

"The most immediate impact was that we didn't have to be confessing our failures every week," Luke said. "We quickly got to the place where we were having a good time together, spending our time praying about our ministry work so that God could direct us more effectively. The entire focus of our meetings shifted because we had moved on from survival mode. We could focus on the things in God's heart.

"Over the long haul, I guess you could say our obedience led to promotions from God. You're already familiar with my work with worship teams and House of Prayer intercession. The other two guys are now senior pastors at their own churches and doing phenomenal jobs."

I'd say that was a great report.

While I didn't do much fasting during my battle for purity, I've done quite a bit since then. Let me share some of my experiences to help you start on your way.

You can find many books out there on fasting and dive into water that's as deep as you like. However, I can assure you that when it comes to fasting, you'll learn much more by doing it than by reading about it.

What does fasting look like in practice? Luke's guys did one- or two-day water fasts, and by water fast, I mean they drank only water. No food.

When my mother-in-law, Gwen, was diagnosed with terminal cancer, I did water fasts every other day for thirty days. I ate normally but not heavily on the off days. I also cut out of work early to intercede for her life for an hour at my church. It was a rough month, but it was an honor. I wouldn't let this great woman and dear friend go to the grave without a fight.

I didn't struggle at all during that month-long fast. I figure I breezed right through it because of the gravity of the situation. But in general, I must admit that fasting has always seemed scary to me. For instance, I attended a church that held a twenty-one-day fast every January to pray for national revival and regional breakthroughs in the kingdom of God. For the first ten years I attended this church, I didn't participate in the fast. I was simply scared of the pain. I felt guilty—and a bit of a sissy—for not being a part of this. I didn't like those feelings.

God must have agreed with me. He'd been drawing me toward obedience in the nicest of ways for ten years, but even my long-suffering Father has His limits. After a decade of losing that argument with me, He got tough and honest with a clear message: *You can fast for your sake and the sake of your family and your business ventures. You can fast for Gwen's sake and for her love and imprint upon your children. But year after year, you refuse to fast for My purposes or for My desires and emotions.*

I was shot through the heart. God was right. I could fast for my sake but never for His sake. What did that say about my love for Him?

As you might expect, I wrestled with myself in the wake of His challenge.

Do I even believe in this fasting stuff? And if I do, why wouldn't I do it for Him?

Am I really a man of the Spirit and a man of intercession, or am I an imposter, posing for the show?

I hated all my answers and every implication of that lost decade of fasting, so I had no choice. I took the leap, albeit with much trepidation. I'm especially embarrassed that I had to text my pastor a couple of times a day to sort through my fear of failure on each of those twenty-one days.

But I did it. I finished the three weeks, and it was good.

What was my plan? It was simple. In the morning, I drank:

- 14 oz of V8 Original vegetable juice
- 6 oz of Bolthouse Farms Green Goodness fruit and vegetable juice
- 6 oz of Bolthouse Farms Strawberry Banana fruit juice

For lunch, I drank:

- 14 oz of chocolate milk
- 6 oz of Bolthouse Farms Green Goodness fruit and vegetable juice
- 6 oz of Bolthouse Farms Multi-V Goodness Cherry fruit juice
- For dinner, I drank:
- 14 oz of white milk
- 6 oz of Bolthouse Farms Strawberry Banana fruit juice
- 6 oz of Bolthouse Farms Multi-V Goodness Cherry fruit juice

That's it, for twenty-one days, along with plenty of water. (I chose the Bolthouse Farms brand because it seemed to have less sugar than other brands, which made it more suitable for fasting.)

A purist would say that my fast wasn't a fast because I included juice. Well, it wasn't a twenty-one-day water-only fast, that's true. It's also true that I have a friend who has regularly done water-only fasts in January. On the other hand, medical advice generally suggests anywhere from twenty-four hours to three days is the maximum you should go without food.

Let me be blunt here. Fasting isn't a contest to see how brutal it can be or how much tougher you are than I am. It is an obedience issue. I was after God's heart and didn't want to be a sissy anymore—in His eyes or mine. I didn't care what anyone else was doing, nor should you.

Besides, I can assure you that this juice fast wasn't easy. I lost twenty-five pounds in twenty-one days, which is plenty rigorous enough for my tastes. But more importantly, I felt humbled before God, which was the entire point.

To God, fasting is about turning to Him, embracing the pain, and humbling your heart to allow Him access to change you. That's why my favorite passage on fasting in the Bible is this from the book of Daniel:

> In those days I, Daniel, was mourning for three weeks. I ate no delicacies, no meat or wine entered my mouth, nor did I anoint myself at all, for the full three weeks. On the twenty-fourth day of the first month, as I was

standing on the bank of the great river (that is, the Tigris) I lifted up my eyes and looked, and behold, a man clothed in linen, with a belt of fine gold from Uphaz around his waist. His body was like beryl, his face like the appearance of lightning, his eyes like flaming torches, his arms and legs like the gleam of burnished bronze, and the sound of his words like the sound of a multitude. And I, Daniel, alone saw the vision, for the men who were with me did not see the vision, but a great trembling fell upon them, and they fled to hide themselves. So I was left alone and saw this great vision, and no strength was left in me. My radiant appearance was fearfully changed, and I retained no strength. Then I heard the sound of his words, and as I heard the sound of his words, I fell on my face in deep sleep with my face to the ground.

And behold, a hand touched me and set me trembling on my hands and knees. And he said to me, "O Daniel, man greatly loved, understand the words that I speak to you, and stand upright, for now I have been sent to you." And when he had spoken this word to me, I stood up trembling. Then he said to me, "Fear not, Daniel, for from the first day that you set your heart to understand and humbled yourself before your God, your words have been heard, and I have come because of your words. (Daniel 10:2–12, ESV)

I love this passage of Scripture because of what the angel did *not* say to Daniel. He did not say, "From the first day you began *fasting*." Heaven doesn't view fasting primarily through a physical portal as we do—the empty plate and feeling starved.

From the angels' perspective, they don't so much see us "turning away from food" as they see us "turning toward God." After all, the angel didn't speak about the delicacies, meat, and wine that Daniel had been avoiding but was instead enamored by how Daniel had humbled himself and set his heart to understand.

That's what angels see. And what God wants to see is the kind of fast that humbles you and opens your heart to Him. He wants to get at the deep things in you that He cannot get to any other way but through fasting. And He gets access to my soul more deeply when fasting than at any other time.

Here are a few more details about my first twenty-one-day fast so you'll understand what to expect as you embark on your fasting journey.

The first two days were simply white-knuckle days for me. It was hard to stop eating. *You won't die*, I thought, which I took to heart. By the third day, though, I felt like I was physically moving into a new place. It's hard to explain, but not eating became less difficult.

The fourth morning brought a deep, spiritual breaking in me as I entered my prayer room to worship. I didn't even know I had a hardened heart, but my callouses began dropping away like autumn leaves. I absolutely could not lift a single word of worship to God without heavy tears pouring from my eyes as my apathetic spirit broke again and again. That spiritual sensitivity took over my worship and prayer times for the rest of my fast.

I must note, however, that around day seven, my mood took a horrible hit, like I was going into emotional shock.

I'd expected that my biggest struggle would be the lack of food, but the hit to my emotions was far more substantial. Until you fast, you have no idea just how much your social life revolves around food. I couldn't duck out with Brenda for lunch. At dinnertime, if Brenda and whoever was around were eating a full, delicious meal, I sat there sipping on my milk and juices, trying to feel like I was a part of things when I wasn't really a part at all.

I felt isolated not eating with my family. Crushed. Deeply humbled. Yes, I know how weak that sounds, but I was surprised by its impact.

The worst part of the fast was the terror that I would fail and have to start over from day one. So I broke things down into little chunks. Could I get through the afternoon? Yes, I could. And then I'd shoot to make it till bedtime. Step by step. That's how I did it until twenty-one days were over.

In closing, let me repeat a line I heard from a pastor one time about fasting:

"Fasting enables you to grow your yes to God."

Your obedience in fasting is connected to your breakthrough. That's a fact. If you're out to tip the scales in your favor when fighting life's battles, you can put more of your will on your side of the scale with fasting.

Most of us will keep fasting up to the point of discomfort, but as soon as it starts to hurt and be an inconvenience, we start whining, *I'm going to break this fast. Why do it anyway? I don't need to get all radical about this stuff.*

But fasting works for a fundamental reason: Your will matters in the affairs of men, and the depth of your heart's agreement with heaven is often the deciding factor.

On the other hand, if you only agree with God to the point of discomfort, all the enemy must do is touch you with a bit of pain and you'll be looking for a shortcut out. Fasting removes that possibility and creates a more significant buy-in in the human heart and a greater willingness to embrace the pain of obedience.

There's no better way to allow God to get at your flesh and to bring it to the surface than to go without food. Fasting brings your flesh under subjection and your spirit and soul to the forefront so God can change you. The scales of history—your history, your family destiny, your national history—all stand in the balance.

Fasting is not just about skipping food; it's a way to come under the lordship of Jesus Christ in a fresh way while allowing God access to your heart like nothing else will.

Trust me, fasting is powerful. I don't claim to fully understand why, but I know that it is.

Whether it's for one day or three weeks, humble yourself. Grow your willingness to obey God and give Him deeper access to your heart through fasting.

It'll change your battle and your life.

8

The Mind

I sit in a black leather chair and open this red leather Bible every morning. When I get up and close this Bible, I am lied to continually the rest of the day.
—Steve Farrar, author and founder of Men's Leadership Ministries

Lies are everywhere. They'll destroy your destiny in God and keep you trapped on the outer threshold of the Christian life, where mediocrity flourishes and sexual sin thrives.

As you have likely figured out, absurd cultural fallacies can cloud your mind and cause outright confusion. One of my favorites is one you've heard already: *Your ticket into manhood is going to bed with a girl.*

Even worse, your internal narratives often teem with lies, which can paralyze you and your relationships. Here's another good one: *Since I'm a fraud and don't have what it takes to make it in this world of men, I've got to hide who I really am.*

Simply put, these lies must be silenced if you're to build a soul that can support a sexually pure life. There's only one way to neutralize them, which Steve Farrar inferred in this chapter's opening quotation: you *must* read the Bible.

Perhaps you were expecting something more profound and innovative, a cutting-edge Stoeker original that devastates the enemy on purity's battlefield. Maybe you're thinking, *Fred, I know I'm supposed to read the Bible. I've heard it a couple of dozen times already. Enough! I get it!*

Here's the rub: even though you know that studying God's Word can neutralize the world's lies, you've been satisfied with living on the mediocre middle ground and muddling along without reading a daily dose of Scripture.[1]

---

1. Of course, you can certainly listen to an audio version of the Bible.

You still aren't approaching your Bible as if your spiritual life—and your sexual purity—depends upon cracking open God's Word.

Remember, I've established that wrong thinking allows sexual sin to root deeply in people's lives, so it should come as no surprise that a sinful mind is hostile to God. If your mindset is hostile to God, your willingness to win this battle will be thoroughly suspect. For your level of purity to change permanently, reading your Bible is a prerequisite. You must renew your mind and take on the mind of Christ by reading your Bible *every day.*

Now, I get it. Reading goes against the grain for a lot of guys. Most men aren't inclined to read the back of a Cheerios box, let alone the Bible. Women are much better readers: studies reveal that Christian women read five times as many books as men.

But here's the problem: if you're not regularly reading God's Word, you can't align your mind to the truth. You can't meditate upon God's precepts to find practical applications of the Word for your life. Instead, you'll keep taking cues from a deluded, misguided culture, stacking up layer after layer of pain, wounds, and stress over time. When the lies remain, so do the chains. You'll never be free.

It's mind-bogglingly common for men to avoid daily time in the Word, but no matter how prevalent that is in our congregations, it'll never be normal. Remember, the Bible defines what is normal for us. Several verses from Psalm 119 perfectly illustrate the normal Christian heart when it comes to Bible study:

> Blessed are those who keep his statutes
> and seek him with all their heart—
> they do no wrong
> but follow his ways.
> (Psalm 119:2–3, NIV)

> I will walk about in freedom,
> for I have sought out your precepts.
> (Psalm 119:45, NIV)

> I reach out for your commands, which I love,
> that I may meditate on your decrees.
> (Psalm 119:48, NIV)

> I have more insight than all my teachers,
> for I meditate on your statutes.
> I have more understanding than the elders,
> for I obey your precepts.
> (Psalm 119:99–100, NIV)

Your statutes are my heritage forever;
they are the joy of my heart.
My heart is set on keeping your decrees
to the very end.
(Psalm 119:111–112, NIV)

These five passages give you a taste of normal from God's perspective. When taken together, they beg a crucial question: Do you have a normal hunger for God's Word?

Now I'd like you to read the entire text of Psalm 119,[2] which can be used like a fabulous, revealing mirror to check your heart.

Finished reading? Now I'd like to hit you with another pop quiz:

1. Do you ache to read your Bible?
2. Are His statutes the joy of your life?
3. Is your heart set on keeping His decrees to the very end?
4. Are you walking around in total freedom today because you've sought out His precepts?

If you can't reply with an emphatic yes to all four questions, your heart toward the Word isn't normal, which will gravely impact your battle for purity. By this point in the book, it's probably easy to see why, but indulge me anyway as I go through this again.

Since you took the time to read Psalm 119 (if you haven't, here's your second chance), I want you to reflect on the psalmist's standard reaction to hardship.[3] Whenever the going got tough, his response was to rest peacefully in his meditations and his understanding of God's Word.

What about you? When the going gets tough, do you naturally wait and rest peacefully in your meditations? Few of us do so, I reckon. For most of us, it's far more likely that when the going gets tough, the tough go masturbate.

We don't rest in our meditations. We rest in our *medications*. In short, we turn to drugs. I used to handle my battles that way, a reaction to life's stresses that never felt right to me, even *before* I committed my heart to Christ. I knew instinctively that real men don't fight their battles this way. I didn't like my responses to life's conflicts, even then.

Herein lies the crucial connection between Bible study and winning your

---

2. I know I'm asking a lot since Psalm 119 is the longest psalm as well as the longest chapter in the Bible.
3. The author of Psalm 119 is unknown, but most scholars agree that it was written by David, Ezra, or Daniel.

battle for purity: If you don't consistently read your Bible, you won't have the deep, intimate relationship with God necessary to turn away from the false intimacy of masturbation when life becomes difficult; neither will you have the enriched understanding of God's Word necessary for you to rest peacefully in your meditations.

But, Fred, God doesn't seem to ever reach out to me!

You've got it all wrong here. You're waiting on God to begin pursuing you, but He already did that years ago when the Father:

- sent His Son to die for you and your sins (see John 3:16);
- ripped apart the veil of the Holy of Holies, top to bottom, to give you personal access to His throne and a personal relationship with Him (see Matthew 27:51);
- offered you salvation while you were still a sinner (see Romans 5:6–8).

When will you return the favor? He sought you in costly ways so you could have the relationship with Him you've been longing for, anytime you'd like. But this relationship is like any other one—when one person pursues, the other must respond appropriately.

God made the first move, and now it's your turn.

To form an intimate relationship with the Lord, you must pursue Him in return. Don't keep waiting for more from Him. Move toward Him with relish and desire:

> You will seek me and find me when you seek me with all your heart. (Jeremiah 29:13, NIV)

The Amplified translation of this Scripture verse fleshes things out a bit and provides you with another mirror for self-inspection:

> Then [with a deep longing] you will seek Me *and* require Me [as a vital necessity] and [you will] find Me when you search for Me with all your heart. (Jeremiah 29:13, AMP)

Your next necessary move won't be outlined any more clearly than that. If you're not searching out the Bible with a deep longing like this, you're not pursuing Him with all your heart.

God yearns for you to pursue Him passionately. That doesn't mean He's asking you for much. He simply wants you to turn and open the door so you can spend some time with Him (see Revelation 3:20). If you do, you'll find Him because He wants you to find Him. He wants you to have the intimacy and understanding you've longed to have with Him, but the ball is in your court. Remember, He made the first move here.

Perhaps you're feeling this way: *I want that deep longing Jeremiah talks about, but I'm simply not feeling it. I can't search for Him with all my heart if I don't feel that longing first, right?*

Wrong.

This kind of inverted thinking is common though. Our culture teaches us that "right actions must come from right feelings," and until you have the right feelings in place, you're doomed to a useless waiting game. But that's just one more lie.

The opposite is true: "Right feelings come from right actions." In other words, if you're not feeling it but want the right feelings to develop, start taking the right actions in faith. It is no different with Bible reading than with what I wrote about one-on-one worship in Chapter 6.

Think back to what I wrote there. I took the right actions for four weeks, in faith, before the right feelings broke out in my relationship with the Lord. My pastor took the right relational actions toward God for six weeks, and then the Holy Spirit delivered intimacy and connection to him. My daughter Laura took the correct steps toward God for a rugged fourteen weeks before she felt anything in return, but then the Holy Spirit finally moved in her life.

Rather than worry about how you're feeling today about reading your Bible, develop an action plan and get started. Start with the understanding that you're not approaching Bible study as a "spiritual discipline" *per se* or adding one more thing to your daily to-do list, like early morning workouts at the club. Neither is this a competition where you strive to read more than the next guy at church so you can better position yourself on the spiritual social ladder. You shouldn't even approach this as an effective attack vector in your battle for purity. (We guys can think so strangely about reading our Bibles!)

Daily Bible reading is not only a *spiritual discipline*, but it's also a *relational commitment*. More like courtship, perhaps. For you guys, remember the days when your wife was your fiancée. You stumbled across the most amazing beauty and were determined to make her your wife. From that day forward, you never let the sun set without calling her or reading her texts and thumbing responses back to her each day.

It wasn't a forced discipline. No one crabbed at you to put it on your to-do list. You simply *committed your heart* to building a relationship with her. Those right actions, with time, brought about even deeper feelings as you got to know each other better. That's how great relationships are built.

Glenn Packiam, a Malaysian-American musician and pastor, said it nicely in a social media post:

Calling it "spiritual discipline" can fool us on two fronts—we can think it's all about discipline when it's really about the training of desire; and we can think it's our work when the Holy Spirit is actually the lead agent. We participate; we cooperate; and that participation and cooperation can feel like discipline. But the end goal is the rehabilitation of longing, the transformation of desire—and that is what the Spirit does in us.

Isn't that beautiful—the "training of desire"? You've been waiting for the right feelings to show up before you begin, but those feelings will only come *after* you've stepped out and into a relational commitment. Once started, your desire will be transformed, and the Holy Spirit will rehabilitate your longing for the Word as you go.

A few pages back, God used the mirror of Psalm 119 to examine your level of desire for Him and His Word. If you got a poor grade on that pop quiz, Scripture reading is your antidote. You needn't grit your teeth and get all disciplined. Simply turn toward Him. Commit to the relationship.

Daily Bible reading is about building oneness and intimacy with your Beauty. It's a matter of turning aside to spend time with the lover of your soul and court the One who finds you so precious that He died for you.

It's time to rise up and read.

But, Fred, I am busy with work and the kids. I simply don't have the time to add this to my busy life.

I'll venture you never said anything like that to your fiancée when you were courting her, but I understand busyness. I raised four kids and ran my own business for decades, building it from scratch. Since we're all busy, it's only right and proper that you count the costs beforehand.

Still, when it comes to renewing the mind and dumping the lies, it all comes down to this: Do you love God with all your heart? Do you require Him as a vital necessity in your life? If you don't, you need to turn and commit relationally so that the Spirit can rehabilitate your desire and form a normal heart in you. If you don't find time to search the Word, you won't find Him *or* your sexual purity. You need intimacy with Him for long-term victory over sexual sin.

I'm not in this to win a Sunday school prize for getting the most men or women to read their Bibles. I'm not your pastor, and I wouldn't take the job if you offered it, no matter how high the pay.

I *am* your mentor, however, so here's the bottom line: I've been sexually pure for over thirty years, and you probably haven't been. I know what it takes to win and, so far, you don't. So it makes eminent sense for you to listen closely to what

I have to say, which can be summed up with this statement:

> Bible reading is crucial to building your soul and essential to winning your purity battle. You may somehow scrape together a short-term victory without reading your Bible and connecting deeply with Christ in this way, but you won't find decades-long victory without it.

Maybe you have this question: *How does reading the Bible on my own, by myself, ever bring me into an interpersonal, relational intimacy with God?*

Because there is no such thing as reading the Bible by yourself. Ever. It's impossible to do so by definition. Consider the following verse from the Gospel of John: "In the beginning was the Word, and the Word was with God, and the Word was God" (John 1:1, NIV).

We know that the Bible is the Word of God. The Bible explicitly teaches us that Jesus Christ is also the Word of God, only in the flesh. That means that when you are reading the Word of God, you're literally engaging in a personal encounter with the essence of Jesus Christ.

I said it like this in my book *Tactics*:

> The Bible is a living document and extremely active in shaping the thoughts and attitudes of your heart (see Hebrews 4:12). Recall, too, that Jesus is the Living Word of God, in the flesh (see John 1:14). Therefore, an encounter with the Bible is an encounter with Jesus.

This point is critical to understand. You will always be as close to God as you want, and the simplest way to get close to Him is through reading His written Word. Every time you crack open a Bible, you get into His presence. To be close to the Lord, you must seek these Scripture encounters with Him with all your heart.

Now, I'm not saying that you will have a take-your-sandals-off-because-you-are-on-holy-ground moment every time you read your Bible, but I *am* saying that you will personally encounter Him each time. Most of the time, it will be less like a burning bush and more like burning logs in a campfire. It's like you're sitting around with your closest friend, sharing your heart.

Having said that, I must manage your expectations regarding this process early on, much as I did in Chapter 6. Remember, I didn't immediately connect with the Lord when I began my one-on-one worship. Similarly, I didn't sense that warm campfire connection with Bible study in the beginning either. Neither will you, most likely, but that's okay. In fact, it's to be expected.

For one thing, it'll take time for the Holy Spirit to train your desires and rehabilitate your heart. For another, passionate relationships are only built over time as two friends consistently spend time together and learn about each other. This one will be no different.

Speaking of time, when we looked into worship back in Chapter 6, we did a bit of time travel to the early years of my marriage to better understand the one-on-one process. I told you exactly what I did—the good, the bad, and the ugly. I shared how the intimacy of worship blossomed naturally in my life over time and shed light on what you might expect when you turn toward a deeper communion with God.

Let's now take a trek back even further in time to Brenda's days as a teen, long before she met me. She'd been trying for years to read her Bible from cover to cover in one year, starting in Genesis and finishing with the book of Revelation. She never accomplished her goal, not even once.

Enter Fred Stoeker stage right through the matrimonial portal. Since I was newly committed to Christ, I'd never read my Bible cover to cover in a year either. In fact, I'd never even heard of such a thing. So, during our first year of marriage, I merely sat in the grandstands and watched in bemusement as Brenda failed miserably one more time.

Of course, the Holy Spirit soon cornered me and stabbed me in the heart: *She's broken over this, Fred. Get with it! You are the spiritual leader of your home, but so far you haven't lifted a finger to help her win.*

That was a jarring challenge to my manhood! He was right. I couldn't let Brenda flounder like this. I *had* to come through for her. After pondering the matter, I figured the best way to help her win was to lead by example.

With January looming again and Brenda mobilizing her heart for another try, I shared my plan to be her wingman this time. She was greatly encouraged.

Too encouraged, I'm afraid. I was no help as I failed miserably in my first attempt. Brenda and I both went down in flames. Some wingman!

Another chilly January rolled into Iowa the following year, and we again took flight together. This time, I hit my target squarely and would start a five-year streak in which I would read the entire Bible all the way through. This string of victories finally worked its magic in Brenda. My example so inspired her that she finally made it through her Bible for the first time during that fifth year. She's been reading her Bible cover to cover annually ever since.

While I finally scored a massive victory for spiritual wingmen everywhere, setting an example for Brenda had a far more significant impact upon me than it did upon her. First, the Holy Spirit was rehabilitating my heart, and without that, He would have never been able to train my desire for a sanctified life in Christ.

Without a rehabilitated heart, I may have never engaged in my battle for purity, as I would have robbed God of the opportunity to express His thoughts on the matter. Had I not heard those thoughts around our biblical campfire, I'd have never learned enough about His nature and His ways to persevere through the pain of the battle to win.

Summing up, my relational commitment to Brenda and *her* Bible reading victory eventually led to my own richer relational commitment to God, all due to experiencing God each day through the written Word.

Let's return to a fundamental concept I first mentioned in Chapter 5. Every Christian—everyone who is "born-again"—has his Father's DNA. That comes from God. But only the *mature* Christian has the Father's character. That comes from yearning and learning to think and act like Him. This is what Christianity is all about.

It's time to add that I never would have developed His character had I not chosen to dig deeply into the Bible. How else could I learn to think and act like my heavenly Father? So I'll say it again: It's time to read the Bible, and it's time to read the entire Bible in a year.

The Internet makes it easy to read your Bible over twelve months. Daily reading schedules abound in cyberspace. You can also purchase *The One Year Bible* in different translations that starts on January 1 with the first chapter of Genesis, the first chapter of Matthew, a few verses from the book of Psalms, and a verse from Proverbs.

The truth is that any approach will do if you commit to it. For Brenda and me, our favorite method is using the daily reading schedule that chronologically takes you through the Bible, which I believe delivers a richer historical perspective. Still, we've only discovered the chronological method more recently.

I'd like to finish this chapter by sharing how the Holy Spirit renewed my mind in four distinct ways, by sharing scriptures that shaped who I am today. I do this in the hope that you'll better understand why daily Bible study is foundational to your sexual purity, just as it's been to mine.

Here are the four ways:

1. My annual reading of the Bible allowed the Lord to reveal Himself to me in the broadest possible way and begin shaping His character in me.

I can't say that I noticed any huge change in me during that first year of reading, but about halfway through the second year, it felt like a new dawn broke in my understanding of the Word. Knowledge is built upon knowledge.

I could remember what I had read the first year, connecting many historical dots in my mind. Best of all, I was reading everything for the second time, so I was getting to know the Lord, my Friend, much better, as this verse attests:

> For you were once darkness, but now you are light in the Lord. Live as children of light (for the fruit of the light consists in all goodness, righteousness and truth) *and find out what pleases the Lord.* (Ephesians 5:8–10, NIV; italics added for emphasis)

With the growth of knowledge came revelation after revelation about my character and how it stacked up against my Father's character. As we spent time together reading, He'd confront my mind continually with His truth, often in the form of pop-quiz questions. In fact, if you flip open my Bible, you'll find the letters "PQ" scrawled next to the challenging verses He used to test my character and renew my mind.

God was never nasty with the questions. We were more like a couple of guys around a campfire, remember? And He didn't just focus on one topic—like sexual purity, for instance. The quizzes would pop in from any direction on any possible topic.

As you read, the most important thing to do is approach God's Word with a humble, open heart. You might consider praying the following before opening your Bible each day:

Lord, what do You want me to change in my life?

What are You asking me to do in my character?

As I read, can You show me what this is supposed to look like in real life?

Let me demonstrate how simply the quiz process works. After reading a particular verse, a question would hit me that I had to answer. Here are some examples from my "PQ" inscriptions in my Bible:

God's Scripture Verse

Confident of your obedience, I write to you, knowing that you will do even more than I ask. (Philemon 1:21, NIV)

Fred's Pop Quiz

Is God so confident of my obedience that He can count on me to do even more than He asks? What evidence have I given Him lately that He can count on me like this?

God's Scripture Verse

But about the Son he says . . . "You have loved righteousness and hated wickedness; therefore God, your God, has set you above your companions by anointing you with the oil of joy." (Hebrews 1:8a, 9, NIV)

Fred's Pop Quiz
Do I love righteousness and hate wickedness as Jesus does? In what ways do I show that?

God's Scripture Verse
So, as the Holy Spirit says: "Today, if you hear his voice, do not harden your hearts as you did in the rebellion, during the time of testing in the wilderness." (Hebrews 3:7–8, NIV)

Fred's Pop Quiz
Am I listening more to those in rebellion around me, or am I listening more to God and forging my own path of obedience? Am I keeping my heart soft toward the Lord?

God's Scripture Verse
Pray for us. We are sure that we have a clear conscience and desire to live honorably in every way. (Hebrews 13:18, NIV)

Fred's Pop Quiz
Are you absolutely sure that you have a clear conscience? Do you desire to live honorably in every way? What are your recent actions that prove it?

God's Scripture Verse
"He himself bore our sins" in his body on the cross, so that we might die to sins and live for righteousness; "by his wounds you have been healed." (1 Peter 2:24, NIV)

Fred's Pop Quiz
Do you live for righteousness, Fred? Or are you still going astray?

God's Scripture Verse
After removing Saul, he made David their king. God testified concerning him: "I have found David son of Jesse, a man after my own heart; he will do everything I want him to do." (Acts 13:22, NIV)

Fred's Pop Quiz
Am I doing everything God wants me to do—like David?

God continually critiqued my mindset because He wanted to renew it and confronted me because He loved me. If He hadn't done that, who would have?

That's an excellent question to ask because you've got to regularly hear a voice calling out to you from the heavenly realm since this world has no answers and no love for you. You've got to be in His presence so that He can challenge you, even if it's for only fifteen minutes a day. I can honestly state that committing to read my Bible from Genesis to Revelation each year was the most important thing I've ever done spiritually besides learning how to worship in my basement.

2. My annual reading of the Bible taught me that "obedience" is the Lord's love language.

If you are Christian and married, chances are good that you've heard of Gary Chapman's book *The Five Love Languages*, a *New York Times* bestseller for the last fifteen years. In his book, Gary offers an actionable approach to sharing and receiving love. His goal is to help you find a deeper and richer level of intimacy with your partner.

The Bible also offers an actionable approach to showing love to Christ so that you can find a deeper and richer level of intimacy with Him. It's called obedience, which is the Lord's love language:

> In fact, this is love for God: to keep his commands . . . (1 John 5:3a, NIV)

> You will have these tassels to look at and so you will remember all the commands of the LORD, that you may obey them and not prostitute yourselves by chasing after the lusts of your own hearts and eyes. (Numbers 15:39, NIV)

> Whoever has my commands and keeps them is the one who loves me. The one who loves me will be loved by my Father, and I too will love them and show myself to them. (John 14:21, NIV)

> They claim to know God, but by their actions they deny him. They are detestable, disobedient and unfit for doing anything good. (Titus 1:16, NIV)

Clearly, the Lord's love language is obedience; so if you want to show your love for Him, obedience must be central to your approach. By nature, we don't care nearly enough about obedience, so we need to continually examine our lives in light of Scripture to know His ways better so that we might better please Him.

The Holy Spirit helps us with this when we read the Bible daily because the Word is the Holy Spirit's teaching language. He chased me with this verse for months, challenging my love for Christ, especially in light of my sexual sin:

> "Why do you call me, 'Lord, Lord,' and do not do what I say?" (Luke 6:46, NIV).

He wasn't mean about it. He was simply relentless. He needed me to wrestle with the truth. If I loved Christ, why wasn't I obeying Him?

Eventually, wrestling with this question led me to engage in the battle for purity. I'm confident that if I hadn't been reading my Bible through once a year, I would not have heard the Holy Spirit challenge me like this. Then again, I was reading with the proper attitude too.

You must always come to the Bible with the assumption that when you don't agree with God, He's right and you're wrong. You just haven't figured out why you're wrong yet. Once you take on that assumption, you will have the humility of mind necessary for God to reveal the truth to you. Do so by lifting up this prayer: *God, instruct me. Change my mind. Help me to be free.*

Obedience is His love language. Obedience means you love Him more than you love yourself. You are never the exception to the rule because there is no exception to any divine rule. Don't be the single man (or woman) who says, "I went ahead and had sex with my girlfriend (or boyfriend) because I prayed about it, and God said it was okay." That's not possible.

Or don't be the single guy who says, "We know we shouldn't have sex until we're married, but we're married in our hearts, so it's okay."

Ugh.

There is no exception to a divine rule. He is either God or He isn't. You either love Him and His ways or you don't. Your obedience will reveal your love.

3. My annual reading of the Bible allowed Jesus to reveal lesser-known corners of His heart.

Colton is a fine athlete and a graduate of a private Christian college who recently wrote after watching me on YouTube:

> The Bible says nothing about avoiding sexual foreplay, so everything short of penetration is all good. This view is fairly objective, insomuch as the puritanical restrictions you're describing really aren't laid out in Scripture anywhere, so, by definition, your views are adding extra rules above and beyond what's written in black and white. I'm not commenting on the merits of those extra restrictions. I'm simply saying that those are your restrictions, not God's.

I replied with a simple sentence: "Go and read the first four verses of Ezekiel 23, and then get back to me."

I never heard from Colton again. If he ever cracked open his Bible to check out that portion of Scripture, he'd have read this:

> The word of the LORD came to me: "Son of man, there were two women, daughters of the same mother. They became prostitutes in Egypt, engaging in prostitution from their youth. In that land their breasts were fondled, and their virgin bosoms caressed. The older was named Oholah, and her sister was Oholibah. They were mine and gave birth to sons and daughters. Oholah is Samaria, and Oholibah is Jerusalem." (Ezekiel 23:1–4, NIV)

In this passage, God used sexual foreplay as a metaphor for the spiritual apostasy of His chosen people, one of the things He hates most. His attitude toward fondling virgin breasts is unmistakable. Everything short of penetration is *not* all good, and the Bible says quite a bit more about sexual foreplay than Colton thought.

When it comes to sexual purity, you're not going to learn what pleases the Lord while sitting around the pub drinking craft beer with the guys, nodding your buzzed heads sagely to tripe like, "Anything short of penetration is all good."

Come to think of it, you won't learn very much by sitting in church once a week either. Pastors rarely cover obscure verses like this one from Ezekiel. Besides, they're too scared to preach on sexual topics from the pulpit. Trust me, if you don't commit to a daily schedule of reading the entire Bible cover to cover in a year, it's unlikely you'll find your way into the book of Ezekiel either.

Colton never did. That's why he thought the Bible said nothing about sexual foreplay. Trapped instead by cultural lies, he's poised to make another treacherous dive into sexual sin the next time he meets someone special. That's certainly not God's will, but this is:

> Do not conform to the pattern of this world, but be transformed by the renewing of your mind. Then you will be able to test and approve what God's will is—his good, pleasing and perfect will. (Romans 12:2, NIV)

An annual reading of the entire Bible will take you into the deepest corners of the Word. Without that experience, you might think that "the Bible teaches nothing about sexual foreplay" too.

What a disaster it would have been to teach that to my kids! Instead, I could show them the truth in black and white. It's much easier to stand against the pressure of the world when the truth is so clear.

You are the spiritual leader of your home. People are counting on you to know what you are talking about, so find out what the Bible says. Don't ever claim that the Bible says nothing about a topic unless you've read the entire Bible yourself. The more times, the better. It's a matter of integrity.

4. My annual reading of the entire Bible allowed Jesus to redefine manhood for me.

My earthly father claimed that I wasn't a man and would never find a place in the world of men because I didn't have what it takes. Eventually, *his* narrative about me became *my* narrative. As I discussed earlier, my quest for manhood was soon broken, hopelessly tied to my sexuality.

My narrative began to change when I started reading my Bible annually. In short, my heavenly Father's narrative took center stage in my life, and my dad's narrative began fading to whispers.

I couldn't believe how many new and jarring scriptures rushed through my eyes that first year! I'll bet your experience will be the same for you, no matter how long you've attended church. This verse, for instance, rocked me to my core:

> With eyes full of adultery, they never stop sinning; they seduce the unstable; they are experts in greed—an accursed brood! (2 Peter 2:14, NIV)

This was me. My eyes never stopped looking and lusting. Fantasizing about girls seemed like a natural, normal part of my manhood. It never occurred to me that there could be another path, yet God called such thinking "accursed," especially in the context of a verse that I'd read a few weeks earlier:

> You have heard that it was said, "You shall not commit adultery." But I tell you that anyone who looks at a woman lustfully has already committed adultery with her in his heart. (Matthew 5:27–28, NIV)

God showed me that real men don't handle their sexuality this way, nor do they search for their manhood in this manner. His will was clear on the matter:

> It is God's will that you should be sanctified: that you should avoid sexual immorality; that each of you should learn to control your own body in a way that is holy and honorable, not in passionate lust like the pagans, who do not know God . . . (1 Thessalonians 4:3–5, NIV)

I was no longer a pagan. I was God's adopted son, and He'd printed a new ticket into manhood for me through obedience in battle. Real men establish their manhood on purity's battlefield by *not* using their sexuality:

> Run away from sexual immorality [in any form, whether thought or behavior, whether visual or written]. Every *other* sin that a man commits is outside the body, but the one who is sexually immoral sins against his own body. (1 Corinthians 6:18, AMP)

> But among you there must not be even a hint of sexual immorality, or of any kind of impurity, or of greed, because these are improper for God's holy people. Nor should there be obscenity, foolish talk or coarse joking, which are out of place, but rather thanksgiving. (Ephesians 5:3–4, NIV)

> Flee the evil desires of youth and pursue righteousness, faith, love and peace, along with those who call on the Lord out of a pure heart. (2 Timothy 2:22, NIV)

> [Treat] older women as mothers, and younger women as sisters, with absolute purity. (1 Timothy 5:2, NIV)

God even gives us a role model of true manhood. Job handled his sexuality exactly according to God's Word:

> In the land of Uz there lived a man whose name was Job. This man was blameless and upright; he feared God and shunned evil. (Job 1:1, NIV)

Job certainly didn't have eyes full of adultery as I did:

> I made a covenant with my eyes not to look lustfully at a young woman. (Job 31:1, NIV)

His declaration later in the same chapter made it quite clear that he had faithfully kept this covenant with his eyes:

> If my steps have turned from the path, if my heart has been led by my eyes, or if my hands have been defiled, then may others eat what I have sown, and may my crops be uprooted. (Job 31:7–8, NIV)

God confirms that Job was victorious on purity's battlefield by bragging about Job's character to His archenemy, Satan:

Then the LORD said to Satan, "Have you considered my servant Job? There is no one on earth like him; he is blameless and upright, a man who fears God and shuns evil." (Job 1:8, NIV)

Wouldn't you like the Lord to say that about you? We would all like to hear that.

You will never outgrow the need to renew your mind. Nobody reading this book is so enlightened that he or she has it all figured out. You've got to start with humility of mind and allow God to continually challenge the way you think through regularly reading His Word.

I'm deeply concerned for believers who aren't hungry for more knowledge and understanding. I can vividly recall what it was like living without God's truth and wisdom. How embarrassing to think back to those days! When I lived by my own wits and desires, I made a huge mess of my life. But hearing from Him through His Word changed everything for me, and I've never found a better substitute for renewing my mind.

So find a place where you can quiet your soul, turn to Him, and wholeheartedly pursue His heart and character. Allow these daily encounters with Jesus to translate into intimacy as the Holy Spirit trains your desires and rehabilitates your heart for Him. Finally, remember His promise to you: *You will find Me when you seek Me with all your heart.*

It's long past time for you to do the spadework necessary "to construct a soul in accordance with the new life God has put within" you, as Oswald Chambers wrote.

I said this in Chapter 5 but let me repeat it here: Until you take responsibility to renew your entire soul, three things will happen:

1. Your spirit won't have complete ascendency in your life.
2. Your manhood won't fully develop.
3. You'll never have total victory over sexual sin.
4. Without that renewal, your soul will keep saying yes to your flesh and no to the new life in you. Instead, move toward a manifest spiritual maturity where freedom reigns.

PART III
Every Man's Destiny

We are now at the midpoint of *Battle On, Battle Over*, so let's take a breath and review the message and goals for the book, as laid out in the Introduction.

In that preamble, I shared that the apostle Peter declared that your faith is as precious as the faith of any of the apostles, and that Christ's divine power has given you everything you need for a godly life through your knowledge of Him. These deposits promise an escape from your illicit sexual desires and are foundational to your destiny as a sexually pure man or woman. Peter asserted that your faith would never be fruitless or futile if you work to mature it in the following ways:

> [Since you have the Lord's divine power], make every effort to add to your faith goodness; and to goodness, knowledge; and to knowledge, self-control; and to self-control, perseverance; and to perseverance, godliness; and to godliness, mutual affection; and to mutual affection, love. For if you possess these qualities in increasing measure, they will keep you from being ineffective and unproductive in your knowledge of our Lord Jesus Christ. But whoever does not have them is nearsighted and blind, forgetting that they have been cleansed from their past sins. (2 Peter 1:5–9, NIV; words inside brackets added for clarity)

To help you add knowledge to your faith, I promised to spotlight a major vulnerability in your sexuality that sets you up to fall into sexual sin, one that's prominent in both men and women. We did so in the first five chapters of this book.

While Peter implored you to make every effort to add knowledge, self-control, and perseverance to your *faith* (see 2 Peter 1:5–9) so that you might escape the corruption of this world, he also exhorted you to make every effort in your *life* to be found spotless, blameless, and at peace with the Lord (see 2 Peter 3:14).

As part of that effort, Oswald Chambers urged you to push past the threshold or boundaries of the Christian life and deep into its center, building yourself a healthy soul (will, mind, and emotions) and a genuine, intimate connection with the Lord to replace your need for the false intimacy delivered through porn and masturbation. Such a soul offers rock-solid foundational support for sexual purity and the full development of your manhood in Christ.

I then concluded:

> Your destiny rests on these truths, not upon the cultural lies bandied about your church, your work, or your exercise club. You are *not* a slave to depravity or to the sexual urges that have mastered you in the past (see 2 Peter 2:19). Your destiny is to walk in the divine nature, well above the sexual fray. It is your destiny to walk in the truth that your brother Peter worked so hard to help you remember.
>
> Since Peter made every effort in his letter to you to remind you that you must be diligent in maturing your precious faith so that you can be free from this battle, and since I'm making every effort in this book to give you the rest of the knowledge you need to establish self-control and perseverance in your life, will *you* now make every effort to apply this knowledge and to be found spotless, blameless, and at peace with your Lord in your sexuality?
>
> I hope so. Freedom is glorious, and freedom is yours to establish.

So your destiny awaits. *Will you now make every effort?* That question hangs over the head and heart of every man and every woman. Sure, by this point of the book you've learned where you stand today, and you know the choices you must make to win.

But while that insight gives you a leg up here, the decisions won't make themselves, my friend. And admittedly, these are not easy choices. I know. I made these choices myself. The decisions to add knowledge, self-control, and perseverance to my faith required my every effort, right to my core, just as Peter suggested.

Ah, but the glories of freedom! Oh, my word. You likely have little idea of the magnificent impact these choices will have upon your destiny, your family's destiny, and the destiny of the local church. I didn't understand the potential impact at the beginning of the battle either.

But I sure do now, and it's time to share what I've seen. Over the following three chapters, I'll reveal what's out there beyond freedom's gates, out there where your destiny awaits.

The prodigious spoils of this war are staggeringly rich, so be encouraged. Boundless freedom calls.

9

Sexual Purity and Your Personal Destiny: What Do *You* Want?

I want you to always remember that life's most meaningless statistic is the halftime score, and as far as I'm concerned, it's always halftime.
—Meadowlark Lemon, Harlem Globetrotter

Whether you are twenty or forty or sixty years old, the first half is now over when it comes to your purity. The score is what it is. It's halftime, and you have adjustments to make.

The current score—the extent of sexual sin in your past—means nothing now. The second half—God's call on your future—means everything. Your decisions today, in the present, will determine how your future plays out.

Perhaps you're older and you're muttering, *It's too late for me. My kids are already out of the house.*

It isn't too late. There's still plenty of time left in the game. It's only halftime, remember? Make your adjustments, and then teach your sons how to teach your grandsons. Hey, you've got this!

Remember, the New Life is in you, so get out of the locker room and back on the field of play. Halftime adjustments are *always* in order and are *always* yours to make at any time, at will, so make them. But first consider this: *What do you want for yourself as the second half unfolds from here?*

I can tell you what I wanted. I wanted to be able to look God in the eye again. That's pretty much it. And I remember thinking that if I couldn't get that, I'd settle for gathering some frontline intel on the purity battle that I could pass on to my son Jasen so that at least *he* could look God in the eye one day and forever escape that pornographic prison cell that I'd come to know too well.

At the time, I didn't know what was possible. In retrospect, my expectations were low and I wanted too little, but that's understandable. Even picking up meager crumbs from beneath the King's table would have meant the world to me. *Anything is more than I deserve*, I figured.

I didn't know that a man *could* go decades without flipping through TV channels or surfing the Internet for something hot and sensual. I didn't know that a man could successfully redefine his family name and trust his sons to cheerfully join him in that pursuit. I wasn't aware that a man could go decades without offering the enemy a sexual beachhead in his life that would compromise his spiritual authority over his home. I didn't realize that a man could stop crippling his connection with his wife for good instead of derailing their destiny together.

You have a tremendous advantage over my situation back then as you look ahead and make those halftime adjustments. You will know what's possible because I'm about to tell you. Trust me, that knowledge alone can dramatically affect what a man wants. My son Michael can attest to that, and his story's a good example for you.

Years ago, my youngest son, Michael, fourteen at the time, rushed into my bedroom one morning at 2 a.m., his voice twisted in anguish. "Dad, Dad, I need to talk to you!"

I wasn't the least bit happy to see him at that moment. Because of a tight book deadline, I'd written late into the night and had finally stumbled into bed at midnight, only two hours earlier. Worse yet, I knew the alarm was set at 4 a.m. so I could shower and grab my bag for an early flight to speak at a men's retreat.

Still groggy, I grunted, "Son, I'll call you in the morning between flights to talk about it. I promise. It's two o'clock in the morning. Just go back to bed."

"No, Dad, please! I can't wait. I've got to talk to you right now. Please!"

Ugh. I flung the covers back and rolled upright slowly, squinting blurredly into his eyes. Brenda had stirred, but I didn't want to awaken her fully. When I saw the agony etched all over Michael's face, I knew this couldn't wait. "Okay, son, let's head to the family room. We can talk there."

After splashing my face with a bit of water and flopping down heavily into my favorite chair, I listened as Michael poured out his heart about a vivid and deeply distressing dream he'd just had, speaking so fast and furiously that I could only catch every other word he said. I never did quite comprehend the dream or why and how despair and panic had gripped him so tightly around the throat, but I *did* pick up enough to realize that this was the perfect moment to lay out the complete history of our family tree and what God was planning for it.

I began with the generational sin passed down from my grandfathers and father that had strangled the joy out of my life as a young husband. I shared how I often looked into his brother Jasen's two-year-old eyes and burst into tears when I realized he was condemned to walk the same path I had because I couldn't believe that I'd ever be free. I confided that I didn't know how to protect him either.

I disclosed the impact of my Merle Hay moment and my decision with God to fight for the Stoeker name and our family tree. I also described how Jasen chose to join me in this great destiny by opting out of the popularity game at school and standing up courageously for purity in both high school and college. I reminded Michael that Jasen often stood alone when ridiculed by his peers. I told him every story I could think of about my battle, about Jasen's decisions, and about the new family destiny that Jasen and I were crafting together. I could tell that Michael was hanging on every word.

Finally, as the chimes of our mantel clock bonged their way past 3:30, I wrapped things up this way: "Michael, once I'd won my battle for purity, several years before you were born and when Jasen was just starting school, there was finally one Stoeker living on this earth in the way God called us to live. By God's grace, I'd reversed course. The Stoeker name no longer meant pornography, adultery, and divorce. Now it meant purity, fidelity, and holiness. And you know what? When Jasen got older and teamed up with me, then there were two of us. If you join us, Michael, there will be three."

By now the anxiety in Michael's face had evaporated. Something new had settled in its place. He was a genuine man, and his heart was captured by this charter to conquer. Here was a big battle to fight—something inspiring, a warrior's call.

"When you and Jasen are ready, you'll both get married," I continued. "Perhaps Jasen will have a son with his wife, and perhaps you'll have a couple more with yours. Once the both of you teach your boys the truth, there will be six Stoekers living this way. When they have *their* sons, perhaps there'll be twelve, and before long, there will be twenty-four Stoekers out there walking in sexual purity and carrying our name well."

I paused. Michael's eyes had now glazed over, captivated by the possibilities. Then, in a resolute, steady voice, he declared earnestly, "I want that, Dad. I want that!"

What an incredible moment. I'll never forget that noble look in his eyes as he stepped up into his family destiny.

In those early morning hours, I portrayed *everything* possible for Michael. My youngest son knew he wanted it all. Fixing his eyes on Jesus, he ran the race marked out for him with perseverance and threw off everything that could easily hinder or entangle him along the way. Scorning the shame and ridicule that come from living differently, Michael never found a price too dear to pay and never moved his finish line up closer to shorten his race. Because men ache to fight big battles and live great adventures, he never wavered as he grew through high school and college.

Throughout his thirty years, there have been no false finish lines for Michael. He carries the Stoeker name well. He carries the title "Christian" just as well.

In sharing Michael's story and the others in *Battle On, Battle Over*, I'm portraying all that is possible for *you*, just as I did that night for my son. Do you remember what he said so clearly?

"I want that, Dad. I want that!"

So what do *you* want? As you ponder that question, let's return to the words of Oswald Chambers one more time:

> Many of us prefer to stay at the threshold of the Christian life, instead of going on to construct a soul in accordance with the new life God has put within us. We fail because we are ignorant of the way God has made us, and we blame things on the devil that are actually the result of our own undisciplined natures. (*My Utmost for His Highest*, May 20 devotional)

You not only know now what's possible to achieve in this battle, but you also now know how you're made. Do you want to stay at the threshold of the Christian life, on the outside looking in? Do you want to keep putting your sin down to the devil's account, or would you prefer to remove those addictions and corrupted neural pathways you have built with your own undisciplined actions over time? Do you really want to keep calling yourself names and blaming your actions on some imagined perversion in you, or are you finally ready to build your soul by following the new life God has put within you?

You can, you know. And it will be worth the battle and the discipline. I have never once regretted my decision to fight. Neither have Jasen or Michael. God gave us a broad charter to get out and conquer, and we *did* conquer, together.

The late Iowa Hall of Fame wrestling coach Bob Darrah once said, "You will always have pain in life, men, but at least you get to choose which kind of pain you'll endure—the pain of self-discipline, or the pain of regret. It's your choice, but always remember this: The pain of self-discipline lasts for a moment. The pain of regret lasts for the rest of your life."

Please, embrace the pain of self-discipline like a champion wrestler. When it comes to building your soul, leave it all out there on the mat. If you do, you'll never experience that lifetime of regret, wondering, *What might have happened had I just walked with God completely in my sexuality and my relationships with women?*

I've escaped that pain of regret because I answered God's call. I pushed through in the battle, and it's been worth every disciplined moment. Freedom is a crazy, wondrous thing.

If you're an athlete, you've tasted the pain of self-discipline somewhere along the way, at least for a while. We often choose self-discipline for our own reasons, perhaps for glory that won't last past graduation. When I played football, I would spend hours upon hours running hills and stadium steps in 90 degree weather and 90 percent humidity to be one of the best in the league that fall. Those afternoons were brutal, but the pain was momentary. They led to the results I wanted, and I've never regretted a single drop of sweat to this moment.

Have you ever charged over a hot gridiron or gasped up some awful hill? Honestly, I have no idea where you've been or what you've done. Your past is opaque to me.

But I absolutely know where you stand *today*. You're decked out in full battle array on a much higher field of play, and everything's played for keeps out there. It's long past those days in school when you might have chosen to discipline yourself and sacrifice for what you wanted for some short-term personal glory. It's *now* time to sacrifice for what you want for those around you in life, for keeps, and for God's glory.

Nobody wants lifetime regrets from *this* field of play, so choose well. Your kids need you to win this battle. Your wife's only hope to have a normal marriage, with a normal intimate connection, rests in your following decisions. So make your adjustments, press through in the second half, and win.

I remember my days of battle well. I wanted to finally establish my manhood, once and for all. Men become men in times like these. What you do over these next months and seasons will define your manhood, your life, and your earthly impact. The battle may seem brutal at first, but it's momentary. You must choose one form of pain or the other, after all. So choose the right kind.

After all, we are living in critical days.

> Because of the increase of wickedness, the love of most will grow cold
> . . . (Matthew 24:12, NIV)

Jesus was referring to how Christians would feel toward Him in the days before His return. I don't know if we are living in the last days, but I *do* know that our current days are exactly like the Lord's description of those last days by at least one criterion. When I was a young man, the percentage of women regularly looking at porn was minuscule. These days, though, I can walk onto a Christian college campus and find 87 percent of the female students sopping up porn at least once a week. That's a *tremendous* increase of sexual sin within the Christian community. You can bet your house that the level of sinful behavior is just as high, if not higher, in today's broader culture.

And that increase of sinfulness has many of us on our faces before God these days. Intercession groups and houses of prayer are popping up worldwide, crying out for revival and cultural renewal. I lead such a group at my local church.

But as my friend the late Bob Phillips once said to me, "People *want* revival, but they *need* holiness." So even as I'm crying out to God to send national revival, I'm also moving deeper into what I need to be as a man and what my family needs from me—holiness. You must move deeper too.

We shouldn't be seeing an increase of wickedness among Christians today. We *should* be seeing Christian men and women making every effort to purify themselves. After all, we have everything we need inside to do so, as you very well know by now.

The grace is there. The knowledge is there. You now know how you're made as well. You have two vulnerabilities in your sexuality that you need to defend but, gratefully, *only* two. You have the knowledge from *Every Man's Battle* to deal with the first one, and you have the knowledge from this book to deal with the second one.

And if you need more understanding, the Holy Spirit will be right at your side, whispering as much truth as you need, right when you need it. So, again, we return to that question formed out of Michael's decision over fifteen years ago as a fourteen-year-old:

What do *you* want, my friend?

I think you know.

I think it's time—time for you to rise up and make everyone in your life forget your first half of play. It's time for you to come through as a man and as a warrior, regardless of what the guys around you may choose. Most of all, it's high time for this battle to be over.

So get out there, my friend.

Make every disciplined effort.

You won't regret it, not now, not forever.

10

Sexual Purity and Your Family Destiny

He established a testimony in Jacob and appointed a law in Israel,
which he commanded our fathers to teach to their children ...
—Psalm 78:5, ESV

Setting a new mark for yourself and dumping porn and masturbation will change your life and transform your family's destiny.

Let me share again what my dear friend Patrick Middleton, the sexual addictions counselor, said back in Chapter 4:

> I deal with a lot of men, and it never fails that the men with deeper sexual issues also have uninvolved or missing fathers. Their sexual issues are directly and severely impacted by their dad's failures as a father to connect with them. That's because there's a point in the development of a boy into a man—say from eleven to thirteen—when the boy needs to move into a deeper relationship with his dad ...
>
> I know this sounds a bit weird, but I've never found a better way to say it: Dad has to be close enough to his son to be able to call the "heart of a man" out of the boy.

That's exactly what I did in my home. I stepped in close enough to my sons, Jasen and Michael, to call the heart of a man out of my boys.

It wasn't by luck. It wasn't by accident. It was a conscious choice I made. As a result, they never used the arena of their emerging sexuality to sort through their questions about manhood. Skipping that counterfeit path altogether, they stayed on the straight and narrow and never formed dependencies upon porn and masturbation. Instead, they found the genuine ticket into manhood, and it sure wasn't going to bed with a girl.

Whether your son grows into manhood with or without a dependence upon porn and masturbation really depends a great deal upon you as his father. Your connection with him and, even more importantly, your decisions regarding your *own* sexual purity will make all the difference in your son's destiny. The trailhead of my firstborn Jasen's path to manhood began with my early personal decisions on purity, and those decisions played out continually in Jasen's life as he matured to manhood.

You'll see this clearly as I share our battle saga, fought together as father and son. I'll start by taking you back in time to a young father in his late twenties—me—who barely knew his head from his feet as a dad and was struggling to find his legs as a parent.

Only two years earlier, Brenda's obstetrician laid my newborn son into my arms for the first time. As I looked deeply into two tiny dark eyes peeping out of that glorious little face, I felt the weight of the world settle upon my shoulders. Then a searing thought rocketed into my consciousness: *I've just been given the responsibility for another human's soul!*

We named him Jasen. He was my firstborn son, the beginning of my strength, perfect in every way. But those same loving little eyes also tortured me because they were challenging me to alter our family's destiny.

Those days remain stark and vivid to me to this day. Jasen loved to have a stick in his hand, like a young prince shaking a miniature scepter over his kingdom. A Matchbox car would be curled tightly in his other hand as he'd amble awkwardly over to me with his treasure, an adorable grin wrapped loosely around his drippy pacifier. Though he couldn't speak yet, I could read those glowing eyes as easily as the Sunday paper: *Daddy, you are my hero! I want to grow up to be just like you!*

I loved him so much. There were many times when I'd sweep him into my arms and wrestle him around for a while. But when we were home alone together, I'd often burst into hopeless tears when I thought of the future that lay ahead of him.

No! Please don't become like me!

As Jasen grew day by day, the truth of my family's generational curse became all too real to me. Both of my grandfathers left their wives for other women, and at least one of them showed signs of an addiction to pornography. My dad left my mom for the sake of many mistresses, and he never kicked his habit of looking at girlie magazines. When he died at the age of seventy-one, I found a stash of pornographic magazines in his desk drawer.

As I grappled with the reality of my family history, I suddenly realized that only three years before Jasen's birth, I was still buried in porn, I was sleeping with girl after girl, and I was essentially engaged to marry two of them. I was certainly carrying on the Stoeker way with women at the time.

Every time I looked into Jasen's yearning eyes, my heart broke a little more. He was the next boy out of the gene pool, flesh of my flesh, but I knew that my continuing sexual sin—since I still enjoyed fantasizing about soft-core pictures of half-naked women—would one day doom him to the same lifeless, heartless jail cell that sucked the souls out of my dad and my grandfathers, who writhed until death freed them from their tortuous chains. I remember holding Jasen tightly and crying out inside, *Son, I can't save you from this prison! I'm not your hero! I can't even save myself! Don't grow up to be like me!*

I thought of all the times I'd wake up at dawn, wide-eyed and shrieking silent screams at the ceiling: *God, why were You so mean to me? Why did You give me a son? You know I can't save him from this mess. Why didn't You give me daughters! You are so cruel! I can't help him, and You don't care!*

Well, God *did* care, and He'd already chosen a date to show me exactly why He'd given me a son. It happened on a bright blue Sunday morning in Iowa. That morning, I figured I'd ease Jasen out of his car seat, carry him into the church nursery, and slip happily into a pew next to my pregnant wife, who was glowing in beauty. Then we'd sing a few songs, absorb the sermon, and grab some Mexican food at Garcia's with Bill and Allison and Jasen's little pal Heather.

That's how my Sunday mornings usually went, but on this particular day of worship, I had no clue that God would use the sermon to quiet the silent screams within me and change the course of my life—and Jasen's—forever.

In his sermon, Pastor Ray Johnson introduced us to Jehonadab, a man mentioned only twice in the Bible. The first time was in connection with a warrior named Jehu, who was about to replace the sissified King Ahab and his witchy queen Jezebel.

God was sick of Ahab and Jezebel's wretched leadership and charged Jehu to take down their kingdom by moving quickly through the nation to butcher everyone politically tied to their reign. Jehu had just put one city to the sword and was on his way to the next on the list when he spotted Jehonadab in the distance, walking along the road.

Jehu knew all about Jehonadab, who stood out throughout Israel as a godly man, perhaps in the same way Billy Graham did when he was alive. *This is my chance to show off in front of this great man,* thought Jehu.

Standing in his chariot, he roared up to Jehonadab and yanked on the reins to stop the horses in a cloud of dust. "Come ride with me today!" Jehu urged. "See my zeal for the Lord!"

Jehonadab shrugged his shoulders and stepped into Jeru's chariot. He rode into the evening with this warrior, tagging along as he butchered the reigning class for the Lord.

Jehonadab was not mentioned again in the Bible until the book of Jeremiah, a passage destined to shift the channels of my life and destiny dramatically:

> This is the word that came to Jeremiah from the LORD during the reign of Jehoiakim son of Josiah king of Judah: "Go to the Rekabite family and invite them to come to one of the side rooms of the house of the LORD and give them wine to drink." . . . Then I set bowls full of wine and some cups before the Rekabites and said to them, "Drink some wine." But they replied, "We do not drink wine, because our forefather Jehonadab son of Rekab gave us this command: 'Neither you nor your descendants must ever drink wine.' . . . We have obeyed everything our forefather Jehonadab son of Rekab commanded us. Neither we nor our wives nor our sons and daughters have ever drunk wine . . ." (Jeremiah 35:1–2, 5–6, 8, NIV)

Obedient children impress God, and He was so pleased with Jehonadab's offspring that He used them as an example to His people:

> Then the word of the LORD came to Jeremiah, saying: "This is what the LORD Almighty, the God of Israel, says: Go and tell the men of Judah and the people of Jerusalem, 'Will you not learn a lesson and obey my words?' declares the LORD. 'Jehonadab son of Rekab ordered his descendants not to drink wine and this command has been kept. To this day they do not drink wine, because they obey their forefather's command. But I have spoken to you again and again, yet you have not obeyed me.' " (Jeremiah 35:12–14, NIV)

While that was an important word for any day, that wasn't the teaching that impacted me on that Sunday morning. Instead, a little-known fact *outside* the direct text slammed home God's message to me. Everything became clear after Pastor Johnson asked us, "Do you know how much time passed between the day that Jehonadab rode with Jehu and the day Jeremiah asked his sons to drink wine with him?"

Fifteen hundred people heard his question that day, and if even one of us knew the answer, I would have been surprised. After a pointed pause, he answered his own question with emphasis.

"Three hundred years!"

I literally fell back against the pew in shock and awe, as if a comet had blasted through my chest.

Three hundred years? I gasped. *Are you saying that a father can live such a great example before his kids that his descendants could still be following his example three centuries later?*

Flabbergasted, my mind raced as the sermon faded to background noise. *Would this work with porn in the same way it worked with wine?* I mused. *Could it be that if I lived rightly enough, then my descendants three hundred years from now might be saying, "We have obeyed everything our forefather Fred commanded us. Neither we nor our wives nor our sons and daughters have ever looked at porn"?*

Oh, my word! God's truth captured me, and my mind exploded with the possibilities right there in the pew. If I could just manage to win this battle and get my children to follow after me, my impact upon my family could last for centuries, not just a generation or two.

I took a long look at my family tree in my mind's eye, standing gnarled, twisted, barren, and fruitless against a gray, lifeless horizon. Its tortured, dark, sinful form had defined the Stoeker name for generations: Adultery. Mistresses. Pornography. Duplicity. Drunkenness.

Suddenly, it struck me. *This could be the watershed moment in my family's history!* Since I was the only male of my generation, the only one who would carry the Stoeker name forward into the future, I could be the difference. Every man in the generations before me may have lived one way, but if I won this battle, every man after me could live another way.

Now things were really heating up in my heart. Even though my family tree was ugly and twisted beyond comprehension, I could regenerate new life through the pruning of God's grace and my obedience. The future of my family tree was now up to me. Where my family name once meant "adultery, mistresses, and porn," the Stoeker surname could mean "holy and true, and chasing the purposes of God" in the future. I could sprout and grow lush, lovely green branches out of a gnarled, lifeless tree for future generations.

Suddenly, I was seeing every man's battle in an entirely new way. I wasn't just involved in some puny border skirmish over what I could or could not look at or what I could or could not touch. It wasn't about my grouchy Father asking me to show Him my hands to make sure they were scrubbed clean of sin. God had just shown me why He'd given me a son, and what's more, He'd just offered me a wide-open door of adventure and impact.

It was about my manhood and my destiny. It was about fighting a big battle to redefine my family name. It was about finally becoming everything my adoption into Christ promised I could be. It was about choosing to be my wife's hero and not her nightmare, defending my beauty Brenda and impacting my family now and into future generations.

I knew this was the defining moment of my life. My heart was stirred to the core at the thought of living out this great adventure! There would be no more posing as a man of God, teaching Sunday school in public and masturbating in private. I was off to war—to destroy my family's oppressor and *be* a man of God rather than *seem* like one.

I knew I was heading into enemy territory with the Almighty's charter to conquer. No wonder my heart was soaring. I'd finally found a place where I didn't have to turn the other cheek, where real men could strap on their pads and get after the task at hand. A place where headbutts were definitely in order.

But just as suddenly, I hesitated.

I know what you're thinking. *How could you? Why would you hesitate with God's charter in hand and a game-changing vista rolling out before your eyes?*

While it seems silly now, at the time I suddenly realized that I wasn't going to be able to do this all by myself. In order to truly redefine the Stoeker name and redirect my family destiny, someone else would have to step up and ride into the battle with me. Only one person could join me: a stubby-legged, drooling little kid who thought I was his hero.

But how could I count on him to join me in this destiny, or any other son I might have, for that matter? I had struggled in this wretched sin for years. Even before I was saved, I hated what I was doing and tried to stop—but failed miserably without God's grace and power.

I knew that winning this battle would be the costliest thing I'd ever done, but I wasn't too sure I was willing to risk all the effort necessary to win when my destiny depended upon a decision that Jasen might or might not make some ten or twelve years into the future. My dependence upon Jasen left too much uncertainty hanging over me.

So I waffled back and forth, counting the costs again and again. *How can I be sure that Jasen will follow the right path? I can't change the destiny of my family tree all by myself. Someone will have to stand up and say, "I'm in too, Dad." But how can I be sure he will?*

This went on for months. God had swung the door wide open for me, but I wouldn't step through. Finally, my exasperated Father in heaven reached the end of His rope and challenged my manhood one morning in prayer with these chilling words to my heart:

Are you going to be the one to drive that stake into the ground right here and change the direction of your family tree, or are you going to leave the job for someone better than you somewhere down the line?

My heart shattered on the spot, and I broke into tears. His words ripped into my soul when He spoke into my inner being that day. It hurt me desperately to think that there might be a Stoeker somewhere down the line who loved God's purposes more than I did (even though that was a good thing, of course).

My mind was racing once more. I thought how I'd spent my whole life in sports trying to prove that I had what it takes to be a winner, a guy you could count on in the clutch, but now I wouldn't even step onto the field. Would I slink back and allow some guy "down the line" to be more committed to God's purposes than me—and finish the job that was mine? I couldn't do that. This was *my* family tree and *my* battle to fight. I didn't like the thought that someone else would have to restore my family name because I wouldn't step into the fray.

But far worse than all that, I knew what lay ahead for Jasen. If I didn't man up and fight this battle, God would one day have to lay the same awful and challenging charge before my precious son. In my mind, I pictured the Lord speaking to my son in this way:

> *Jasen, are YOU going to be the one to drive that stake into the ground right here and change the destiny of your family tree, or are you going to leave the job for someone better than YOU somewhere down the line? Your dad didn't have what it takes to be a man. Do you?*

That thought sealed it, and that's all it took for me to enlist for the front lines. My precious son wasn't going to fight this brutal battle alone; I was going to charge the enemy line first. Still, I must be honest: I fully expected to lose the war. I really did. But that no longer mattered because win or lose, I figured I would at least learn some things along the way that I could pass on to him—crucial intelligence that would help him finally put the Stoeker name right.

So the time for counting costs was over. No matter how miserably I might fail in the field of battle, it was *my* battle and Jasen was *my* boy, and he wouldn't have to fight this horrid thing by himself.

It was time to fight, no matter the cost.

Freedom or bust, the first thing I had to do was face up to the raging war at hand. Could I come through when it mattered most? Would I come through in the clutch?

My destiny as a man depended upon my actions. My *family's* destiny also hung in the balance. This was my moment.

As the Lord would have it, I finally engaged the battle just a few days later. While driving home and checking out a skimpily clad jogger sweating her way up Merle Hay Road—and allowing my eyes to roam and lust over her glistening body—I broke down in tears once again. Pounding my fists onto the steering wheel, I shouted, "It stops here. I don't know how to build a covenant with my eyes, Lord, but I'm going to learn. I'm not going to live like this anymore. It stops here!"

I drove a stake deep into the ground and tied myself to it. There would be no more running. In due time, and by God's grace, I soon stood victorious over my enemy in this ruthless fight. Against all odds, I completed my side of the bargain.

Today, it's your moment to shine. Are you going to drive your stake into the ground? I hope you do because *your* life in Christ and *your* family's destiny depend upon it.

As you ponder your course of action, I want you to notice something. Interestingly, God Himself framed this battle as a fight for manhood when He addressed me on the issue when I was in prayer that morning:

> **Are you going to leave the job for someone better than you, somewhere down the line?**

He needed a man. A warrior. Someone in my family line willing to arise and to walk through the necessary suffering to get it done.

In other words, the Lord's challenge to me that morning in prayer was not so much a tug on my guilt as a disobedient Christian son but a jarring yank on manhood's chain. It's crucial for you to see the difference. This battle is just as much about your integrity as a man as it is about your integrity as a Christian. God wants you to see things this way.

God has always been clear about this, but most of us miss it. It isn't and never was simply a moral issue. I had to learn that the hard way. Learning to control my sexuality was crucial to my development as a man, and it will be the same for you as well.

So let's couch this decision in terms of your manhood. Are you going to fight this great battle here and now and join God in this great adventure of a lifetime? Will you man up and defend the beauty (in my case, Brenda) and the weak (in my case, toddler Jasen)? Or will you flee the scene and let them fend for themselves, like my dad did to my mom and me, choosing his porn and his mistresses over us?

Don't take that route. You must be willing to lay it all on the line and pass the ultimate test of manhood.

You are a man, and that means something special. Your heart was created uniquely for battle. Think back to every plastic machine gun you bravely brandished as a boy and every game you suited up for against your crosstown rivals. Every male heart yearns for a battle to fight, an adventure to live for, and a beauty to save, and this battle for sexual purity lays all three possibilities before you. You're built for moments like these. This is *your* moment. So what are you going to do?

I know what I did. I engaged the battle.

And against all odds, I won.

And because I won, an interesting thing happened when Jasen entered his adolescent years. My decisions shaped his. Even though I agonized for a long time whether Jasen would follow me into this fight for our family destiny, I needn't have worried at all. Jasen stepped up early, at puberty, and joined me in every man's battle. He accepted the challenge without a peep of protest. Though there was overwhelming peer pressure in the world around him, he engaged the battle as naturally as breathing.

Hold it a minute! You're telling me that Jasen got on board like it wasn't a big deal? Like it was the normal thing to do?

That's what I'm saying and, as a matter of fact, it *is* the normal thing to do.

Normal? But practically no one makes a choice to flee from sexual immorality anymore. Why do you say it's the normal thing to do?

Let's freeze this frame and talk about this topic of "normal" for a moment. We must do this because the answer to the following question is crucial: Why *do* I call Jasen's choice to live a pure life "normal"?

Simple. Because God calls it normal. God measures normal by what is common in His *Word*, not by what is common in the *world*. It will always be normal for Christian men to save sexual foreplay and sexual intercourse until marriage, no matter how uncommon it may be to find anyone who is "saving himself" in the present culture around you. It is God who defines what's normal, not us.

It seems we're always calling what's common "normal." For instance, if you're a Christian guy living anywhere in North America, you're likely peeking into other people's bedrooms and watching them having sex regularly.

That's not true, Fred! I'd never do a creepy thing like that.

Think again. Most men do that sort of thing all the time. It's called "streaming" or "going to the movies." Watching others have sex, whether you're sitting on your living room couch with a TV or a handheld device or inside a movie theater, makes you a voyeur—a Peeping Tom.

You might not think of yourself that way, but this behavior *isn't* normal for a Christian, no matter how common this practice is with those in your congregation. Nothing can make it so, whether you're sitting in plush seats sharing an enormous tub of delicious buttered popcorn with your girl or kicking back at your place, watching a sex-soaked, raunchy R-rated film on Netflix.

Christians are normalizing wickedness everywhere. Our salt is losing its saltiness and is no longer good for anything (see Matthew 5:13). Recent surveys even reveal that porn use is acceptable Christian behavior in North America, like it's no big deal, despite God's clear stance on the issue. In short, what's common in our culture has become the new normal.

But not to God. He'll always measure "normal" in relation to His Word. He'll keep using words like "sin," which means "missing the mark." What mark are we missing?

The mark set by Jesus. Jesus was the Word in the flesh, so He was and is the most normal person ever to walk on planet Earth. Are you walking out your life as normally as Jesus did?

As Christian men, we must measure from this mark. Why? Because "becoming normal" is what Christianity is all about. If you don't become normal like Jesus, you will constantly trample and hurt those around you emotionally, especially those you have pledged to love the most.

And given the definition of manhood we're using here, "becoming normal" is what *manhood* is all about as well. How can you ever expect to protect any beauty in your life if you're lusting, having affairs, or being a Peeping Tom? Stop listening to your culture, no matter where you live. Jesus sets the mark that you mustn't miss, especially when it comes to manhood.

And that, my friend, provides the answer to my earlier question. Jasen chose to walk out his life as normally as Jesus did, and that's why I call Jasen's choice to join me in battle "normal." It was a normal step into manhood for a young man like Jasen because that was the mark of normal that Jesus set for us when *He* was a young man here on earth.

Since Jesus set the normal marks of manhood, just like He sets the mark of normal in every other area of life, let me ask this fundamental question: In Jesus' view, what is a guy's normal ticket into manhood?

That's easy to answer, and I can illustrate it through Scripture. You may recall that at the age of twelve, the age when Jewish boys became men, Jesus was in Jerusalem for Passover with His family. When the ceremonies and festivities were over, families began heading back home, filled with joy and laughter. At the end of the day, a long way down the dusty road, Mary and Joseph realized Jesus wasn't with their group, so they rushed back to Jerusalem in a panic. Jesus was at the age of manhood. Did they find Him searching out His manhood with a girl, rolling around in the hay in the back of some secluded barn, searching out His ticket into manhood through His emerging sexuality? Hardly.

His parents discovered Him talking with the religious leaders. When they asked Him why He hadn't joined the caravan for the trip back home after the festival of the Passover, He seemed slightly perplexed, as if the answer should have been obvious to them. He was, after all, a man now.

"Did you not know that I must be about my Father's business?" He asked His earthly parents.

To Jesus, there was only one ticket into manhood: being about His Father's business. That's the mark He sets for all of us, and that's your ticket into manhood as well. If you're a Christian, being about your Father's business is the *only* ticket in town.

Sure, the counterfeit ticket of going to bed with a girl is the one guys use most commonly these days, but hitting culture's mark should mean nothing to you because it's a false mark. Choosing sexual purity is the mark of manhood and the path to manhood in God's world. It's normal for His sons.

That's why I said all the years of worrying over whether Jasen would follow me and join this fight for purity were silly, and I needn't have worried a bit. When Jasen became a young man, it was *normal* for him to choose to be about his heavenly Father's business, and his earthly father's business, as long as I was engaged and active in teaching him and connecting deeply with him as father and son.

Under those circumstances, Jasen naturally stepped up into manhood and helped me redefine the Stoeker name, and he carried that name well, all the way to his wedding day.

As you consider all these things in relation to your family tree, remember Jehonadab's impact upon his family tree and the promise that holds for you as head of *your* family. When it comes to your sexual purity, this is not just an individual decision you're making. Your decision to be about your Father's business will have a significant impact on your family's future and your children's destiny.

In fact, think beyond your children, my friend. These days, I'm thinking about my grandchildren. Consider my granddaughters, Halle and Linnea. As of this writing, Halle is thirteen and Linnea is eleven years old. They're so feminine, so nurturing, and so loving and kind. Halle is brilliant and courageous, and Linnea is so beautifully sweet that sugar is sour by comparison.

Sometime around the year 2035 or so, they could very well meet the men of their dreams. Because of my decision fifty years earlier in 1985, they can enter these relationships knowing with absolute certainty that a husband can commit his sexuality so completely to his wife that even his eyes are kept solely for her. They will understand that a husband can commit his masculine heart so completely to God that he'll willingly tie himself to a stake in the ground and fight for his family's purity.

I haven't yet attained the three hundred years of impact that Jehonadab did in his family line. After all, new chapters are still being composed by my children, Jasen, Laura, Rebecca, and Michael, and there will be others to come after them somewhere down the line.

But I *can* already see the impact of my decision in 1985 rolling out fifty years to Halle's and Linnea's weddings in or around the year 2035. And suddenly, Jehonadab's three hundred years of impact upon his family tree doesn't seem so out of reach for mine.

So please, let that thought inspire you as a parent, as well as this verse of Scripture:

> Therefore, since we are surrounded by such a great cloud of witnesses, let us throw off everything that hinders and the sin that so easily entangles. And let us run with perseverance the race marked out for us . . . (Hebrews 12:1, NIV)

Sure, each of your children will have to run their races for purity on their own, but with your stand and God's help, they won't be heavily burdened by generational sin from the beginning like I was. You can vaporize the family curses and free them to run further and faster than you ever dreamed possible.

Give them a vision.

Hand them the baton.

Teach them to carry the name well and to run and win.

This is part of your role as a man. It's part of authenticity, of being who you say you are, even when you're alone in your room with your computer or smartphone.

Carrying the family name well is what destiny is all about.

I was there to see what victory looks like in the family arena with my own eyes.

I'll never forget the afternoon I sat in the first row with other family members for the marriage of Jasen and Rose, listening to Pastor James Christopher talk about the meaning of covenant in marriage. Facing the young couple and four hundred people filling the pews, Pastor Christopher said this:

> Well, we're coming up to that special moment—the kiss—that we all look forward to at the end of every wedding. But before we do this, let me share something with you. This is certainly the moment we're always waiting for, but it's especially true regarding this couple. Many of you

may not realize that this couple really *has* waited until marriage, and this is going to be their very first kiss.

The crowd gasped audibly.

What did he just say? Did he say what I thought he said?

The fact that Jasen and Rose mutually decided to wait until they were pronounced husband and wife to share a kiss surprised me, and it certainly surprised everyone else in attendance that afternoon. I can't imagine how rare it is for *any* couple to get married without ever having kissed. I never taught Jasen to do that, and frankly, it wouldn't have even occurred to me to ask that of him.

Pastor Christopher, with a grin, continued by saying this:

> We just talked about what a covenant relationship means before God. Now let's look at how the Lord's temple completes the picture of a marital covenant for us.
>
> In the temple, there was a veil at the entrance to the Holy of Holies. In order to go beyond that veil and worship the Lord, the high priest had to first enter into a blood covenant with Him. What's interesting is that in the original language of Scripture, the word used for worship was *proskuneo*, or "kiss." In other words, only the man in covenant with God could pass beyond the temple's veil and "kiss" the Lord in worship.
>
> This couple's relationship has followed that same pattern as they've approached their marital covenant, and I think the Lord is very pleased with that. When it comes to relationships between men and women, God is clear that a man must be in covenant with a woman before he goes in to her.
>
> As a man, Jasen has willingly waited until this moment, the moment he's entered into covenant with Rose. He has accepted the position of high priest for her, and he has accepted the responsibility of representing her before the throne of God as leader of his family.
>
> Now that he has done so, his wait is finally over, and that special moment has arrived. Since Jasen has just entered into covenant with Rose, he can now go beyond the veil—her wedding veil—and kiss his bride.
>
> So now it is with especially great pleasure that by the power vested in me by Jesus Christ, His Church, and the state of Iowa, I now pronounce you husband and wife. Jasen, you may kiss your bride!

As Jasen joyously wrapped bubbly Rose into his arms and their lips met for the first time, our exuberant guests burst into spontaneous, boisterous shouts of jubilation for this heroic young couple.

But not me. Sure, I had a big smile on my face, and I was extremely happy, but I was simply too mesmerized by it all to make a sound. Instead, I was filled with unadulterated awe for a grinning, handsome young groom standing in the spotlight on this day. Jasen had run his race and finished the course. There he stood, standing regally and victoriously at the top of the podium, a spiritual gold medal draped invisibly around his neck.

From those earliest days of puberty to this grand, triumphant moment at the altar, Jasen had never touched a girl's body in dishonor, whether on a couch in a dim basement or inside a car with fogged-up windows on a lonely rural road, or even in his private single-bed Iowa State dorm room. He was the same man of integrity, the same man of his word, wherever he happened to be. That's manhood, and because of that, he never left a girl worse off for having known him, from puberty right on up to his wedding day.

Because of that, one and only one thought kept reverberating through my mind and continued to echo across my heart repeatedly throughout the wedding reception: *Jace, you're a greater man than I ever dreamed of being. You are the finest man I know.*

I meant every word then, and I mean every word today. It was never more apparent than on Jasen's wedding day that sex was not a man's ticket into manhood but his ticket *out*. It was so easy to see.

It was also easy to see that God's work in my family tree had been extraordinary. Consider this. When I was twenty-three years old, I had four girlfriends simultaneously. I was sleeping with three of them regularly, and I was essentially engaged to be married to two of them, wrapped up tightly by the generational bondage of my family tree.

Only one generation later, and at that very same age of twenty-three, my exultant son Jasen was sweeping freely up the center aisle, hand in hand with his radiant wife, Rose, having just kissed a girl for the very first time. The generational curse was disintegrated.

What a huge change of behavior between two Stoeker men! Every one of my dreams for a massive move by God in my family tree had just come true before my very eyes. The Lord had changed our very destiny as a family and had literally, in a single generation, returned my family tree to normal.

Catching this vision—and keeping in mind that your decisions today will impact your family for generations—will change everything for your family.

Sometime after the wedding, I was sitting in Pastor Christopher's office, talking about that day and what it all meant.

"Fred, what strikes me," James began, "is that one of the things you carry as a father is this vision for the family crest—the family line. When you fought for your identity as a young Christian man, you had an understanding of this unlike anybody I've ever known. You weren't just redefining your identity, but you were redefining your lineage, the Stoeker name. Your boys had a father's voice speaking into their lives, but it wasn't just a call to resist sin. You were building in them an identity: *Hey, you're a Stoeker. We're going to change the family name together.* For you, it wasn't about just resisting what was chasing you from the past. Instead, you kept talking about the *future* and who you all would be together. That was such an essential part of this."

"I appreciate those words, Pastor. But I think you know exactly why I did what I did, don't you?"

"I do, and that's why you need to share this vision with others because a man's life is not just about *his* identity but about changing the lineage—the line that your forebears laid down in the past. I say that because we each produce after our own kind, if you know what I mean. If I see myself as this messed-up sinner, then I will keep sinning and struggling to get righteous. If I see myself as a righteous saint, sometimes struggling with some sin but primarily a righteous guy, then I will produce after my own kind. That's why every father must cast a vision of the future and fight for that, not dwelling upon what he used to be."

"Catching that vision changed me from the inside out, forever," I mused with him.

"I bet it did. I love this line in Andy Stanley's book *Visioneering*, which says, 'What could be, is an idea. What should be, is a dream. And what must be, is a vision.' You knew what *must be* in your family. You see, vision speaks to our deepest destiny. When you spoke at the men's conference a while back about reforming your family, it made my heart burn, especially that part where you spoke of every person in your family line being different from here on out. Visions speak to those deep aspirations within us that are wired there by God. There's a knowing, deep within us, that strikes at something."

"That's what I did with my boys," I said.

"Your daughters too," James kicked in. "Sure, you put the message of your books into them naturally because you live out your books at home. That's who you are, day in and day out. But you also added an element that really got them away from just white knuckling it against sexual sin. You instilled in them an identity, an essence of knowing who they are so that whenever they walked out the door of your home, they were no longer scared of the enemy. They weren't being chased every moment by the thought of *I hope I don't lust today!*"

I shifted in my chair. "I didn't want them to go through what I went through. It was awful, lust's hold on me and the sense that Satan had my number," I said.

"With your kids, it was just the opposite," James continued. "They knew the enemy was scared of *them*. People like this have their destiny in hand. That's what you've instilled in your kids. I think the difference is always the father's voice. I'm talking about your voice and, of course, the voice of the Father. It was that intimacy with you and with Him. You were both encouraging fathers who believed in them. I think that was the crucial element."

"Honestly, Pastor, I never thought of it in such lofty terms back then, but I can tell you, it all burned in me exactly like that, inside and out," I mentioned.

"Fred, whether you made the connection or not, what you've done in your family is what God Himself did in establishing a testimony in Jacob, His own family. God established a whole history, testimony upon testimony, for Israel. As it says in Psalm 78, that became their legacy. God called on them to share with the coming generations what God did for them and what they as a people meant to Him.

"He did it so that they wouldn't turn from Him. He was saying that sharing the family history *in* God keeps their walk with God alive. If we never share our testimonies, then we forget that God is a miracle-working God, and everything just becomes life as normal.

"It strikes me that your sons don't let people define 'normal' for them. It doesn't matter what people say to them, mocking or not, because you've so thoroughly defined their identity in Christ and as a family in the home."

"Yes, that's true," I said. "I'll never forget the time I was speaking in Miami. I'd just gone through the whole history of Jasen and me and the change in our family destiny from the podium. As I finished, I remember coming down from the stage and sitting down next to Michael, and he put his head on my shoulder and started sobbing. Before long, he turned and hugged me. 'I'm so happy to be part of *this* family and *this* destiny,' he said. Let me tell you—there were tears in my eyes too."

"Exactly!" James exclaimed. "Remember Esau? He traded his birthright for a pot of stew. But think about what Michael said to you in his tears. Is Michael ever going to trade that destiny, that deep thing he sees God building in the Stoeker family, for a quick fling in the back seat of some car, like some measly pot of stew? No way! He's not going to trade his inheritance for one lousy sexual meal."

As you can see, it's not inevitable that a young man will get hooked on porn and masturbation and the emotional dependence that comes with it. As fathers, we can always make the difference. If we refuse to believe that the cultural flotsam and debris swirling about us must sink our families, we will parent proactively and walk a different path.

Once I'd won my battle, I refused to believe that my sons had to be bound as

I had been. Even before I became a father, the following verse got me thinking about the dramatic possibilities we have as parents:

> You will not fear the terror of night, nor the arrow that flies by day, nor the pestilence that stalks in the darkness, nor the plague that destroys at midday. A thousand may fall at your side, ten thousand at your right hand, but it will not come near you. (Psalm 91:5–7, NIV)

While this verse isn't typically used in parenting classes at church, no verse had a more profound impact upon my vision as a father than this one. What God's Word said to me here was this: *No matter what is happening in the society around you, it needn't touch your kids.* This was a game-changer for me, and I clung to it with my life.

I didn't have to tolerate what so many parents endure! While every other guy in the youth group might slide his hand up under his girlfriend's bra, that plague needn't stalk my sons. Ten thousand girls may let their boyfriends' hands roam their bodies, and a thousand may fall into bed at our sides, but it will not come near my girls.

That keystone truth enabled me to raise four sexually pure children amid a sensually drenched culture. None of it entered my home. Jasen strode to his wedding altar having never once masturbated.

The pestilence of sexual impurity is stalking ten thousand young men standing at your right hand today, but it needn't touch you or your kids. Taking this stand as a parent will force you to engage your kids early on this topic and fight for an alternative path forward as a family.

That step of engagement is the vehicle that delivers their genuine tickets into manhood. Being about their Father's business will keep them from forming an early dependence upon porn and masturbation that stunts their growth as men.

That's what you want as a father and as a man. It's essential because that decision will not only impact your family but will also influence everyone else around you, as I'll explain in my next chapter.

11

Sexual Purity and Your Church's Destiny

Why don't men play the man? Why don't they offer their strength
to a world desperately in need of it? For two simple reasons: We
doubt very much that we have any real strength to offer, and we're
pretty certain that if we did offer what we have, it wouldn't be
enough. Something has gone wrong, and we know it.
—John Eldredge, *Wild at Heart*

When I think about the possibilities we have as fathers to impact our
families' destinies, I can't miss how Jasen's approach as a young husband
and father was so different from mine, even though he was as heavily strapped
with financial pressures early in his marriage as I had once been.

The story is short but poignant. Jasen was married with two girls and desiring
a third child. Along with the typical costs of raising kids, Rose had brought
some leftover college debt into their marriage. Their first house, a lovely little
blue one, had become a money pit. Toss one totaled van into the mix and a
financial noose tightened swiftly around Jasen's neck. He was having difficulty
breathing under that load and needed a new job that paid more money.

The trouble was, Jasen was an engineer. He liked to have everything in its
place and in order. Uncertainty? He didn't like that, not one bit. Caution was
his middle name, and so the decision to look for a new job scared him to death.

So where did Jasen run in the face of his financial stress?

I'm sure you remember where *I* ran when the financial noose tightened
around my neck, and Logan raced down that same road as his throat tightened

up. But not Jasen. Remember, he never used his emerging sexuality to search out his manhood when he was a teen. He never used that counterfeit ticket as his shortcut to manhood. He was a genuine man and knew how to play the real man in his life. Real men have no dependence on orgasmic stress relief. Real men have a dependence on God.

So Jasen ran to God in prayer and worship, and he asked the Lord to join him on his great financial adventure. My son then stepped up and made a courageous but scary decision to leave a safe but less-than-challenging job at a Fortune 100 company to take on an extremely challenging position with a smaller private firm but with much higher pay.

He took that heroic leap to provide for his family's future and protect them financially today. He had no idea how his choice would turn out, and he was scared white by the magnitude of making such a bold move. But he faced his decision head-on with the Lord. That's what real men do. This act drew the hero out of my "take the safe way" son.

You see, Jasen's destiny as a man was changed long ago when he was a boy. His father—me—eradicated the pestilence of sexual sin and drug-like dependency it inspired from his childhood home and cleared a wide-open road into manhood. So a man was born from the word go.

Your decisions today absolutely matter, for decades, to everyone around you. If you allow this pornographic pestilence to go unchecked in your home, remember that this contagion can't be constrained by the walls of your home. This pandemic-like plague will ride right into your children's homes, infecting them too. In fact, it'll ride right into your local church along with you, impacting even *its* destiny.

Sure, inside the isolation cell of our sin, we think we can quarantine it all. We whisper our lies to ourselves repeatedly, clouding our understanding.

What's the problem with a bit of porn and masturbation? I'm under grace! I'm forgiven! Besides, nothing I do in the privacy of my own home affects anyone outside of here.

But these are lies. Those polluting effects of your sin churn on through the waters of your church community as inexorably as an oil spill. For example, let me pull back the curtain on the inner life of one Midwestern church to show you what I mean.

One Saturday morning a few years ago, I stepped into a church unlike any I'd ever seen. I say that because the men I met were unlike those in nearly any church in this nation.

I speak with some authority because when I travel to speaking engagements, almost every church rolls out pretty much the same for me. Whenever I walk into a foyer or atrium for the first time, the men of the church are generally on guard, holding back. They aren't rude. It's just that they all seem, well, nervous.

I get it. They're edgy because of the subject matter of *Every Man's Battle*, and they wonder if my laser eyes can pierce into their souls, fearing I'll bellow out the truth: "You, sir, were masturbating just last night on the basement couch at precisely 11:32 p.m. as you watched Cardi B twerking up a storm. You need to be here today *so* much!"

Listen up, guys! I cannot read your minds, but even if I could, I'm a good guy. I'd never call you out in front of your friends. I promise.

But this church was different—and I mean that in a good way because I walked into another world that morning. Nearly every guy who greeted me—and there were a bunch—held their chins up and their chests out, topped with big, warm smiles. There wasn't a trace of shame or guilt inside that building.

It was the craziest thing I had ever seen. That just doesn't happen when I show up to speak at a men's conference.

And then an old axiom came to mind: *You can always tell the condition of a culture by the state of its men.* On that Saturday morning, I could easily tell the condition of that church culture by the state of its men. They were flat-out manly.

When the weekend conference was over, I sat down with the pastor of the church, Travis, to find out how in the world this happened. The story he told me was quite revealing.

When Travis began leading his five-hundred-member church, he noticed a troubling pattern. Men weren't stepping into leadership roles, and Travis knew that a church needs men in leadership to be healthy.

"What I noticed is that I would continually ask the men in my church to help us out, and they kept saying no," Travis said. "After a while, I got really frustrated. I thought about going up to every one of them and saying, 'You seem like a good guy, and I need you to help me. What's up here?'

"I was trying to figure out why in the world they kept saying no to me when I needed them to be leaders. They clearly liked the church. I even checked their giving records, knowing people will only give to a church they truly believe in. They were giving. But still, they never wanted to help with anything, from teaching Sunday school to heading up a Life Group in their homes. If one or two *did* step up, they only wanted to usher. I got the impression they were okay with that because ushering was not that spiritual in their eyes," Travis explained.

"The more I prayed and thought about it, the more I was sure that they didn't believe their private lives matched up with the way they knew they should be living, and so my men were disqualifying themselves from serving. They didn't want to step up into leadership where things might get uncovered. In leadership, you're accountable, closer to the pastor and closer to the hands-on ministry that's going on."

I was interested in hearing more and nodded to Travis to explain further.

Travis took a breath. "They knew what they were doing in private, so when

I'd ask for men to step into leadership, they'd respond negatively in their hearts, saying, 'There's no way I can do that, Pastor. Some things I can do. I can go out and make more money and I can give you that money. After all, that's what I know how to do, and God seems to smile on my ability to make money. I can help single moms with their cars or use my power tools to bless the church, but when you ask me to teach Sunday school, go on missions trips, or head up a small group, I can't do that. I'm not qualified to step above the threshold of usher. Sorry about that, but that's how I feel.' And even with ushering, it was *no, no, no* most of the time," Travis said.

"What caused all this self-disqualification?" I asked, figuring that sexual sin lay at the root.

Travis had reached the same conclusion. "They didn't say anything out loud to me, so I had to get to it in a different way. That's because few guys were going to say to me, right out of the blue, 'Uh, Pastor, I'm looking at porn,' or 'My marriage is a mess . . . we never have sex, so I must get release in other ways,' or 'I'm self-medicating my frustrations by looking at porn and then getting off.' Sexual sin makes guys think they're the creepiest, sickest people ever. The guilt and isolation beat them up.

"A few of them finally admitted that this was going on. Since I knew this really is every guy's problem, I figured sexual sin was at the root of my male leadership problem. If I could address the guilt by getting them free and address their isolation by teaming them up to fight this battle together, I knew my men would finally quit self-disqualifying and answer my call to lead."

"So what happened?" I asked.

"I preached on this topic several Sundays and then started quite a few purity Life Groups, and boom, guys started stepping up right away. As they began to win their battles with sexual sin, they started realizing God could use them. It was the greatest breakthrough for our men's ministry that you could imagine."

Hearing Travis explain how things went down was fascinating to me. After all, I felt the difference in his men the moment I entered the church foyer.

"But how exactly did you come to this realization?" I asked. "Guys don't like to talk about these things directly, so was there a key moment in time when the guys made things clear to you?"

Travis reflected, then pressed forward. "I think the key moment was when I took a risk and explained my own struggles to some of the guys. I told them, 'Guys, I lust too, and I have to repent of that.' Another time, I said, 'Yeah, I have to bounce my eyes every time I go to the gym.' Basically, I opened up about myself first.

"They were shocked that I did. They were like, 'You do?' Like they just thought I could walk into the gym without noticing the women in skintight clothes and curvy figures in yoga pants. It was so comical, but that's what they thought.

"It's strange being a pastor, Fred," Travis continued, chuckling. "Even when I lost weight, they thought I had simply prayed and lost weight miraculously. They thought I didn't have to be disciplined in what I eat or how much I work out like other people do. Literally, they were like, 'Seriously, you have to avoid sweets too?' It was ludicrous. There was this misperception that somehow a pastor doesn't struggle with anything even remotely like other guys do. No wonder they were disqualifying themselves and didn't want to get too close to me in some leadership role.

"So I kept being as transparent as I could. I kept telling them, 'No, no, no. I'm like every guy—we're *all* facing this.' That's when the lights came on for them. They breathed a collective sigh of relief and finally began to let their guards down. They could finally talk to me in real terms. *Okay, Pastor, what is normal when it comes to sex? Where's the boundary of temptation? Where's the line where I cross into addiction?* They had a lot of questions. They needed sound teaching."

They sure did. Once the dam broke, though, their transparency was breathtaking, exposing the depth of the problem in full view. Pastor Travis had assumed that most of the guys were living in a "normal but tripping up every once in a while" sort of range.

"But that wasn't true," he told me. "I soon discovered there was a percentage, maybe 10 to 15 percent, who flat-out told me, 'I cruised for hookers last night' or 'I hire call girls on road trips.'

"I was stunned, Fred. Inside, I gasped, *Oh my goodness! You did? But you're in our church! Like seriously?* Or they might say, 'I spent $500 on pornography last month.' Hearing that sort of stuff shocked me. As a pastor, I was embarrassed. I suddenly realized that I had been *so* naïve and blind about the men in my congregation. I mean, I figured there were married men out there in the world who cruised for hookers and spent five hundred bucks a month on porn websites, but I didn't know that guys like this were in my *church!*"

Travis was really getting animated.

"I had assumed that most of my guys were in the 'normal struggles zone,' but now I realized many of the guys lived far beyond that. They were deep in the 'yielding to the flesh zone,' and there was a significant percentage of men—nice, good guys—who were just flat-out 'controlled by the flesh.' I wondered how many pastors out there were as naïve as I'd been. That foolish assumption about my men was devastating to my call as a pastor and to our call as a church. It kept them from getting the help they needed from me."

"'Devastating' is the perfect word for it," I commented.

Once this behind-the-scenes truth clicked in Travis's head, he knew he had to get all this under control so he could begin raising up leaders in his church. While looking for a first step to take, he received an answer from a guy in his congregation.

"I'd just preached a series of sermons that included sections on sexual sin," Travis said. "A guy from our church came up to me after the series was over and said, 'Hey, I've never heard a church pastor be that honest, so let me be honest too. I got some help from an intense purity ministry here in Minneapolis, and it helped because I was full-on addicted. In fact, my wife had finally caught me, and I was going to lose my marriage, so it was a very good thing I found that ministry. Would you be interested in having them do some of their stuff here in our church?'

"What an amazing opportunity! His words seemed more than a simple coincidence to me, so I didn't hesitate in my response. 'Sure. That would be perfect,' I said.

"That shocked him once more. He said, 'Most pastors would just say, "Not our guys! Our guys don't struggle with this sort of stuff." I'm amazed you're saying yes, Pastor.' "

At that moment, Travis was overwhelmed with joy, grateful God had recently opened his eyes. He knew God was about to mount an all-out rescue.

"Granted, even then I didn't fully realize how many of my guys were controlled by porn and sexual sin, or even how many were on the edge between yielding and being controlled. But I turned the corner and ran with God on this, come what may. We started an 'Every Man's Battle for Purity Ministry' boot camp, and I basically got up in front of the whole church and said, 'Everybody struggles with this. If you don't, you're lying. Because of that, every guy, married or single, should be here.'

"When I added that *all* the pastors were required to be part of this new ministry, every attitude changed. *Every pastor is going?* they thought. It was a huge breakthrough when I admitted that *every* pastor struggled too. The isolation and guilt began to evaporate immediately. We started that ministry with a one-day intensive, which then birthed the boot camp that we did every morning from 6:00 a.m. to 7:30 a.m. for three days.

"During that first Saturday intensive, we discussed lust, pornography, uncontrolled sexual desires, and the damages that those things will do. We told the guys flat-out that this is where Satan has you trapped, but three days of boot camp would give them the tools to fight it.

"Every guy received a copy of your book *Every Man's Battle*. After going through the first couple of chapters, the guys shared their testimonies, and then there were prayer times. We gave them an opportunity to write down all the things they had done wrong sexually, which was difficult, but then we asked them to talk about what they had written with a friend—a purity partner. Next, we set out a paper shredder and told the guys they could go at it, declaring, 'God, we *know* that You've forgiven us, although our sins keep wanting to come back into our minds. We *know* we have been forgiven. We confessed them to You, we confessed them to a brother, and now we shred this list.' And then from there, we had them sign up for the Purity Groups."

I thought this was fantastic. "At first, how many Purity Groups did you have?" I asked. "And how many men were in a Purity Group?"

Travis said there were anywhere from eight to twenty guys in each Purity Group. "We wanted a couple of dozen groups, so we asked, 'Please tell us the three times you can meet on the sign-up sheet.' We had groups scheduled for nights, mornings—whenever. As each told us his first, second, and third choices, we slotted each guy into the best time for him.

"Our Purity Groups, as well as our Addiction Groups, are our only Life Groups allowed to meet on campus. Normally, we want all our Life Groups out in the community to be salt and light, but we felt that we didn't want guys sitting at a Panera restaurant trying to get honest and vulnerable while fearing somebody might overhear them. So we asked the guys to meet here at the church. Each group got together for about ten weeks, and they'd also pray with each other daily as accountability partners, which helped remind each guy what he was trying to do."

"Were the guys supposed to do any homework?" I asked.

"They sure were. We asked them to read a certain chapter in *Every Man's Battle* and to be prepared for the discussion questions during those ten weeks."

After putting out a schedule of Purity Groups for his men, I wondered what its impact was on their willingness to step into leadership at church. After all, Travis had said that his men had been disqualifying themselves from leadership on a broad scale.

"Okay, Travis, so you waded right in and soon had all these men battling this thing together. What happened? Were they interested in stepping up to help at church almost immediately, or did that take some time?"

Travis considered my question for a moment, then spoke. "The first thing we saw was immediate camaraderie building up among the men," he replied. "They were no longer isolated. They no longer felt like they were the only guy struggling out there. That was huge! Then the next thing I saw was men stepping up all over the place. Men leading men, men leading Life Groups, and men going on missions trips. It was a stepping up across the board. Some guys were like, 'Hey, now that I've brought my sin into the light, I can jump into leadership.'

"It was almost comical to me, but that's one thing I've learned about us as men. We are quick forgivers of ourselves. We can compartmentalize, of course, which can be bad and good. It isn't helpful when you can compartmentalize and give yourself a pass on your sin, saying, 'I'm only bad when I'm on the road.' We can compartmentalize like nobody's business and forget what we did and instead focus on how good our intentions are—even while sinning.

"But this trait can also work in our favor. As soon as you've asked for forgiveness, you can get up from there and say, 'Where do you need me, Pastor?' As a man, you realize you don't need a track record to ask that question, whereas a woman might ask, 'Well, how long has it been since your last stumble? Maybe you ought to wait a year or two and prove you are worth.'

"But a man's attitude goes like this: 'If I said I'm moving forward, I'm moving forward today.' Even if he falls, he still intended to be pure and holy. As a group, it works out the same way. They jumped up and stepped into leadership a lot quicker than I expected they would."

I nodded because what the pastor was sharing made sense. "This story fits everything I saw when I first arrived here, Travis. Stepping into the foyer, I immediately recognized a difference in the health of your men. No one was averting their eyes from me or looking down in shame. Everybody, even those who told me later in the morning that they were still struggling, had their chests out and their chins up. The camaraderie was strong, with a lot of smiles and friendship evident among your guys. Later, as the morning rolled forward and I listened to their testimonies, I saw men who had once been weaklings in the face of sexual sin now leading the charge. They were now men to be reckoned with, men of obvious character and fierce spiritual strength."

"We've worked hard on the camaraderie," Travis explained. "One of the first rules of our Purity Ministry was that your Life Group couldn't just go through *Every Man's Battle* and talk about purity all day or all night. We made it mandatory for them to go out and do some fun things together because men need good, fun things to do with other guys. Some groups went out and did paintball. In my group, we chose to race go-carts and then go out for Buffalo wings afterward. We had a blast! Some guys said, 'I've never had such good, clean fun with men before.' That was great to hear, but isn't that sad? That's why these outings were so huge in their impact.

"We wanted guys hanging out for a couple of hours, relaxing and realizing that there were other guys in the church they could hang out with. We had guys get into fantasy football leagues together. We had guys who went on camping and fishing trips, or they golfed together and had a great time without all the drinking and coarse sexual talk. This was a good thing. Life-changing, really. Our church culture has never been the same."

"I'm sure it hasn't been," I commented. "In my experience, when guys start hanging out with other guys, the battle for purity turns in our favor because isolation and shame are at the very root of the issue. This genuine intimacy with each other *decreases* the desire for the false intimacy that comes from porn and masturbation. Did you notice that in your guys? Did they say things like, 'Man, it seems like all the friendships I've built here have made the entire battle easier'?"

"Yes, all the time," Travis replied. "Having a friend makes all the difference in the world. Let me give you an example. I went to Russia recently on a missions trip, and I usually travel with my wife, Hannah, or another guy in our church, just for the accountability. This time, my wife canceled at the last minute, so I had to travel alone. When I got to my hotel in Moscow, the first thing that happened when I walked into our hotel lobby was that I got approached by a swarthy-looking Russian dude. His English was quite good. He looked at me and asked, 'Hey, do you need a hooker?'

"I replied, 'Dude, I don't need a hooker. I'm a pastor.' He practically sneered at me. 'Whatever,' he said. 'Pastors need them too.'

"I wasn't going to let that statement go by without challenging it.

"'No, they don't!' I exclaimed. I thought that was the end of the matter until I went up to my room and turned on the television. There was porn on the first channel, right in my face. I turned off the tube and said, 'Man, I've got to go for a walk.'

"I hit the streets, and it looked like there was a porn explosion in Moscow. There were magazines with naked women on the cover at every kiosk. There were beautiful bodies everywhere I turned, so I texted my purity partner back in the States and said, 'Dude, you've got to hold me accountable. I'm in an onslaught attack—help me!' "

What a story. I was impressed with Travis's transparency. As a pastor, he showed how it should be done: admit you're being bombarded, seek accountability, flee from temptation, and tell others what you're doing.

"When I'm transparent with my experiences to the men, they're all in," Travis reflected. "These guys are there for me, and I'm going to be there for them. And this is what I need to be strong for my guys, to be strong for my fellow pastors—this kind of transparent commitment and passion in the battle. By now we are unified. We are one. So yes, having an accountability partner helps, but so does having groups of guys battling together.

"As a matter of fact, I just talked to a friend in another state who fell into an immoral relationship," Travis continued. "My friend said, 'Travis, a guy needs someone in his life to whom he can say, "That woman is way too attracted to me, and I'll admit that I'm way too attracted to her. When I walk by, I look at her. I gaze. I daydream.' "

"Tragically, he went on to say, 'I wish I had you closer in my life because the entire time, Satan's voice was working on my mind. I could have silenced the enemy's voice by hearing your voice.' This was a great insight, and it helps explain why teaming up changes the battle completely."

I asked Travis if the Purity Groups had any impact on the growth of his church.

"Fred, when you are a larger church, like we are now, church growth is always limited by the number of leaders you can raise up. If you don't have the leaders, you can't handle the Christ-followers or the nonbelievers that God wants to send you. So whenever you do anything that increases the number of leaders you have, it increases the number of people your church can minister to. That's the key to growth!

"Now, when you're a small church, you need fewer leaders, so a lot of pastors can afford to overlook a purity ministry for men. If your church has one hundred people, then a pastor and a couple of deacons or elders are probably all the leaders you need. But if you've got three hundred or five hundred in your congregation and most men are self-disqualifying, you've got a problem. That's why I couldn't grow my church, no matter what I did.

"But when we started our Purity Ministry, the men got healthy and began stepping up in droves. We are up to over five thousand people now, with multiple campuses all over the city, but that's only because we have the leaders we need to handle what God sends us. The Purity Ministry has had everything to do with that.

"I know that growing from five thousand to ten thousand will also depend on how many leaders we can raise up. Even though we've had great growth, we never treat the Purity Ministry as a 'been there, done that' situation. This ministry continues to be a central part of our church culture because everything rides upon the sexual health of our men. Because of that, I've made it mandatory for guys to go through our Purity Ministry to become members of our congregation. If we can keep men from disqualifying themselves, we will always have the leaders we need, and we're only going to grow because of it."

I had a question. "Were there other sins you've seen in your men that led to widespread self-disqualification? Or was it just sexual sin?"

"I've *never* seen one other reason!" Travis replied. "I mean, a guy can be a bad husband, almost abusive. He can be embezzling money. I've seen many guys living a dual life in other areas, being completely unethical in business or rotten as husbands, but they still don't see these as disqualifiers from leadership in the church. If you think about it, it's scary that they *don't* disqualify themselves because of these other sins.

"But sexual impurity always seems to gnaw on every guy's conscience in a unique way, and we won't allow guys to step up into leadership until they deal with it. I would say to any pastor that it's a huge mistake to pretend that sexual sin doesn't exist among your men. You will never have enough leaders until you correct that mistake in your thinking.

"One of the things I love about our church is that people will visit and say, 'Boy, your men really step up.' Guest speakers tell me all the time that they can't believe how many men are in our church. And they are right. We have a ton of men in our church."

Which prompted another question. "So what's your theory on that? Why is your church so attractive to men?" I asked.

"Here's how I see things. Because men are swamped in sexual sin across this nation, and many are avoiding leadership in their congregations, women have been forced to take their place, resulting in feminization of the church over time. For most guys across this nation, the church looks feminine to them, the church feels feminine, and the sermons are feminine. Many men have a mental picture of Jesus petting sheep, always turning the other cheek, and floating through life peacefully in nice white robes. The guys are groaning inside, saying, *Man, maybe my wife can love Him, but I can't flow with this at all. I'm not like that, and I don't want to be like that either.*

"But that's not who Jesus is or what the church is supposed to be. If we help the guys get clean, I can cry out, 'We aren't going to pet sheep! No, no, no! We're going to take this city, and we're going to take this world.' They can make a trip to the Amazon jungle basin to build a church, a place where they don't shower, and they all come back with beards. When other guys see them upon their return, they respond, 'All right, sign me up! I'm in!' The church won't be feminized when men step up.

"And that's vital because a feminized church keeps men trapped in their sin. The typical guy believes that if he tells his wife he struggles with lust, she'll think he is a pervert. He's pretty certain that if he tells his pastor that he struggles with lust, he'll also call him a pervert, and that pastor will side with his wife. Do you see what I'm saying? The two of them would gang up on him, so he's thinking to himself, *It's bad enough that I've got my wife on my case. I'm not telling you anything, Pastor!* The men of my church were shocked when I didn't gang up on them after they opened up to me. Instead, I said, 'I feel your pain.' "

"That must have blown them away!" I mused out loud.

"To a man, they all said, 'You do?' And I'd say, 'Not only do I feel your pain, but we are in this thing together, and God has a plan for our lives. Let's chase the visions *He* has for us instead of the things of this world.' That's masculine. That can't help but sound like a great adventure to a guy's ears. That's perfect because men need to be on a mission."

"That *does* sound masculine!" I gushed.

"Listen," Travis said. "I sometimes get criticized for having goals as a church and as a pastor. But I don't think goals are wrong because men are made for conquest, and if we're to engage men, they need a target. We men are goal chasers—and as men, we're created that way, to be conquerors. When guys are in a church that's all about conquest, goals, chasing down the enemy, conquering, going out and starting another campus, winning another neighborhood or city for Christ, or going on another missions trip and constructing another building, they're shouting in unison, 'Yeah, let's go!' They like that!

"But when a church is passive, and the pastor doesn't address their sin and allows the men to stay isolated, only a few men will still attend there. Even those attending will look for an excuse not to be there, and when they *are* there, they'll want to get out early."

All this made perfect sense to me, but I wondered if Travis had initially been worried about bringing up the topic of sexual sin, especially from the pulpit.

"You know, Travis," I began. "I've heard pastors say, 'Well, I can't talk about this. The women will have a cow, or there may be children around.' But obviously you disagreed. You went ahead with it, so whatever those concerns were for you, you figured the women in your church would rise above them. Was that your thinking?"

"Women are always the concern, but I had to risk grace and push forward anyway, despite the concerns. The destiny of our church depended upon it," Travis conceded. "Let me be completely honest here. I could go forth boldly from the pulpit because I had already talked to my wife, Hannah, about this. A couple of years before I got open with the congregation about my struggles, I got open with Hannah. She was shocked, but I also remember the unforgettable moment when she exclaimed, 'Oh, Travis, our poor sons are growing up in a world that's even worse than your world! We have got to protect them from being tortured even now, as youngsters. And we've got to help the men in our church protect their kids too.' "

Obviously, Hannah got it, to her credit.

But while she got it, Travis knows that many pastors *don't* get it, so he had some final thoughts for all of us. "Let me say to pastors first that I think you're doing a great disservice to your men if you don't take steps to help them in their biggest struggle. Why would you leave the biggest issue off the table? Get to the basics—sexual sin—because that's where all men live. Deal with that one, pastors. When you do, you're helping your men live in victory.

"To the rest of us men, I would say this: if your church doesn't tackle this topic head-on, maybe you could have the courage to start a Life Group on your own. But get your pastor's blessing first. You're going to need that because without the pastor's blessing, your group could be seen as a bunch of deviants when, in fact, it's just the opposite—a bunch of heroes trying to live holy and follow God's teaching on sexual purity in the right way.

"If your church does offer Life Groups or a men's ministry that deals with sexual sin issues, don't give excuses for why you're too busy to join them. You're flirting with a danger that could ruin your marriage if you don't get this lust thing under control. Why would you *not* show up to that event? Why would you *not* show up to get the help you need? Why would you *not* show up to help your brothers win this war? Every guy knows that's where he's battling, so why not address it head-on rather than avoid it or give excuses? Get up and kill it.

"Let me tell you—nothing breeds complacency in Christians like sexual sin and the self-disqualification that follows. But transparency breeds relationships, and those relationships give us access to the freedom of the gospel.

"The secrets you hold to yourself are the very ones the enemy uses to lock down your life's destiny. He keeps you in hiding behind those secrets."

As Travis spoke, I thought of my pastor, James Christopher, who's just as open and transparent as Travis. James once said it this way: "I've got a policy. The enemy can never blackmail me because I will always share openly about what's going on in my life, right from the pulpit. And if you ever come up to me and say, 'James, I heard something negative about you,' I'll reply, 'Yes, but you haven't heard the worst of it. Let me share the rest of it with you!'

"So why do I say that?" Pastor Christopher continued. "Because that keeps me free. I'll never get an envelope in the mail saying, 'Pastor, if you don't send us money, we'll share the truth we've found about your life.' My life's always been an open book. Sometimes I question myself when I get home after church on Sunday mornings and whine, *Oh, James, why did you say that during your sermon?* But, hey! It keeps me free."

And freedom, my friends, is what the Christian life is all about.

In our next section, Brenda and I will discuss why every man's battle is best fought together as a team, as husband and wife, because finding sexual purity is not just every man's battle or every woman's battle.

It's *every couple's* battle.

PART IV
Every Couple's Challenge: Establishing Genuine Interpersonal Intimacy

As we move into this fourth and final part of *Battle On, Battle Over*, I want to remind you once again about the power of relationships in this battle. Your destiny as a man and as the leader in your home depends upon the depth of your relationships. You ignore them at your peril when you're on purity's battleground.

As I've pointed out, sexual sin is often nonsexual at its roots, so establishing a close, intimate relationship with God is a pivotal step toward long-term victory because having a deep, genuine connection with the Lord replaces the need for the false intimacy from porn and masturbation. Since it's crucial to produce a close, intimate relationship with your spouse for the very same reason, let me turn the spotlight on you and your spouse in this part of the book.

In my experience, every man's battle is best fought as a couple. The common goals behind this great adventure can draw two together like nothing else. For this reason, when Brenda and I decided to team up as authors of *Battle On, Battle Over*, we resolved to fashion a resource that could be *read* together as a couple and *applied* together as a couple. We are confident that the stories we share and the teaching we communicate will launch numerous profound heart-to-heart conversations between a husband and wife that will help create a deep, interdependent, interpersonal connection.

Granted, creating a marriage *with* sexual oneness and *without* sexual sin is a weighty challenge, considering the vast differences between men and women.

But that only means that as you read *Battle On, Battle Over* and discuss it together as a couple, you'll need to intentionally risk unconditional transparency and take a chance that the other will offer lavish grace in return.

Still, the rewards of these risks are bountiful and limitless, so allow Brenda and me to use these following five chapters to explore these vast challenges with you. As we do, we'll review the appropriate attitudes and actions you must take on as a couple to establish an enduring triumph on the battlefield and in your lives together as Christians.

We'll do this by *modeling* it for you. Let's face it, modeling behavior in book form is problematic at best, but we feel that by sharing actual conversations between successful husbands and wives on this topic, we can go a long way toward illustrating the one-on-one respect and humility necessary to win this victory together. If conversations like this have been rare in your relationship, make it a point to change that reality.

Humility is indispensable in the process. You need a human mirror in your life, someone who loves you enough to say, "Hey, your slip's showing," or "You have a blind spot in your perspective." Your humility will free your spouse or partner to reflect on what he or she is seeing.

Without humility, it's easy to get defensive regarding your sexuality, your desires, and your disastrous, degrading mistakes. Resistive, defensive attitudes will shatter your mirror on the spot. Once you go there, she can't help you, and he can't help you.

Humility is being willing to be known for who you are today, at this moment, both good and bad. You're owning your weaknesses and refusing to pose for the crowd or make yourself look better than you are. Thankfully, humility is easy to understand and even easier to do once you set your mind to it.

Look, humility can be embarrassing, but that's okay because with humility comes real freedom. Freedom to love. Freedom to know and to be understood. Haven't you always yearned for that? We always have, and humility is the only door in.

Please watch for the humility in the conversations that follow. Use these conversations as an accountability partner of sorts. When your conversations don't match the transparency and humility portrayed here, and your mirror has withdrawn in frustration, then face the truth head-on. You're being a harsh jerk or a loud, noxious clown. Admit that to yourself. It isn't that difficult if you want something more in your relationship.

Soon, you'll grow as one and enjoy the most wonderful conversations of your life.

And winning the battle, in tandem, as a couple.

12

A Heart-to-Heart with a Pair of Couples

From Brenda

Fred was spot-on when he wrote in *Every Man's Battle* that navigating marital intimacy within the covenant of marriage can be "complicated and fraught with challenges in the best of circumstances." I'll say!

In this opening chapter of the fourth part of *Battle On, Battle Over*, I'm sharing two penetrating heart-to-heart conversations to generate valuable and crucial discussions between you and your spouse regarding sexual oneness in marriage. Take time to read them together. Take time to open your hearts, just as these two couples did. Allow these couples to serve as healthy examples of communication in marriage. Then jump in and follow their lead.

In a moment, I'll share a relevant exchange I had with Fred about the navigation of marital sex, which happened while we were biking under beautiful blue spring skies on our favorite local trail. Before I do that, though, I must first share a conversation that Fred had with Joe, a wonderfully transparent pastor and friend from Missouri. This happened after Fred spoke at a men's purity event held at Joe's church one Saturday morning as the two sat in his office afterward to unwind. That's when this young pastor shared a hair-raising tale about a significant turning point in his sexual relationship with his wife:

> A few years ago, I sat down with my wife, Megan, and said, "Honey, I'm dissatisfied with our marriage. I feel like we're just roommates."
>
> I told her that it felt like sex was a chore to her. "Hey, before you were our kids' mother, you were my *wife* and my *lover*," I said. "I need that

person back in my life. That's the person I made a vow to. That doesn't mean we're going to carry on sexually like before—I mean, we're not twenty-three anymore. But guess what? We ain't in our eighties either."

When we had this heart-to-heart, I was in my thirties, and I knew only one thing—I didn't sign up to have a roommate. Something had to change, and I was willing to risk every bit of pride and lay my heart completely on the line with her. That's when I said, "Here's what's happening, sweetheart. Since we don't have sex that often, I masturbate to make up for it."

Megan was surprised. "Oh, really?" she said.

"Yes, really. And I don't want to masturbate anymore. It's sad when a buxom girl in a beer commercial is more alluring than you are when you walk by the TV in your sweats, mumbling, 'I hope you're not expecting anything tonight.' I adore you, sweetheart. I need your partnership in this."

I guess I got her thinking. I told her, "Look, I'll do my part. I'll romance you. I'll bring home flowers. I'll do whatever you need from me. But no one else in the world can fulfill this need in my life. There's no one else that God will allow me to connect with to meet these desires. You may not understand this, but you signed up for this 'privilege' to fulfill me."

Her response to the word "privilege" surprised me, as it seemed to strike her between the eyes. She got really quiet and lost in her thoughts.

Suddenly, everything I'd said hit her at once, and she began crying like crazy. I held her close while she processed it all with me. We talked and talked, and then she finally said, "Okay, I'm in, but here's what I need from you." She listed several things, like making sure I was attentive to her when she told me about her day.

"Great, you can count on me," I replied. "And here's what I need from you."

We got into the nitty-gritty together. But, Fred, the most important thing for you to understand is that when I told her how I was feeling about our love life, she was utterly shocked, especially about the masturbation.

Fred was intrigued and asked Joe to tell him more.

You see, when we were processing it together, I even shared some of the things I thought about while I masturbated. I wanted to help her understand what I'd been going through sexually on my own, all by myself. She was completely blown away. "You really think those things while you're doing it?" she asked.

"Yeah, and all guys in our church think the same way when they do the deed, but they don't want to do it anymore either," I replied. "They want their wives to be their lovers, just like I want you to be mine."

There was something else I had to tell her too. "You know, sweetheart, a low-cut dress on another woman is still a low-cut dress. I've got to bounce my eyes just like anybody else."

"Really?" she replied.

Once again, Megan was astonished. "I had no idea! You men must live in torture!"

"*Yeah!* You're getting it now."

After the meeting of their minds and hearts, Megan responded as beautifully and gracefully as any woman possibly could in that situation. She upped her game big-time, and without a doubt, Joe couldn't have been happier. As her sister in Christ, I'm in utter awe of her graceful response to his risky confession and his dreams for their marriage together.

But Joe's story didn't end there:

Fred, I got to thinking a little more about all this. Since I talked to Megan and things turned out so well, I knew I needed to help the rest of the guys in my church too. I started by speaking to the Women's Bible Study one evening, accompanied by Megan. Once again, I was as transparent and open as I knew how to be, just like I've been today with you. I started by saying, "Hey, ladies! Here's the deal. Your husband is open to having sex with you two or three times a week instead of masturbating."

And they were like, "What?" They were absolutely dumbfounded. I'd say that about half the women in that Bible study were flat-out freaked out by what I said. Since Megan had responded to me so perfectly, I wasn't expecting that. I was also surprised that their responses were all over the board. In fact, some were quite negative.

After the Bible study, some of the wives went home and brought up what I said to their husbands. When a few of these guys confessed and agreed that they didn't want to masturbate anymore, their wives stuck their heads straight into the sand.

Don't talk to me anymore about this, and let's just pretend this conversation never happened. You just do whatever you've got to do because I don't want to deal with it.

These guys were naturally devastated by this response. They were stunned that their wives could seem so cold-hearted. They'd say, "Sweetheart, I'm trying to live purely, and now you're telling me that you don't want to help me and that you prefer I go off alone and masturbate?

And you won't even *talk* about it?"

Other wives were repulsed to their toes, spitting, "Oh my goodness, you're masturbating? I don't even know if I want to give myself to you anymore because I now know you're just a stinking weirdo."

Of course, a few ladies, like my wife, said that even though they didn't entirely understand everything that was going on, they were willing to help their husbands.

Here's what I've been trying to get at, Fred. Even though my wife responded well to this situation, she was still freaked out by how visual guys are. I think all the other wives were too. Megan said, "You mean all those years when I was a teenage girl and I didn't think anyone was looking at me . . . now you're telling me that they *were* all looking at me?"

When I nodded, she could barely take it in. "Wow! Why did God make us so different?" she asked. Then she just sat there mesmerized, shaking her head.

Fred, let me tell you, we had a fantastic time discussing *that* question, and it got me thinking about how we men, and we as a church, don't do a very good job of explaining to women the way men are wired, how visual we are, and why we're programmed that way. As a pastor, I'm still working on this one too.

For instance, I didn't talk about this in my last sermon series on marriage because I didn't feel right raising this topic in front of the whole church with kids being in there. But I can certainly see myself talking about this again at one of our marriage retreats, and soon.

The truth is, I don't think married women understand that their husbands are visual and *want* to see them naked and are delighted by their bodies. I also think there's a second reason women can't see that, and it's because many of them are not happy with their own bodies. From what I've read, most women are pretty disgusted with their bodies and the way they look to others. I've even heard stories of beautiful professional models who have plastic surgery to make themselves practically perfect, and yet they're *still* disgusted with their looks, which is the craziest thing to me.

But because most wives seem to share these same feelings of disgust, they can't even imagine that their husbands would *ever* want to look at them. Because of that, they don't want to give themselves to their husbands in bed either. They don't even want to give them the slightest thing to look at.

But guys are dying, saying, "Honey, I love you. I *want* to look at you. I'm created this way."

Since we don't do a good job of explaining how men are wired, we end up with all these fine Christian women fighting *against* the very thing they should be helping. When they don't want to appear naked and give him a visual peek, they are actually fighting against the way their husbands are wired. Does that make any sense at all?

It's absurd. We pastors need to assure them, "Look, he loves you, and he made his vow to you, so he will be *delighted* in you. He loves you more than you realize. He thinks you're beautiful, wrinkles and rolls and dimples and all. You're his *wife*, for heaven's sakes!"

If only every wife could see how delighted her husband is in her! If she could only believe that she is secure in his sight, I think she would be more abandoned in love and sex because she would realize, *Hey, he really does delight in me. I'm not this imperfect thing that he had to settle for.* I badly want the women in my church to understand that.

Joe is a fantastic pastor, isn't he? He cares about vital things. I love his perspective.

Fast-forward to a beautiful afternoon when Fred and I were happily biking together, and I noticed that Fred had gone silent for a while. That wasn't unusual with this deep thinker of mine, so I kept pedaling away until he asked, "Brenda, can you help me with something that's been puzzling me for a while?"

"Sure, what do you need?"

He described the conversation with Joe that I just shared. Then he made this observation to me: "You know, the thing that's puzzling me is the open rebellion against Scripture in the attitudes of some of those wives, especially the ones who shut down the conversation, leaving their husbands standing out there in the rain. I mean, they *are* Christian women, but they didn't care a fig about what the Bible says about having regular sex in marriage. How can that be? Why don't they respond with grace like Megan did to Joe?"

"It makes perfect sense to me," I responded.

Fred couldn't have been more astonished. "It does? But you're the godliest woman I know! How can you understand their position when it seems so unbiblical?"

"Because I'm a woman. Here's the thing. You are a guy, and you're visual. It's difficult for me to truly understand how much you like to look at my body, even at my age, and it's even harder to comprehend how you can take one look at me and want sex, even if we've been fighting for a few days. That doesn't make sense to me at all because I'm a woman, and my sexuality is relational. I *never* look at you when you're getting out of the shower and instantly want sex. But when our relationship is happy and strong, I do desire sex with you."

Fred came to a stop, and I pulled up alongside him. "So the reason I don't understand these women is because I'm a guy and my sexuality isn't relational like that?" he asked.

"Exactly," I replied. "These women probably have husbands who are poor leaders in the home, or they're selfish and don't understand their wives or help them when they should. Those wives in Joe's church have zero interest in helping their husbands sexually because they don't have a genuine relationship together with their husbands. Because of that, the husbands aren't the least bit sexually attractive to these wives. The thought of having sex with them two or three times a week is appalling."

Fred frowned pensively. "I kind of understand what you are saying, but I'm still a bit confused. Remember when I had such a bad temper when we were first married? Why did you still have sex with me regularly back then?"

I smiled. Fred had asked me an excellent question.

"Because you only had that one real flaw," I replied. "You were understanding and kind and honoring in many other ways. Even then you were a rare man, and I loved you dearly for caring so much for me."

"So what about today? You like sex with me because you love me?"

"Yes."

"But not because it's exhilarating?"

"No. I mean it is exhilarating and all that, but I like it because I love *you*. You are everything to me and have been so good to me. You have always treated me with such respect and honor. That makes you sexually attractive to me, and that's why I like sex with you."

Fred was still slightly perplexed. "So you wouldn't like sex with me if you didn't love me and if our relationship was weak?"

"You got it," I replied bluntly. "And that's precisely why I can say I understand those women so perfectly. Sure, the Bible says what it says about sex, and as wives, we're called to obey. Like Joe said, wives are commanded to make themselves available for regular sex, probably two or three times a week, and wives have no biblical right to do otherwise. I get that and understand why you are puzzled by the wives' harsh attitudes at Joe's church.

"But remember, the Bible also talks about husbands loving their wives sacrificially until they blossom and shine, just like you've done for me. As a woman, I'm puzzled that these men are so rebellious about *that* bit of Scripture. If they loved their wives sacrificially, I assure you that it would make them very sexually attractive to their wives. But I want to make the point that this whole sexual equation isn't quite as simple as you and Joe are making it out here. When a wife holds back on sex and says she doesn't even want to talk about it anymore, it isn't always her fault, and it isn't always rebellion either."

Fred nodded thoughtfully, but I was really warming up to the topic now. "Women are created to be responders. When a husband loves her sacrificially, she will respond happily in bed. When a husband is demanding and controlling and forcing her to submit all the time like a dictator, she will avoid sex at all costs. Who wants to have sex with a dictator? Or with someone who isn't the least bit sexually attractive to her? Fred, would you want to have sex with a woman who has ugly warts covering her entire body?"

"Ugh. No!"

"That's because you are visual, and ugly warts don't trip your sexual triggers. But we're relational. Why should we want to have sex with someone we have no genuine relationship with? A husband like that will never trip his wife's sexual triggers. If he worked on the relationship, he would make it far easier for her to think about having regular sex with him."

The lights were finally clicking on for Fred. "Hmmm. I'm getting it now. But don't wives still have to obey the Scripture about regular sex?"

"Yes, but when husbands don't love their wives sacrificially, it makes everything much harder. Offering regular sex becomes almost impossible for her. That may not be *right*, but I understand it perfectly.

"You see, while it might sound strange to you as a guy, that particular Scripture [1 Corinthians 7] about not depriving each other of sex isn't the key issue here, at least not from our point of view as wives. If there is no regular sex in a marriage, there is something undoubtedly wrong, but the husband shouldn't look to solve things by pounding his wife over the head with that passage of Scripture. That's undoubtedly the wrong approach.

"His first step should be to sit down with his wife and to ask her to share the three worst ways he treats her—you know, the things that make him sexually unattractive to her. If he then sacrificially heals the relationship, I think the sex part will take care of itself. If he wants her to like to have sex with him *inside* the bedroom, she's got to like him personally *outside* the bedroom. He's got to quit trampling her heart."

I then concluded our conversation this way. "Fred, think about it. You're having trouble understanding the wives' responses to Pastor Joe because you aren't relational in your sexuality, while I'm having no problem understanding it. I promise, you could ask any woman on this bike path, and she would tell you the same thing: *If you want me to have regular sex with you, sit down with me and ask me how you can treat me better!*

"Without question, this should be every husband's key first step in fixing things in the bedroom, but the funny thing is that this step doesn't even *occur* to most guys because they aren't relational. It's quite sad when you think about it. Since they are visual, they think they've got to get into the gym to lift weights and lose weight to be more attractive to their wives. But a six-pack of abs is useless if they're still being brutish and trampling their wives' hearts, so they are running down the wrong path."

I wrapped our conversation with this thought:

"You told me that Joe's been using *Every Man's Battle* in their men's groups to help the guys with their sexual sin, and that's great. But if he really wants to get those guys' wives to respond sexually after they've read *EMB*, he ought to start using *Every Man's Marriage* with them, which will teach those guys how to heal their relationships and quit trampling their wives. Nothing will make them more sexually attractive to their wives than this."

And I don't want to masturbate anymore.

Amazing. Joe's appeal is, beyond question, the most transparent, perilous, delicate, and profoundly piteous plea I've ever heard from a hurting husband. Has there ever been a more courageous man? Such bold and extraordinarily heroic action, taken to reclaim his future for the sake of their original dreams together. What leadership! What transparency!

And the truth is, no husband should have to masturbate anymore if the couple, together, ensures that three things are taking place in their marriage:

1. The husband is taking on his wounds and learning to deal with the pain and stress in his life in partnership with his wife and the Lord.
2. The wife is graciously taking on the privilege of providing the interpersonal intimacy he earnestly desires in bed.
3. The husband is making himself sexually attractive to his wife by setting out to romance her again and by ceasing to trample her heart with rigid or lazy attitudes in the home.

Moving ahead will require courageous, transparent, heart-to-heart communication from both sides and tremendous respect for the natural differences between the husband and wife in their temperaments and emotional makeup. These differences must be honored.

I hope these two heart-to-heart conversations have sparked necessary and compelling discussions between you and your spouse regarding your connection in your marriage, sexual and otherwise. If things aren't the way God wants them to be today in your marriage, you can always change things together. Perhaps that's the most significant thing about life in God and something you can count on as you engage in the battle together.

In our next chapter, Fred and I will describe what happened when we counseled our friend Jim, who was winning every man's battle but *losing* every couple's battle.

13

Jim's Plaintive Plea

Now the LORD God said, "It is not good (beneficial) for the man
to be alone; I will make him a helper [one who balances him—a
counterpart who is] suitable and complementary for him."
—Genesis 2:18, AMP

As you know from the last chapter, I was struck to the core by Pastor
Joe's heartrending cry: "Sweetheart, since we don't have sex that often, I
masturbate to make up for it. And I don't want to masturbate anymore."

What Joe said was so vulnerable and beautifully transparent. Yet, in my
experience, many wives don't see it that way and simply bark back, "If you don't
want to masturbate, then don't. It isn't my issue!"

Things aren't remotely that simple.

Pastor Joe's vulnerability here reminded me of our friend Jim, who had
experienced much early success in his battle for purity after some counsel with
Fred and me one autumn. I was at home with Fred a few months later when
he dropped by to talk. My husband welcomed him in with a big smile, and I
joined them in the living room since Jim wanted to hear my perspective as well.

"Hey, Jim, how's it going?" Fred asked cheerfully. I could tell my husband
expected to hear more good news.

"Things have gone well in the battle," he replied. "My eyes are under control,
and my thoughts are much cleaner."

"Fantastic!" Fred was beaming.

"I'm feeling much closer to God," Jim continued. "The problem is that I'm
feeling a lot closer to my wife too."

"That's a problem?" I asked with a grin, thinking that was usually a good thing.

"Well, Samantha doesn't have much interest in me sexually. It's weird,"

173

he mused. "I don't think it's personal. She simply has little need for a sexual relationship and doesn't give it much thought. It also seems hard for her to be receptive sexually if there is anything out of the ordinary going on, whether it's something with the kids, concerns about friends, church things, whatever."

I appreciated how Jim was opening up and leaned in to hear more.

"I've been working harder to encourage her," he continued. "I've been talking more with Samantha about what's going on at home, helping her with her chores, and doing nice little things like when we were dating, but still no luck."

"Does she understand how this is affecting you?" I queried.

"We've talked about it, but she doesn't seem to get it. Maybe she doesn't *want* to get it. I don't know. She often says she's just not in the mood. She also seems put off by how my sexual needs can seem more physically driven than heart-driven at times."

"Women aren't as much like that, and we can find that unromantic," I admitted.

"I'm sure that's true. But as I've explained to Samantha, even in those times, I love her passionately. I want only *her* to be the one to fulfill those needs, but saying that doesn't help. Nothing changes."

Jim sighed deeply. "Monday was especially discouraging. Due to MLK Day, we didn't have to work, but our kids still had school. Samantha asked me over the weekend what I wanted to do on our day off together, and I expressed an interest in being intimate. When the kids left for school, I showed some interest again, but she ignored me. The day turned into furniture shopping, errands, a lunch together, and a return home in time for when the kids jumped off the bus. Look, it's not like those things were bad, but I felt almost insulted that she would rather go to a furniture store than share thirty minutes in bed with me."

"Of course, you did," Fred said. My husband knows how crushing and dishonoring that feels to a man. Wives often give this little thought because they don't experience things this same way.

"My attraction to my wife is getting stronger than ever because of my purity," Jim continued, "but I'm ashamed to say I've tripped up and fallen into 'self-relief' a couple of times lately. I'm afraid I'm going backward. I suppose the point of my marriage is not for me to get my sexual needs met, but I can't help feeling heartbroken. I just don't know what to do next."

After some more discussion, Jim headed back out to his car. Fred waved goodbye as he drove away. Then, as he shut the door, he shook his head sadly as he recalled Jim saying, "As I've explained to Samantha, even in those times, I love her passionately. I only want *her* to be the one to fulfill those needs, but that doesn't help. Nothing changes."

Jim's statement had torn my heart too. So why don't things change? Here was this heroic husband advancing on purity's battlefront and depending upon his wife for help along the way, exactly as he should be doing. I felt for Jim and the situation he was in. As we've said, a husband's battle for purity is not just every *man's* battle but every *couple's* battle too, though many wives don't see it that way. Jim's wife certainly didn't. She hadn't yet joined him on the front lines, and now his emerging victory was very much in doubt.

As I prepared for bed following Jim's visit, I shuddered at the thought that I could have just as easily made the same mistake years ago when Fred's attractions for me had boiled over in the same way Jim had described his fresh passion for Samantha. At the time, Fred hadn't yet told me that he was fighting on purity's battlefield. All I knew was that he suddenly desired intercourse twice as often, for absolutely no apparent reason, which was quite jarring. Oh, sure, I knew that Fred had a stronger sex drive than I did, but to me, there seemed to be more to all this. He hadn't looked at me quite like this since we were newlyweds.

Since I didn't know what was going on, questions began racing through my mind: *Has he found an aphrodisiac?* I even considered the possibility that he might be having an affair.

What's going on here? He's been telling me how hot I am and patting me on the bottom all the time. Is he having an affair and covering his tracks with all this extra affection?

In the end, I figured he was experiencing something like the food jags I had during my pregnancy when I couldn't eat enough Hostess Ding Dongs. *Perhaps Fred's itch for me is like that and it will be over soon. I certainly hope so!*

But nothing changed over the next couple of weeks. As the higher pace of his appetite showed no signs of abating, it dawned upon me that this might not be just some simple jag or phase. His greater hunger might be permanent!

I began to panic. The next time he looked over at my body with a low whistle, I whipped around in frustration and leveled a finger at him, blurting, "Tell me what I'm doing to be so attractive so I can stop it!"

That moment is hilarious now, in retrospect, but not so much at the time. Thankfully, Fred sat me down on the couch and immediately connected the dots for me. He told me he was starving his eyes of every bit of sensuality in his life except for me.

"All my desires are coming straight at you, and I don't quite know what to do about it yet," he said. "I promise I'll work hard to get back to a sexual equilibrium we can both live with."

Of course, I was beyond relieved that the jag wasn't permanent, but I was also excited that he invited me to ride out such a great adventure with him. Once he explained that he was doing this for the sake of our children and to crush the generational sin in his family line, I was all in. I was certainly willing to allow him the time to find that equilibrium again because we were in this together.

As I climbed into bed and turned out the lights, I remembered the conversation we shared with Jim earlier that evening. What if I'd responded to Fred like Samantha was responding to Jim? Would Fred have ever won his victory? If not, Fred's impact on the destiny of each of our children would have been severely compromised. I know I'd have shared the blame.

Now let me be clear. I'm not suggesting to the women reading this that you caused your husband's porn and masturbation problem. I'm sure those things started long before you met him, and it remains his responsibility. Let me also clarify that regular sex does not cure sexual addictions. If you recall, Fred was still trapped in his sin, even while having a great sex life together with me early in our marriage. Regular sex guarantees nothing.

Still, you *are* one flesh. While you are not at fault for his sin, your attitudes and connection with him—sexual and otherwise—can still dramatically impact his battle for purity. Let me share some thoughts that helped me anchor my heart and body in place when Fred was out there on the battlefield.

First, I believe that helping my husband is my nonnegotiable call from God. It's yours too. According to Genesis 2:18, as a wife you were both created and called by God to walk at your husband's side, shoulder to shoulder, as the original language for "helper" in that verse means "side-by-side partner." I must help lift my husband to Christian greatness when it comes to Fred's purity, and I must never allow him to sink to his lowest sexual nature.

I can't just turn away from Fred sexually because his sexuality is visual, or because his sex drive is much stronger than mine, or because I'm sickened to the core by his sin. Loving the unlovely is at the heart of my marriage because loving the unlovely is at the very core of Christianity. God demonstrated His love for us while we were still sinners (see Romans 5:8). Can you demonstrate your love by joining up with the Lord and with your husband on purity's battlefield and in the marriage bed?

Second, I humbled myself and got educated about male sexuality. Whenever I'm interviewed about what a woman should do after finding out her husband is trapped in sexual sin, I always reply that she must first get educated about male sexuality. I feel so strongly about it that I helped Fred write *Every Heart Restored* to help wives learn how men are sexually wired. If you're ever going to find the grace to come back to your husband's side in the wake of an awful revelation of his sin, you'll need to develop a deep knowledge of male sexuality. This background will help you understand the roots of his sin and how to help him.

Once educated, you'll understand that sex plays a different role in a man's life than in yours. Sex is a man's native language of connection and intimacy. Without it, a man's sense of connection fails and his sense of manhood is quickly drained. Regular sex took on a genuine urgency once I learned this, and why not? I'm Fred's helper and best friend, and he counts on me. I'm not about to send Fred out into a complicated and harsh world feeling disconnected and disrespected as a man. How can he be heroic and fight for our family under those circumstances?

Sure, I want to have regular sex with Fred because that's my call from God, but it is also undeniably in my best interest to do so. With that intimate connection in place, Fred can better pray because he isn't stalked by guilt. He is better able to intimately connect with the Lord for the same reason. In this light, how can a Christian wife afford to "not give it much thought," like Jim's wife was doing? How naïve and dangerous it is for her to allow her "little need for a sexual relationship" to impact her family this way. If you can't do it for your husband's sake, do it for the Lord's sake, for yourself, for your spiritual defense, and for the protection and security of your children.

To our shame as women, we don't always think in terms of obedience, spiritual defense, and protection when it comes to our sexuality. Instead, we think like our culture thinks. That's why we're likely to turn away from God's counsel when handling our sexuality, much like Eve did as she contemplated eating the forbidden fruit from the Tree of Knowledge: *I don't trust God or His commands. He's undoubtedly holding something back from me anyway, so I'll go my own way here.*

This attitude plays right into Satan's hands. He'll do anything to keep us from using our sexuality God's way, twisting our minds with ease like boardwalk taffy.

Think about it. First, before marriage, he does everything he can to convince you that your love relationship *must* involve sex to be genuine. Fred and Jasen co-authored *Hero: Becoming the Man She Desires* to help couples to stay pure before marriage, and it was disheartening to see how many guys wrote them in frustration, opining, "I want to stay pure, but my girlfriend says that without sex, our relationship is no different than a mere friendship. She's not willing to roll that way, no matter what God says."

Then, after marriage, Satan gets us to *avoid* sex so that our relationships are as much like mere friendships as possible. He gets wives thinking, *I don't care what God says. It's my body, and I'll only have sex when I feel like it. If my husband presses the issue, then it's sexual abuse.*

That's absurd. Jim practically apologized to Samantha for expecting to get his sexual needs met in marriage. God makes no such apologies because one key reason marriage exists is so that both of you *can* get your sexual needs met in a holy and honorable way.

Every wife is supposed to aid her husband in his battle for purity, as a matter of course:

> But because of the temptation to sexual immorality, each man should have his own wife and each woman her own husband. (1 Corinthians 7:2, ESV)

Even if you haven't seen your husband's sexual purity as every couple's battle, God plainly does. Because of that, a marriage without regular sex is abnormal in God's eyes. He made regular sex a *matrimonial guarantee* to keep our misguided thinking, our exhaustion, and our gender differences from eliminating this vital intimate connection. Consider this Scripture:

> The husband should give to his wife her conjugal rights, and likewise the wife to her husband . . . Do not deprive one another, except perhaps by agreement for a limited time, that you may devote yourselves to prayer; but then come together again, so that Satan may not tempt you because of your lack of self-control. (1 Corinthians 7:3, 5, ESV)

Now, I get that "regular" is a vague term, so let me share how I view things. Regular sex is not doing it every day and probably not every other day. But "regular" doesn't mean once a week, and certainly not every other week or every other month. Remember, sex is a man's native language of connection and intimacy. If you want him intensely and intimately connected to you, you must align your sexual attitudes more closely with his needs for connection.

Regular frequency arises naturally when (1) your heart aligns with 1 Corinthians 7:2–5 and (2) when you realize that sex is not just an act of individual desire or romantic passion but also an act of kindness and mercy from God's point of view. Physical intimacy is a mutual act of relational healing and bonding, delivering protection for your spouse.

Because of this call and the critical part that sex plays in your relationship, God grants neither of you full control of your *yes* or full control of your *no* when it comes to your bodies:

> For the wife does not have authority over her own body, but the husband does. Likewise the husband does not have authority over his own body, but the wife does. (1 Corinthians 7:4, ESV)

Now, I can ignore these truths and even hate them, but I can't change them. My sexuality has never been just mine, and neither has yours. It doesn't matter whose podcast says otherwise. God crafted my sexuality for Fred and his pleasure every bit as much as He created it for me and my pleasure. Biblically, I have never had the right to only use my sexuality at my discretion.

Samantha said she's just not in the mood that often. Seriously? What does mood have to do with it? That's girlish Disney Channel indoctrination and Hollywood messaging. You're an adult woman now. It's time to give up these childish ways of thinking about sex (see 1 Corinthians 13:11).

You're also a daughter of the Most High God and a servant in His kingdom.

You simply must get this right biblically because your marriage and your family's Christian destiny depend upon it. Sex is far too crucial to oneness and connection to be left to the whims of mood. If sex were to happen only when both spouses were in the mood, it would *never* occur regularly, and we could never please God in our marriage bed.

Besides, moods can often change on the spot. As a woman, hugging and touching have a profound impact on me. I've found that if I'm not in the mood, but if I obey God and go ahead sexually for Fred's sake, all the touching and caressing we do early on often changes my mood, and soon I'm enjoying things as much as he is. I've learned to count on that imminent change of mood, and my obedience to God's call has become a blessing to both of us.

Now, I'm not forgetting that Fred plays a part in helping my moods. For instance, he no longer tramples my heart outside the bedroom with his bad temper like he did early in our marriage, so my moods can more easily change inside the bedroom. He never forces me to do anything inside the bedroom that I find sinful or demeaning because doing so would drive my heart away and kill my mood. He also never uses me as an interactive toy on which to explore his selfish pleasures unilaterally on his own, somewhere in his mental fantasies. He studies my heart, and it's clear that my desires are as important to him as his own. In short, he honors my female sexuality in the same way I honor his unique male differences.

I fully understand that your husband may still have a lot to learn. While your sexuality belongs to both of you, he may still think that this means you must service him like some call girl on retainer and that your sexuality is to be used only at his discretion. Sigh.

It isn't easy to craft the right attitudes regarding sex in marriage. Men are as obtuse about female sexuality as we are about theirs. They are especially blind to the relational nature of our sexuality because they simply don't experience it that way. The statement I made earlier would never occur to them naturally on their own: *If you want me to have regular sex with you, sit down with me and ask me how you can treat me better!*

But that doesn't mean your husband is incapable of learning. Remember, he has the same Bible and the same call from God as you do. He can read and understand that his sexuality is also yours and that he must use it to connect with you and honor and pleasure you. He must also care for you and study your heart and listen to you too, because you won't be able to build this marriage bed without him. When he isn't pulling his weight in this arena, he must welcome you to call him out on his behavior.

Building a great marriage bed together takes study and great humility. It gets no easier as the years pass and new challenges are added to the mix, like children, weight gain, menopause, hysterectomies, and other medical issues. But even though these obstacles may slow us on our path to sexual connection, we must never move God's finish line or change the target He's set for us. Throughout your days together, God wants you to pursue each other sexually as husband and wife.

This kind of mutual sacrifice in the bedroom is the entire point, isn't it? Marriage is a team sport where couples must engage in the battle for purity together and find regular sexual connection, against the odds, by selflessly sacrificing, even in bed, to build the marriage of their dreams. Mutual pleasure and mutual sacrifice have always been in God's plans, both inside the bedroom and outside (see Ephesians 5:21).

Fred's godly philosophies of mutual submission in the bedroom have made things infinitely easier for me to help him with regular sex. At the risk of sounding like I'm self-promoting our work, if you've been struggling in this area, I strongly urge you to check out Chapter 23 of *Every Man's Marriage* and read it with your spouse. The ensuing conversations may change everything on a dime.

And now, as we look ahead, there are many ways a wife can come to her husband's side in every man's battle. You'll learn about one more way when we share how Audrey helped Jake in the next chapter.

14

Step to His Side

Next to him was Eleazar son of Dodai the Ahohite. As one of the
three mighty warriors, he was with David when they taunted the
Philistines gathered at Pas Dammim for battle. Then the Israelites
retreated, but Eleazar stood his ground and struck down the
Philistines till his hand grew tired and froze to the sword. The LORD
brought about a great victory that day.
—2 Samuel 23:9–10a, NIV

When a husband tries to hide what's happening with his sexual sin behind
the scenes, it's the worst thing he can do. When Fred first revealed his
battle with sexual sin to me, the fact that he came clean about his sin, on his
own, made it one hundred times easier for me to take it in. The fact that he was
already engaged in the battle made it a thousand times easier.

If he hadn't come clean on his own, and if I had instead discovered his sin
by chance, emotional chaos would have ripped through our lives. Endless dark
questions like these would have incessantly haunted my heart:

- *Would Fred have ever come to me on his own?*
- *Is he truly repentant, or is he just sorry he got caught?*
- *Has he genuinely been convicted by the Holy Spirit?*
- *Is Fred being driven to change from the inside out, or has he merely been
  convicted by me? If so, is he simply responding to the embarrassment of my
  surprise discovery?*
- *How can I trust that he's really in this battle for God's sake and not just going
  through the motions to shut me up and stop my tears?*

Now let me tell you about Audrey, who was one of the fortunate ones, like me. I say that because her husband, Jake, came to her on his own.

You see, Jake had approached Fred for help in the battle. Jake had admitted that his sexual sin was making him tense and angry in the home because of his guilt and anger with himself.

"Audrey has no idea what's going on in terms of my porn use," Jake told Fred during one of his infamous Starbucks meetings. "But she knows *something* is different between us. Like most wives, my wife is very intuitive. She senses some things aren't lining up right, but she can't quite put her finger on it. Of course, I'm way too chicken to tell her what's going on, but there's no question that her gut is telling her that something is wrong somewhere."

"Has she mentioned anything about what she's sensing?" Fred inquired.

"She's asking me a lot about my temper, like why it's flaring up so much lately. I'll admit that practically everything she says ticks me off these days. If she asks me to take out the garbage or dry the dishes, my anger burns, like, 'What's wrong with you, woman?' The weird thing is that I don't even mind doing those chores. My anger isn't even connected to those things."

"Is she noticing anything else?"

"I don't know about her, but I sure do. I have absolutely *no* patience handling the kids. If I look at porn some night, then the next day, the next week, and even the next couple of weeks, I have no patience with her or the kids. I get angry and snap easily. None of them deserves what I dish out. I'm telling you, Fred, I despise all of it—the porn, the guilt, the anger—all of it!"

Fred nodded from his chair. "Yes, I'm sure you do. I know I sure did when I was feeling those same things. But let me explain how common it is for a guy's temper to light up quickly when he's hiding his sin. As the porn and masturbation cycle continues, it creates a negative relational vortex that drives you even deeper into porn and masturbation. Here's what happens as it feeds on itself. First, a guy's disconnection with God always increases. Then, his connection with his wife suffers because he's angry with himself, just like it's hurting your connection with Audrey. Finally, a guy becomes as crabby as he can be with his kids because of his guilt. His connection with them starts to fade, just like it's happening to you with your girls. That's exactly how it happened to me back when I was struggling.

"Which brings me to Audrey, of course," Fred continued. "You need to tell her what's going on with you so that she doesn't wonder why you are so crabby and your temper is out of control. C'mon, she's your wife! She senses something is wrong! Don't leave her hanging emotionally when her heart's troubled by these painful questions and concerns. Since I helped you finally discover the answer as to why you're so crabby yourself, you need to tell *her* so she doesn't have to think she's crazy. Man up, my friend. Real men protect their wives in this way."

Jake pursed his lips. Fred could tell he was processing what he'd said. After a momentary lull in the conversation, he looked Fred straight in the eye, like a man. "Thanks, Fred. You've told me just what I needed to hear. I'll tell her everything as soon as I get home."

Fred often requires husbands to tell their wives about their sexual sin. Sure, Jake was scared, as there were no givens here. He had no idea how Audrey would respond but took in the truth that day and refused to retreat, as many men often do. When Jake had a private moment with Audrey, he stood his ground. He told her about everything he had been doing and how emotional wounds and financial stress were driving his actions. (Note: Here it is again. It is incredible how often father wounds and financial stress are at the root of a man's sexual sin.)

Jake could step up because he understood from Fred that he was dealing primarily with a financial issue, not a porn issue. He could also step up because he was a man and understood this was something men do.

Sometime after Jake had confessed to Audrey, Fred asked him how it went.

"You know, Fred," he began, "I hadn't even told Audrey that I was going to meet with you because everyone knows that Fred Stoeker deals with sexual sin issues. So the first thing I told her was, 'I met with Fred Stoeker.' "

"That was brave," Fred said, chuckling. "What did she say?"

"She was like, 'Oh, good for you!' Fred, it was so weird for her to say that! I thought to myself, *How can that seem good to her? Fred deals with sexual sin!*"

Jake shook his head at the memory and continued. "I didn't know what to think, so once I pulled my jaw off the floor, I pushed ahead and said, 'Honey, I've been looking at porn. It has nothing to do with you. The sex you've given me is just amazing. But you already know I'm dealing with all this horrible financial stress, and Fred says it's driving me to look at porn.'

"Her response completely blew my mind. 'At least we know what it is now,' she said. 'We can handle this together. We'll pray, and I'll stand by you. We'll get through this.' "

"Wow," Fred offered meekly. Now *his* jaw was on the floor. After a moment to collect his thoughts, he asked Jake, "What if Audrey had thought you were looking at porn because she thought you were a deviant? Do you think she would have reacted differently?" Fred and I had counseled couples where this had happened.

"Honestly, I doubt if she would have acted any differently," Jake mused. "I have a wonderful wife. She knew that I had struggled with porn in the past. Back then, she reacted gently, saying she'd pray for me. Then I got free, and life went back to normal."

"Do you think that the fact that you were taking steps to deal with this porn issue helped her?" Fred continued.

"Without a doubt. When I let Audrey know that I had talked to you, she knew immediately that a godly man was speaking into my life. If I had just told her that I was struggling with porn without mentioning that I had met with you, she would have responded, 'What are you going to do about it?' But once I told her I had already spoken with you, she knew I was in it to win it."

"Did she automatically understand the connection between the financial stress and the sexual sin, or did you have to explain it?"

"Somehow, she completely understood. I don't know how, but she got it instantly. She already knew I felt like a failure because I wasn't providing the way I thought I should. It has been a tough couple of years for us, but she also knows who I am in other ways. When I said I wanted you to keep me accountable, that sounded like me to her ears. She felt protected, like she was on familiar ground. That made it easy for her to say, 'Yeah, let's get after this and take care of it together. I'll walk through it with you.'

"Now, of course that was awesome to hear, Fred, but it caught me off guard too. I thought, *Wow, she doesn't look at me as a sexual deviant. She looks at me as a man. Sure, as a man who struggles, but as a real man, one who will get set free.* It was enormously encouraging."

"Did you explain how the temper you were showing toward her and the kids was also related to the porn?" Fred queried.

"I did. I told Audrey that if I looked at porn the night before, I would be furious at myself the next day and take it out on her and the kids. But I took things one step further. I told her, 'Audrey, from now on, you can check up on me when you see me acting like that. You can ask me if I have fallen back into sin and temptation.'

"And you know what? She does that for us now. In fact, she does a lot of things to help us win this battle. She's helping us plan better financially and being a frugal shopper so I don't have loads of stress crashing down on me."

"Fantastic," Fred responded. "Tell me more about the money angle. Once she saw that porn use can be driven by financial stress, how did life change regarding your finances?"

"Tremendously. Before all this, we lived a life where if one of us wanted something new, we just bought it, but later we'd look back and moan, 'Oh, man, we shouldn't have done that.' I'm so glad we don't live like that anymore. Today, we think about a major purchase three or four or five times before buying anything. And if we do make a decent-sized purchase, we shop and shop for the best deal, where before we would have said, 'Let's get it.'

"I recently drove a car dealership crazy because I thought about getting a new SUV a month before doing anything. I wanted to make sure I didn't put myself in that position of financial stress again, where I might fall back into porn.

"Look, it's not that I'm living in fear now. It's that I'm finally living in wisdom. And Audrey is such a wonderful partner in all this. Anyway, when we were looking at the new SUV, Audrey said, 'Jake, I really love this car and really want it for our family, but is this going to stress you out? Because we don't have to get it.'

"Wasn't that beautiful? She was willing to sacrifice that brand-new SUV for my purity's sake or consider a cheaper used one. I said, 'No, I think we'll be fine. We're done paying off the truck, so I know we can take on this van payment.' Now that we're aware of the effects of financial stress, I'm thrilled she loves me enough to run at my side in all this."

In a perfect world, this is how every wife should respond. We were created to be helpmates, to be at our husbands' sides and help lift them to Christian greatness. We were also called to love them as ourselves. Audrey is doing precisely that for Jake.

But in a sense, Audrey had an advantage over many wives because she had a strong identity as a beloved daughter of God, separate from Jake. She also had a strong self-image. She knows her role as his helpmate very well too. She knows that she and Jake are one flesh and that his sin and his battles are also her sin and her battles, so she must be at his side fighting with him if their marriage is to be free from the effects of his sin.

At the same time, she knows she's married to a warrior who fully expects to win.

But not all of us live in that same world. Perhaps you've caught your husband in the act, and, unlike Audrey, you're writhing in pain and surrounded by dark questions. Maybe your husband has never been too passionate about God and isn't much of a warrior like Jake, so you aren't exactly sure if he'll stand up and fight for what's right. When you glance in the mirror and pluck up the courage to admit what you see there, perhaps you recognize that your own sense of identity as God's daughter is a bit on the wispy side, and you aren't all that sure of the Lord's care and support for you when the going gets tough.

After reading Jake and Audrey's story, it probably won't surprise you that a wife's support is the best predictor of success that Fred and I have ever found in the battle for purity. Even if you live in this lesser world, I urge you to find your way to your husband's side. His success in the battle depends a lot on you.

That support is so vital that Fred rarely counsels married men on their purity issues unless their wives are totally on board and they're in counseling together as a couple. When helping men get free, Fred has a nearly 100 percent success rate if a wife saddles up with her husband in counseling. If she doesn't, the rate drops dramatically.

This makes sense if you think about it because you know by now that many of the roots of your husband's sin are nonsexual. As his wife, you know him, and as a woman, you have the insight and intuition to spot his every wound, his every doubt, and his every despair, probably better than he does. I'm sure they're all flashing through your mind right now as you read this.

You can help him connect the dots between the nonsexual roots and his sexual behavior. You can intercede on his behalf for the Lord to heal those wounds. You are a woman. You know how to love. How to support. How to nurture someone in pain.

If life has been dreadfully painful and depressing since you discovered his sin, you may have forgotten that you possess all these traits, but they are all inside you just the same. Sure, your idyllic view of marriage may be ripped apart. You may still be raging in anger. You may have even collapsed emotionally, with waves of tears washing over you again and again. You may have withdrawn your heart from your husband for the longest time.

But your Father needs you to find your way back to your husband's side because your presence will lift his odds of victory dramatically higher. You have the tools inside of you to do the job, and the Holy Spirit is chomping at the bit to help you help your husband, so don't hesitate to come along his side.

At the same time, I understand that you're hurting, angry, and frustrated—and rightfully so. I also understand that he must do his part and be accountable to you and God. There's no substitute for that in the rebuilding process. But if you two stand together as a couple in this battle, your best days may be ahead of you.

I'll share a blueprint for restoration in my next chapter.

15

A Heart-to-Heart with Wives

By now it must be clear that your husband's sinful habits weren't simply some irresponsible entertainment choices that he made on a lark to get some sexual thrills or kill time in cyberspace. If that were the case, you could take on the role of a snarling surrogate mother and lay down the law with withering ultimatums and a flood of broken tears to force him to straighten up and fly right.

Now that you have a better understanding of how he is made and how this stealth vulnerability worked to trap him, surely you realize that his sin is not a case of mere disobedience. But his choices were not frivolous and out of the blue, and they certainly weren't out of character. No, he made those choices in character—a flawed character—spawned from an underdeveloped soul and the shifting sands of addictive neural pathways, wounded emotions, and a will that wasn't aligned with God's.

Since that's true, it'll take more than ultimatums and tears to help him win the battle. You must become his side-by-side partner to help him build out a soul fit for a Christian man, and you must help him replace his need for false intimacy and that numbing medication of masturbation with the genuine article—an intimacy born of tight marital communication and a healthy, monogamous sexual relationship.

I know what you may be thinking: *It's patently unfair of God to expect anything of me at this moment. My heart is shattered and my emotions are scattered to the winds!*

I understand how you're feeling, that's for sure. It's also natural to think this way. After all, you've been tossed onto an unintended journey over churning emotional seas of confusion and despair. Still, we never get a day off in our roles as God's children, and the Lord *is* counting on you, even now, to obey His will.

187

Ready or not, you're the only one close enough to your husband to really help him.

I know you're hurting. You may even feel like your life ended when you learned about your husband's sin. Desperate questions are likely pouring from your wrenched heart. I hope this chapter answers some of those questions and brings a sense of emotional balance to you, especially after everything that's happened recently to you.

Let's start with three basics:

1. Your frustration and anger at his sexual betrayal are natural and fitting.

You needn't feel guilty about your present lack of trust in him. He betrayed you. He wronged you. Most likely, he hasn't been trustworthy for years, all the while pretending that he has been honorable and worthy of your respect. Why *would* you trust him right now? You shouldn't. It wouldn't make one bit of sense to do so. You'll trust him when he's trust*worthy*, which means trustworthy in *actions*, not just in words.

2. To heal quickly, you'll need to study or review male sexuality in depth.

Once you learn more about your husband's sexual makeup and how it differs from yours as a woman, you'll clearly understand why his sin is not about you, some lack of attractiveness on your part, or some imagined lack of love in his heart for you. His sin is about him, his wounds, his lack of manhood, and his sloppiness in his relationship with God. Remember, his sexual sin likely began long before he ever met you. So how could his sin be about you?[1]

3. You must believe that men can become free from all their sexual sins.

Full restoration is not only possible, but it's also God's will, which means it will definitely happen as long as your husband engages in the battle. Of course, he must choose freedom. If he does, he must put his whole heart into rebuilding his soul and full strength into defending the two vulnerabilities in his sexuality.

I know men can get free. Fred hasn't looked at porn in well over three decades, and he hasn't masturbated in over thirty years. I call that freedom, and his freedom has completely restored our marriage. I totally trust him as a man and as a leader. Fred thoroughly turned things around, proving that sexual sin is not forever. A sweeping turnaround can happen for you and your husband as well.

Now that we've reviewed those three basics, let me lay down a blueprint for restoring your heart and your marriage:

---

1. *Every Heart Restored* is an excellent educational resource for understanding male sexuality.

1. You must start by building a thankful heart. Now that his sin is out in the open, be grateful that this mirage of a marriage finally has a real chance to become all the Lord meant it to be. God wants your dreams to come true in your marriage. That's now possible, perhaps for the first time since your wedding day. Focus on the bright possibilities of this new dawn. Work at being thankful.[2]

Be grateful too that you now know that your angry feelings are natural and that his sin is not about you. This means you are free to choose mercy over judgment and can begin to play your God-given role as a helpmate in your husband's life.

2. You must answer God's call to be your husband's helpmate. This is your second foundational point in your blueprint. Your role is to help lift your husband—to boost, assist, prod, or encourage him to Christian greatness, to be Christlike in all his ways. A faithful helpmate will not let her husband sink to his lowest natural levels of behavior, no matter how much she hates confrontation with him or how much he squeals. She will stand up fearlessly and speak freely into her husband's life, refusing to be muzzled. Your husband needs your complete honesty to see the full extent of the damage he has caused. He has blind spots. Help him to see them.

A great helpmate never suspends the laws of reaping and sowing in her husband's life, which would simply enable him to continue sinning without paying the price for his sin. You must help him come clean despite the embarrassment you feel because the secrecy gives this sin its staying power.

3. You must insist that your husband openly admit his sin to another man. This is vital if he's to gain freedom. The easiest thing in the world is to sweep his actions under the rug, but you must insist that your husband stop posing as something he's not because living lies must stop. If he's on the leadership board of your church, he must step down until he's found freedom. He must step aside if he's on the worship team or missions board. There are no secrets in the spiritual realm, and he's draining the power of your church by harboring sin while filling these roles.

My role as Fred's helpmate has been my highest call from God, and the same can be (and even should be) true for you in your relationship with your husband. You are married and your husband's wife. Outside of loving God with all your heart, mind, soul, and strength, you have no higher call than this, not your role as a mother, not your role as a women's ministry leader, and not your role on the worship team.

4. You must guard your motives in your role as a helpmate. Since you want to help lift him to Christian greatness, you should remember his wounds and speak from an "encouraging" perspective, not manipulating him and playing

---

2. For a bit of help, I recommend *Choosing Gratitude* by Nancy DeMoss Wolgemuth.

games. Please recall that emotional wounds are often at the root of his failures, so you must be careful to affirm his manhood, even in a confrontation, which will help heal his emotional hurts rather than inflict new ones.

Since love and restoration must be at the root of your every action, you should review 1 Corinthians 13 twice a day—in the morning when you wake up, and in the evening before you sleep. Allow these soothing words to wash over you, transforming your motives over time through repetition.

Okay, so you have the basics, and now you have your blueprint. Still, let me be frank. You cannot unilaterally control the results of all this, no matter how well you stick to the basics and follow the blueprint. In the end, your husband has control.

Yes, this is every couple's battle. Yes, victory is far more likely with you at his side. But in the end, while you may feel closer to God than he is and may be all-in and fiercely committed to a sweeping triumph, you are *still* only the helpmate. He is the general who needs to be leading the charge. He must choose his responses well, or there will be no change.

Having said that, you can still have a significant impact on the battlefield, especially if you mind some of these helpful "don'ts," which will help him respond more positively to your role as his helpmate:

1. Don't expect long-term results in the short term. Finding freedom is a process that won't happen by next Tuesday. He could very well stumble and fail along the way again. That's a normal part of every learning process. Because of the addictive nature of looking at porn and the subsequent masturbation, this is especially true. So be patient.

2. If he does blow it in the short term, don't seek vengeance. Your lack of retaliation will remind him that you are focused more on his long-term good than your own wounds and pain.

3. Don't belittle him or demean him, especially in public. Be very disciplined in this. Although confrontation is always part of a helpmate's role, wounding him further is not helpful to his purity. Don't use the silent treatment or withdraw emotionally.

Remember, you aren't fighting to have *your* way in his life. You are fighting to have *God's* way in his life.

Suppose you follow the dos and don'ts that I've laid out above. In that case, you can expect to hear and see certain behaviors along the way that will reveal whether or not your husband is genuinely repentant and committed to his purity. You should listen for complete openness and honesty about his sin and see trustworthy acts that signal true repentance.

One example of the trustworthy acts you can expect is that he'll actually read the books you ask him to read, books like *Every Man's Battle* and *Every Man's Marriage*, and he won't dawdle in doing so. (Both books come in audio formats on sites like Audible, so even if he isn't much of a reader, he can listen to them during his morning and evening commute.)

Another example is that you'll see him initiate setting up defenses himself, like downloading and using anti-porn software on his phone (ladderout.com and covenanteyes.com are good ones) or placing his computer or laptop in a high-traffic area without pressure from you. He should also eagerly accept your suggestions to arrange for professional counseling and personally seek out accountability relationships with other guys on his own, with no harping from you. If you don't see these things, he still hasn't repented fully.

In that same spirit of commitment, you'll likely hear him asking you for ideas on what he might do to rebuild your trust in him, and you'll see him attempt to do these things without reservation. If he's genuinely repentant, you should *never* hear him shifting the blame by saying things like, "This problem would go away if you would just have sex with me more often." That too would be a sign of weak repentance and a lack of ownership of his sin.

If he's genuinely sorry for the damage he's done, he should never summarily demand your trust before he's earned it. He should never say, "If you really loved me, you would trust me again." Instead, his genuine patience with the dawdling pace of your healing heart will reveal a deep recognition that *his* betrayal was *his* failure and his alone.

If he's not repentant, you won't see these actions. Instead, you'll likely see the same old things you've seen all along. Be suspicious if he doesn't read his Bible or worship and pray privately. If he doesn't pray regularly with you, that may signal a guilty conscience over ongoing sin. If you've been pleading with him to talk to your teenage or young adult sons about sexual purity but he remains reluctant to do so, that's another red flag.

Of all things, be especially suspicious whenever your husband becomes unusually critical or if he stops pursuing sexual intimacy with you, as both can be reliable indicators that he's pursuing porn elsewhere.

Don't forget to address your own needs. Since you're hurting, you must also help yourself if you expect to restore your heart and marriage. To navigate this unintended journey, take immediate steps like these for yourself:

1. Start by developing a deeper intimacy with God than you've ever known. You may be thinking, *That's easier said than done in the middle of this chaos.* I know that. But it can happen. Start by applying the principles in Chapters 6 to 8 in this book and establish a much deeper connection with God, even during these pressured, crushing times.

2. Understand that you are emotionally vulnerable right now. You must avoid outside male relationships at all costs and refuse to discuss your dreams and desires with anyone of the opposite sex. Protect yourself from an emotional affair.

3. Build close relationships with several experienced women who've completed their unintended journeys in restoring their marriages. Don't allow your husband to forbid you from developing these relationships under any circumstances. He has no right to do that. Remember, he has crushed you. You have every biblical right to seek counsel, and your husband has a biblical responsibility to help you heal in every possible way, even at the risk of others at your church learning about his sin.

If he's embarrassed about his transgressions, his proper response is to stop sinning, not forbid you from getting the help you need. Protecting his false "Christian image" should never take precedence over your genuine need for healing.

And make no mistake about it: small group support will speed your healing. If you can't find anyone in your church to connect with on this topic, Clay and Susan Allen have co-founded an outreach called Avenue just for you. Avenue will help you meet your specific need for peer support and connect you with other women dealing with the same issues. This outreach can also provide small group support for your husband by connecting him with other men in the purity battle.

Let's not forget that these unintended journeys—known for their wrenching trials and blistering betrayals—can make a woman become someone she doesn't want to be. It can also tie her relationship with God into knots. To jump-start your healing process, enroll in one of the small restoration groups at Avenue, where you'll meet other women in your position and connect with them weekly by phone, online, or in local gatherings.

No matter what form your group takes, Susan's *The Healing Choice Guidebook* will bring you eye-opening information that will guide your group through the tumultuous emotions you're enduring while helping you make the necessary life-changing decisions, both little and large, that are essential to healing your heart.

To learn more about Avenue, visit Clay and Susan's website at avenue.works (yes, that's the URL). Click on **Women** and then **Get Help Women**, which will guide you to joining a Healing Choice restoration group. Please email any questions to the caring and confidential women who've already traversed their unintended journeys through the "Get Help Women" link. And take hope! Again and again, my readers have found great help in Susan's capable hands.

4. Finally, make an honest assessment of your sexuality as you continue to assess his. What is your attitude toward sex in general? From God's point of view, are your attitudes normal? Is regular sex happening in your marriage? God thinks that regular sex is foundational for a great marriage:

> But since sexual immorality is occurring, each man should have sexual relations with his own wife, and each woman with her own husband. The husband should fulfill his marital duty to his wife, and likewise the wife to her husband. The wife does not have authority over her own body but yields it to her husband. In the same way, the husband does not have authority over his own body but yields it to his wife. Do not deprive each other except perhaps by mutual consent and for a time, so that you may devote yourselves to prayer. Then come together again so that Satan will not tempt you because of your lack of self-control. (1 Corinthians 7:2–5, NIV)

If you do not have regular sex in marriage—and by that, I mean around two times a week—you're missing the mark in your marriage by God's way of thinking. There is a wound somewhere in your marriage, a warp in your attitudes, or a disrespect of your differences. Something is off-kilter in your husband's approach to you, or something is off in your approach toward him.

Let me remind you of an immutable truth when it comes to relationships. Hurting people hurt people, and if you don't stop the hurt inside you, you'll keep hurting the ones you love the most.

I'm sure you expect your husband to heal, don't you? There is nothing wrong with that. After all, if your husband doesn't heal his wounds, he'll keep right on masturbating and never form a genuine intimacy with you.

But the truth is, you can't expect your husband to heal *his* wounds if you aren't willing to heal *your* wounds. Have you done a self-assessment? Where are your wounds? I've found that a wife's attitudes often reveal the location of her wounds, so let's go through several common attitudes in a marriage that will help you with your self-assessment:

- *I'm okay with my husband masturbating. It takes the pressure off me.*

You have a serious heart issue if you've said this to yourself. You're acting selfishly because God's given you and your body to your husband as a gift of mercy and grace (see 1 Corinthians 7:9), but you've taken it back in opposition to God's will. The pro-abortion lobby has shrieked forever that a woman's body is her own. I'm afraid Christian women have inadvertently picked up this lie and applied it to the marriage bed. Your body simply isn't your own.

- *I shouldn't have to have sex if I'm not in the mood.*

If you've said that, you have a cultural wound and a mindset issue, in the sense that you do not have the mind of Christ when it comes to sexual connection. You are completely missing the big picture and blocking God's dreams for deep, mutual intimacy in your marriage.

- *I hate sex. I was abused as a child.*

If you've said that, you have a wound in your sexuality. There's nothing wrong with *being* wounded, but it doesn't do anyone any good to *stay* wounded. You've allowed a sin *against* you to create sin *in* you by stealing your body away from your husband when it is rightfully his by marriage. Don't shut Christ out of this area of your life entirely, an area He has every intention of healing if you would only let Him in.

Do I understand where your pain is coming from? Absolutely. Childhood sexual abuse, body image issues, premarital promiscuity, or emotional disconnection can make it seem too painful to "go there" again, even in marriage. Perhaps you have shut down sexually, avoiding your husband's sexual advances for years . . . or decades.

But the truth is, that simply isn't how God said things should be in a marriage, and He wants far more for you. He wants to heal that wound. He wants you to find true oneness in marriage.

Perhaps it's time to carefully consider what may be keeping you from enjoying a vibrant, healthy sex life within the context of the marriage bed.

Navigating marital intimacy is tough for all of us because men and women are created differently, and we can barely understand our partner's makeup, let alone easily accept it. Even in the best circumstances, married couples need a ton of communication to get it right. Without that communication, it's far too easy to mislabel "normal male differences" as "negative character flaws." We must never do that because it's always devastating to oneness and unity.

Let me share a couple of stories illustrating how destructive this mislabeling can be to marital unity. Early in our marriage, Fred discovered that I responded to stress and turmoil in ways that he simply couldn't understand. As a quarterback, Fred often barked, "When the going gets tough, the tough get going!" His natural temperament was never like your average quarterback, but more like a fullback or linebacker. His prevailing mindset in life was to lower his shoulder and hit every problem head-on.

I have a different philosophy of life. I'm a peace lover and, by nature, I don't like conflict. When the going gets tough, I retreat to the couch and read a book.

I love a great escape!

During our tumultuous first two years of marriage, how often did Fred return home late after work to find me reading on the couch? Born with a vastly different temperament, he immediately mislabeled this difference as a weakness in me, deriding it as evidence of poor character and resolve. I disagreed vehemently with his narrow assessment.

Our unity was strained until one day when he picked up a copy of *Spirit-Controlled Temperament* by Tim LaHaye. As he read, a light flipped on for Fred. For the first time, he understood that different temperaments exist and are written into our DNA.

The coup de grâce came when LaHaye described my temperament blend in detail and specifically said that it was typical for those with my makeup to retreat to a couch to read a book when life gets rough. Fred was astonished to see this truth in print, but he certainly took it to heart. There was an overnight change in our marriage.

Fred stopped mislabeling our differences as annoying, negative flaws and began to honor them instead, making room for them in his mind, in our home, and in his decisions. He now accepts this one difference *so* well that he often chuckles when he sees me reading on the couch, calling it cute. I know, it's hard to believe. He no longer considers that trait a flaw but a treasured expression of the natural makeup of the woman he loves most in the world.

But do you want to know a secret? I wasn't too good at honoring our differences at first either. A chief issue between us was our differing sex drives. Not surprisingly, that had a negative impact on our marriage.

Fred and I still laugh about the night evangelist Rich Wilkerson spoke in our city. At one point during his talk, he mentioned the obvious visual nature of male sexuality, which I'd mislabeled as an acutely harmful character flaw, and a kinky, perverted one to boot. Imagine my jarring consternation when Wilkerson boldly declared, right out loud from the pulpit of God, that wives must lovingly accept that difference between men and women and use it to their advantage in the master bedroom together.

In the ensuing argument at home after the service, I spat at Fred, "So now I suppose I have to wear some cheap teddy and prance around the bedroom like a saloon girl!"

Not much honor there, I must admit.

But at that moment, I didn't care one little bit. Male sexuality seemed relatively shallow and almost weird to me. After a bit of reading and more discussion with Fred, I soon discovered that male sexuality wasn't shallow, perverted, or kinky. It's just different. And once I understood that sex is Fred's natural language for sharing emotional intimacy with me, it was only too clear why he desired sex more often than I did. He was in love with me, for heaven's sake! Of course he yearned to share his joy and affection for me regularly in that way.

That's no character flaw. That's merely a gender difference written into his DNA. It had to be honored, like every other difference in our marriage.

If you're anything like I was, you probably need a little humility regarding these sexual differences, especially if you've been too narrow in your sexual stance. I don't know what the complications or challenges have been inside your bedroom, but one thing is absolutely certain: If you are aware of your husband's sexual sin, it has made things worse for you as his wife, and now you have some hard decisions to make.

In the middle of your turmoil, it's helpful to take on a more complete and accurate view of God's purpose for marriage. If you're like most people, you see marriage as a place to live happily ever after with your prince, the guy who loves you unconditionally for exactly who you are. But today you're living in the wake of your husband's sexual sin. This limited view of marriage has left you focused entirely on your losses, especially your shattered dreams and lost hope for that happily-ever-after place in your heart. You mustn't stay there.

Take on God's view of marriage. The Lord doesn't see matrimony as a happily-ever-after place. He sees it more as a medical center, a place of healing, and a place where He can upshift the speed of change in your character to light speed. That's because, in marriage, you're living so closely with one another that you can easily detect each other's blind spots.

Character growth emerges rapidly in marriage because blind spots are swiftly exposed there. Your husband can see you more clearly than you can see yourself, and he can open your eyes to your blind spots. What a treasured gift! You'll finally see things in yourself that you could have never seen on your own, things that need fixing, like the fact that *he's* paying a hefty price for *your* reluctance to have sex with him.

When he calls out your blind spots, you'll know where you're hurting him and see where the wounds are in your relationship. You'll feel an urgency to swiftly follow whatever Scripture has to say on the topic, and you'll grow in grace and character. God's matrimonial medical center is good for both of you in this way because marriage is a place where you can heal speedily as you focus on the possibilities and not just upon your losses.

Sometimes God needs to heal your poor character and hard attitude, which means there'll be times when your husband is paying hefty prices for your sin until you grow in grace. But God also needs to heal your husband's character, which means there'll be times when you'll be the one paying hefty prices for another's sin.

So here's the question. Can you patiently hang out in God's waiting room, enduring the pain of your husband's sin while you lovingly wait for your husband's changes to take hold?

Perhaps your marriage has been nothing but a mirage. Perhaps your husband has been your nightmare instead of your dream. It may feel like you are sitting in the darkest period of your life.

But you are still married, which means you're still in God's hospital and not at the end of your dreams at all, no matter how painful life seems right now.

In truth, you're at the dawn of your dreams. I say that because now his sin is out in the open, and the mirage has vaporized. You can now build a genuine marriage in its place, the magnificent one you always desired.

Will you risk intimacy with this man again during this darkest hour before the dawn? Sure, your husband has blown your marriage to bits and defiled your marriage bed with sexual sin. Rubble is everywhere. No one disputes that.

But there are still decisions to make. Will you leave the scattered rubble in place, or will you drag in the heavy equipment and help clean up the mess? Will you rebuild something normal and beautiful in its place, at your husband's side?

Granted, picking through the rubble in sin's aftermath will test your commitment to him and to God—daily. Restoration projects are never easy and always take longer than expected, but you won't be alone.

Now, there's one more thing I want to share. Because of the sexual differences between men and women, forming a consistent and regular sexual connection can be tricky, even in the best times. But you have an irrevocable call to be your husband's helpmate, even in tough times like these. That pressure is a privilege, not a curse. So remember, if you are going to have regular sex in your marriage, you can't afford to wait until the situation is perfect or your feelings are just right to make love. That kind of Hollywood thinking never leads to the regularity that God expects. Consistent sexuality demands personal sacrifices.

In other words, if you are to build normal sexuality in your marriage, you will likely have to respond sexually to your husband *as if* you trust that he's being pure, perhaps long before you *do* trust him. Even if it is hard at first, you'll want to do this because regular sex is vital for building genuine intimacy in your life together. If you can't do it for your husband's sake right now, perhaps you can remember all God has done for you, leading you to do it for God's sake. In my darkest times with Fred, that mindset always worked for me. (There's sometimes a place for a sexual moratorium when breaking a sexual addiction, but only for a short time and only under the direct supervision of a professional counselor.)

Remember your wedding day vow "for better or for worse"? Well, today is probably on the worse side of things, but now is the time to keep your vows to God and your husband anyway. Believe me, you'll see better days ahead if you do.

Getting through this whole sex thing might be easier than you think because the truth is that God's principles extend all the way into the marriage bed, including this principle: *Right feelings always follow right actions.*

So even when I'm not in the mood, I've always found that if I can choose the right action and just get started, it isn't long before the wonder of the human touch has its way with me. Before long, the right feelings find my heart.

I love my husband. His purity is not an individual sport, especially not in a marriage. Since we are one flesh, it's a team sport. I can't afford to let down my teammate and closest friend with an indifferent approach to my life in bed with him, no matter where my wounds lie. Such indifference can cost him dearly on the field of battle, and if he loses, I pay the price too. In a real sense, we both win when we're running together regularly, side by side.

I owe that to my husband and my children.

And you owe it to yours.

As I close this chapter, I want to share an email from Madison to paint a picture of hope for you as you work to restore your heart, your attitudes, and your marriage. Madison made the perfect decision as she stood in a pile of rubble and chose to risk intimacy with her husband once again:

> I won't pretend that this year has been easy. It hasn't been. I won't even pretend that this year has been fair. It hasn't been that either. But I *will* say that this year, our ninth year of marriage, has been our best year ever.
>
> You'd think the opposite would be true. After all, my husband confessed to being addicted to pornography, to lying and deceiving and manipulating me and everyone we knew to keep his secrets, *and* to pursuing a relationship with another woman. We had to go to counseling, join a sex addict accountability group, and talk about the most intimate details of our marriage with complete strangers. Don't these all seem like bad things?
>
> Well, it's all a matter of perspective. Before our crisis of truth, Caden and I never had true intimacy. I'm not even sure he ever really loved me. We certainly had no genuine communication because everything was built on lies. We had a lingering darkness over our home and our relationship. Our marriage was plagued with bitterness, anger, resentment, unmet expectations, and a general lack of love and respect.
>
> But once the truth came out and Caden repented, that darkness lifted, and we began to see each other in a new light. God intervened and worked a miraculous transformation and restoration in my husband and our marriage. We began communicating openly and honestly about

everything. It brought us into an incredible place of intimacy where we connected in a way that only happens between people who have gone to war together. Caden and I went into battle, fighting side by side, which united us in a way I never dreamt possible.

Beyond that, all of Caden's sexual desires are now focused on me, so our sexual intimacy has flourished and has become something we both treasure and enjoy. We're like two kids in love again, getting to know each other for the first time. He is pursuing me now, and I am his only beauty. Who would've thought that my husband would ever become my hero? It's been an amazing adventure, and it's great running at his side. I absolutely love spending time with Caden now.

Sure, we still have days when we struggle. Sometimes someone might say something that triggers a bad memory for me and I am instantly back into pain mode. But now we know how to fight the battle and stand together. We continue to charge the battlefield, and we don't back down because our marriage and purity are things worth fighting for.

Madison's marriage is now normal, and their sexual intimacy is flourishing and treasured by both. That's how it's supposed to be.

Never forget that God's Word and God's ways define "normal" for us. In 1 Corinthians 7:2–5, God declares "regular sex" as normal in marriage, and that declaration serves the same purpose for you as the indicator lights on a vehicle's dashboard. If you aren't having regular sex with the love of your life, something is wrong under the hood.

It may be that you're still struggling with the pain of sexual abuse before your marriage. It may be that your husband never learned how to keep his trampling feet off your heart, so you don't find him sexually attractive anymore because your relationship is on life support. It may simply be that in the rush of raising kids, you've misplaced your sex life. You've become nothing more than dependable roommates who know how to carry their loads around the house, but neither of you knows how to carry your hearts together as one. Please, make healing a priority, and get things back to normal.

Hopefully and happily, you're married, which means that rapid growth and swift change are right at your fingertips, just like they were for Madison and Caden. Focus on the possibilities. They are still endless. After all, consider Madison's words once more: "Who would've thought that my husband would ever become my hero?"

Well, no one, except for the very same God who still thinks your husband can become *your* hero. The best years of your marriage may be just ahead of you. Madison and Caden considered the possibilities, and then they made them happen.

Now it's your turn. Go out and make it happen for you too.

And now, in our final chapter, Fred will share his closing thoughts to men as they step up to engage in combat and sweep to victory on purity's battleground.

16

Defend Your Beauty

Then David said to the Philistine, "You come to me with a sword,
with a spear, and with a javelin. But I come to you in the name of the
LORD of hosts, the God of the armies of Israel, whom you have defied.
This day the LORD will deliver you into my hand, and I will strike you
and take your head from you. And this day I will give the carcasses of
the camp of the Philistines to the birds of the air and the wild beasts
of the earth, that all the earth may know that there is a God in Israel.
—1 Samuel 17:45–46, NKJV

From Fred

W hat does your wife want from you?
The answer is easy: She wants you to answer the cry of her heart. She
wants to hear from you on questions like these:
Am I lovely to you, my husband?
Is my heart worth pursuing?
Can we ride together on a great adventure in God?
She longs to share her secret garden with you, but she doesn't want you
polluting the landscape with the pornographic tastes you've developed in
the darkness of cyberspace. Acting like a porn queen in bed is not the great
adventure she craves. She simply wants to be who she was created to be—a
kindred spirit, a partner to run at your side, and a friend who helps lift you to
Christian greatness. She'll sally forth on your great adventure and push on with
you to win your biggest battles. Defend her heart's beauty as she rides at your
side.

She wants to communicate openly and honestly about every last thing with you and live in an incredible place of interpersonal intimacy. She also wants your sexual intimacy to flourish and to become something that you both can treasure and enjoy together, where *all* of your sexual needs and desires are laid squarely on her (instead of shared with a pixelated nude) and where she'll never doubt that you desire *her* as your one and only beauty. She wants you to lead as you both charge purity's battlefield together. She wants you to be the man who clearly knows that marriage and purity are worth fighting for.

You are meant to be that man, and I'm confident the Holy Spirit has confirmed that to you by now.

So don't make your wife beg for a miracle in your life, wrestling for *years* in prayer for your purity, on her knees before God! You don't need a miracle to make this happen. It's not like you have congestive heart disease or plaque clogging your arteries. Your heart is simply hurting, hardened by your wounds and the stresses along life's way.

So soften your heart.

Encounter God.

Get counsel.

Engage the battle.

And win this war.

This is what your wife needs. She needs you to choose purity and take up God's charter to conquer so that she might ride at your side on this great adventure. She needs you to choose manhood.

In that spirit, I leave you with the *U.S. Navy SEALs Ethos & Code*. When it comes to war, I understand two things very well.

First, as long as there is evil in the world, we will need men like the Navy SEALs. Second, as long as wives ache for purity in their families and peace in their homes, we will need warriors like you with souls—minds, emotions, and wills—aligned to this code. So, without further ado, please consider these words for the sake of your wife and the defense of her heart:

The U.S. Navy SEALs Ethos & Code

In times of war or uncertainty, there is a special breed of warrior ready to answer our nation's call. A common man with an uncommon desire to succeed. Forged by adversity, he stands alongside America's finest special operations forces to serve his country, the American people, and protect their way of life. I am that man.

My Trident is a symbol of honor and heritage. Bestowed upon me by the heroes that have gone before, it embodies the trust of those I have sworn to protect. By wearing the Trident, I accept the responsibility of my chosen profession and way of life. It is a privilege that I must earn every day.

My loyalty to my Country and Team is beyond reproach. I humbly serve as a guardian to my fellow Americans, always ready to defend those who are unable to defend themselves. I do not advertise the nature of my work, nor seek recognition for my actions. I voluntarily accept the inherent hazards of my profession, placing the welfare and security of others before my own.

I serve with honor on and off the battlefield. The ability to control my emotions and my actions, regardless of circumstance, sets me apart from other men. Uncompromising integrity is my standard. My character and honor are steadfast. My word is my bond.

We expect to lead and be led. In the absence of orders, I will take charge, lead my teammates, and accomplish the mission. I lead by example in all situations.

I will never quit. I persevere and thrive on adversity. My nation expects me to be physically harder and mentally stronger than my enemies. If knocked down, I will get back up every time. I will draw on every remaining ounce of strength to protect my teammates and accomplish our mission. I am never out of the fight.

We demand discipline. We expect innovation. The lives of my teammates and the success of our mission depend on me—my technical skill, tactical proficiency, and attention to detail. My training is never complete.

We train for war and fight to win. I stand ready to bring the full spectrum of combat power to bear in order to achieve my mission and the goals established by my country. The execution of my duties will be swift and violent when required yet guided by the very principles that I serve to defend.

Brave men have fought and died building the proud tradition and feared reputation that I am bound to uphold. In the worst of conditions, the legacy of my teammates steadies my resolve and silently guides my every deed.

I will not fail.

That is the soul of a warrior in writing. Make no mistake, my brother, you are built for this battle, *a common man with the uncommon makeup* to succeed and protect your family's Christian way of life and destiny. Since you are a man, you are that *special breed of warrior* ready to answer your Lord's call. This mission depends upon you as you run in His knowledge, grace, and firepower. You're made this way.

So drive your stake into the ground, here and now. Pursue your wife's heart. Pursue freedom, and always persevere as you train for war and fight to win. Lead by example in all circumstances. In the worst of conditions, allow the legacy of your Christian brothers who have won this war and walked in purity before you to steady your resolve and silently guide your every deed.

Refuse to fail.

Soon, the ability to control your mind, will, and emotions, and the actions flowing from a disciplined soul, regardless of your wounds or stress, will set you apart from other men.

And soon, these words will ring from your heart:

The battle was surely on, but now? The battle is over!

A Note Regarding the Open Letters from Fred Stoeker

The primary intended audience of *Battle On, Battle Over* is the married reader, but Brenda and I are confident that single women, single men, and divorced men will also read this book.

For them, we've created this appendix with "open letters" for each group. We longed to offer this guidance within the primary text of *Battle On, Battle Over*, but since this book is primarily targeted at married men and women, we felt it was better to use this format instead, so thanks for your understanding.

Appendix 1

An Open Letter to Single Young Women from Fred Stoeker

The technological innovations of the digital age make pornography so easily accessible that it can be punched up on a smartphone twenty-four hours a day. This instant access to porn means that anyone seeking purity is standing on a slippery slope of skin and smut—truly miserable footing.

This has tremendous implications for you as well. One might be that you are in a relationship with a man hooked on porn, and we will spend most of this letter talking about how to deal with that. The other possible implication is that you are just as hooked on porn as the young men around you.

If this is the case, don't despair! The advice given earlier in this book about waging war on the battlefield of purity applies to you too. Reread it and take it to heart. You are not weird or messed up. You are a Christian with a serious job in front of you: learning to fight for your purity!

Now, if you're serious with a guy who can't stop peeking at naked women, you must understand that an addiction to porn does not set the proper foundation for a healthy romantic relationship. So how do you traverse a path toward matrimony through this pornographic cultural quagmire?

If your boyfriend is hooked on porn and masturbation and you know about it, that's probably prompting a ton of questions in your heart. As the two of you try to sort things out as a couple, you may yearn to talk to your dad about this to find some answers.

Sadly, this digital age is also a fatherless age for far too many daughters. If you don't have a father's voice in your life right now, allow me to take on that role for you in this letter. I'll answer some common questions and tell you the same things I've told my daughters, Laura and Rebecca.

So let's begin our conversation. Perhaps a question like this is on your mind: *If I'm dating a guy and find out he's addicted to porn and masturbation, should I break it off until he's free of his habit?*

I'd say not necessarily. Take a look at God's will for a moment:

> It is God's will that you should be sanctified; that you should avoid sexual immorality; that each of you should *learn* to control your own body in a way that is holy and honorable, not in passionate lust like the pagans, who do not know God; and that in this matter no one should wrong or take advantage of a brother or sister . . . For God did not call us to be impure, but to live a holy life. (1 Thessalonians 4:3–6a, 7, NIV; italics added)

God uses the word "learn" here on purpose. Learning implies a passage of time: a time to make mistakes, a time to learn the triggers that make one stumble, and a time to learn how to crucify the flesh and submit one's sexual desires to God's will.

If you've caught your boyfriend in the middle of this learning process, you needn't drop him at this time. There isn't necessarily anything wrong with him. He's simply going through the learning process that every guy goes through when dealing with these issues. You can play a significant role in his eventual victory by encouraging, prodding, and pushing him toward Christian greatness within your dating relationship.

Of course, this approach can only work if you can keep your *own* sexual boundaries protected from any of his advances along the way. If you're not strong enough to avoid fondling each other or even having sexual intercourse, you must break off the relationship immediately. You're a stumbling block to him, and him to you, and you'll never learn to control your bodies in each other's company. But if you *can* protect your boundaries, you may decide to keep dating him, at least for a while.

But never forget, dating is one thing, and marriage is another. Do not marry a man who's still addicted to porn and masturbation, which leads to the following question:

Is that really fair?

Well, let me answer you with another question. Is it fair for him to ask you to marry when you both know that an addiction to porn does not set a proper foundation for a healthy romantic relationship? If you're valuable enough to him to marry you, let him prove it on the battlefield of purity first. Anyone can *say* he loves you, but those are mere words and emotions. Rather, is he heroic enough to *prove* he loves you, in battle and in action? That's the guy you want to marry.

Are you saying it's possible for a single man not to look at porn and masturbate? And how can guys avoid masturbation before marriage?

Of course, it's possible! Guys can be sexually pure outside of marriage if they want to be, no matter what you've heard. Neither of my sons has ever masturbated, but then again, we taught them early on how to control their bodies and worship the Lord one on one, which establishes a deep and personal intimacy with God that helps protect them. I don't share my sons' testimony to make anyone feel guilty. As my wife often says, guilt is irrelevant. I share it to let you know what's possible.

My oldest son, Jasen, went from puberty to the wedding altar at age twenty-three without masturbating, and my son Michael, who's turned thirty, is following in his brother's footsteps. As an aside, if you and your boyfriend are really interested in learning how to stay pure while dating and if he wants the mindset necessary to keep porn and masturbation at bay, then the both of you should read *Hero*, a book I co-authored with my son Jasen, a guy who lived out a pure life victoriously with his fiancée, Rose, amidst this very sexualized culture.

Getting back to your question . . . since it's possible to be free of an addiction to porn, it isn't unfair to ask your fiancé to find freedom first, before marriage. A guy who doesn't reach victory before reaching the altar often gives up on freedom's call altogether. Please don't doubt me on that. After all, once you marry him, the incentive to change usually drops precipitously, which could transform your marital dreams into nightmares.

But won't his predilection for porn and masturbation disappear once he starts having regular sex with me in marriage?

Don't fall for this lie, my friend. If he's a masturbator before marriage, he'll be one after marriage, in most cases. If you've read the rest of this book, you know that sexual sin isn't always sexual at its root, so you should also know that your marriage bed will not end his habits, especially those that aren't sexual in the first place.

How can sex with you deal with *non*sexual issues? A lack of sex doesn't always cause masturbation, and since sex isn't the root issue, it won't matter how much sex you give your husband. There is something nonsexual driving it all.

If he's dependent upon porn and masturbation to medicate his deeper, psychic wounds, he'll maintain that chemical dependence no matter what you do for him in bed. I know this personally from experience. I had a great sex life with Brenda in our early years of marriage, but I remained addicted to masturbation for deep and painful reasons, despite her comforts.

Look, I recognize that the regular sexual connection in marriage is helpful in the battle for purity. The Bible tells us so: "But if they cannot exercise self-control, they should marry. For it is better to marry than to burn with passion" (1 Corinthians 7:9, ESV). Because of this verse, I recognize that while it may be a rare exception, there will be the occasional guy who needs marriage to find his purity.

But you must also soberly recognize that your fiancé will drag every one of his wounds and all his bad habits into your new home along with the rest of his possessions. If you're willing to marry him while his addictions are still ablaze, you better be ready to jump into bed regularly with a guy who's been gawking at sexually explicit videos and has a porn star's bare breasts in his mind while he's having sex with you.

At the very least, if you do go ahead and marry him despite his porn habit, you better tighten the clamps on his commitment to victory the moment you become husband and wife. After all, if you're willing to offer up your body to help him in his battle, he better be willing to intensify his fight to put his sexual sin out of business on the spot.

My suggestion is that you better know before your wedding that he has what it takes to turn his back on sexual sin and is genuinely willing to do so. But don't take a few promises from him as your guarantee. Never depend upon his promises alone. Remember, the words of an addict mean nothing.

But, Fred, if his promises mean nothing, how will I know if he really wants victory?

You'll know by the fruits of his life with God. You'll know by his actions.

Now, before we dig into what you need to watch for in his actions, allow me to share a couple of foundational thoughts to remember.

First, always remember that as his girlfriend or fiancée, you absolutely have the right to ask him tough questions about this issue anytime, anywhere. Once you're married, his sin will affect the entire household, so a lot is riding on this. You have a right to know, and no secrets are his to keep if marriage is a potential for you. If he battles you on this, this should raise the deepest scarlet of all red flags for you.

Second, make sure you get educated about male sexuality. Hard-hearted women who refuse to believe that male and female sexuality are different generally end up shrill and bitter because their husbands aren't approaching their sexuality like a woman would approach hers.

Well, of course not. They are men! Get knowledge of the inner workings of guys so that you can both approach this issue from a position of truth, not from a position of bitterness and anger and frustration.

Don't expect him to be like a woman in this area of his life. Expect him to be holy. That is your goal.

Let me now offer you a set of keys to watch for and a set of questions to ponder that will uncover his current level of discipline to God's standard of purity from Ephesians 5:3. In short, let's discover together how committed he is to root out every hint of sexual immorality in his life.

1. Watch his level of urgency. If he's not pressing to crush this before marriage, he will drag his sexual sin into your marriage and have much less urgency to deal with it afterward. Listen to his excuses. If he's saying things like, "I'm not as bad as the next guy" or "It's just pictures that aren't hurting anyone," then you know you have a problem on your hands.

2. Watch his eyes. Do his eyes linger on the beer-and-bikini TV commercials during football games—or do those eyes turn away? (Or does he turn to another channel?) Does he feast on the sensuality of shows like *Dancing with the Stars* and *The Bachelor* and get angry if you question him about it? What happens when you're in a restaurant and a hot babe slides past your table?

3. Watch his talk. Does he comment a lot about the appearance of other girls, saying offhand comments like, "Man, she's really hot" or "She's amazingly pretty"? Do his jokes veer toward the off-color?

4. Watch how he treats you. Does he ask you to highlight your cleavage and curves with tighter clothes? Does he buy you gifts of revealing clothing that are far less modest than you would otherwise buy yourself?

5. Watch who his friends are. Who does he hang out with when he's not with you? Who is he talking to these days? Who is holding him accountable to God and asking him tough questions? When it comes to guarding his eyes and his purity, does he mention any training he's received from a father or a mentor? What books is he consuming on Audible, or what podcasts is he watching to help him win this battle? What is he sharing with you about what he's learning?

6. Watch for the motivations behind his sin. Dig into his past. Discover his wounds. Remember, sexual sin is not always sexual at its root.

7. Watch his relationship with his father. What's his relationship with his dad like? Is it stormy? Is he often angry or dismissive about his father? Has he struggled to find his place in the world of men, or is he always out to prove he's tough and has what it takes to be a man?

If the answers to these questions are less than satisfactory, I'm not saying that means you should dump him on the spot. After all, if he's weak in his discipline to God's standards of sexual purity, that may simply mean he's been attending a less-than-dynamic church that rarely addresses the topic of sexuality. In that case, he just needs good training to prepare for marriage.

On the other hand, his behavior may also mean that he has a generally weak Christian character and doesn't love God as passionately as you do or as he needs to.

8. Watch what he's reading. Is he reading his Bible regularly? Does he share what he's learning with excitement? Does he read or listen to Christian books to sharpen his alignment with Christ?

9. Watch his prayer and worship. How much does he care about the back-forty, behind-the-scenes, no-headline aspects of his walk with God—like his personal purity? Does he spend one-on-one worship time with God at home? Or does he slump with his hands in his pockets during worship at church? Does he spend as much time praying and reading his Bible as he does watching television or playing video games?

10. Watch his life. If you point out flaws in his character, does he respond thoughtfully, or does he argue and get angry? Does he love God more than he loves himself? In other words, is he quick to repent and change his behavior, in joy and without frustration?

Is honesty really important to him? If the cashier gives him the wrong change, does he correct her and hand back the extra money? If he backs into another car, does he leave a note with his phone number to make it right? Does lying come easily for him?

11. Watch the responses of your friends and family. They say that love is blind, which means that you may have devastating blind spots regarding your boyfriend that prevent you from seeing critical flaws in his character. Pay special attention to what your friends and family say about him, and be sure to offer them an opening to speak into your life about your relationship. In fact, give them a bullhorn. They won't tell you their feelings if you don't ask, so ask a simple question: "Is there anything you see in my boyfriend that scares you about our future together or looks like a red flag?"

When they answer, pay attention! Research shows that no other single criterion is more accurate in predicting the marital success of a couple than the opinions of family and friends.

Oh, and be sure you don't ask that question with your boyfriend present. Promise ahead of time that you'll keep their answers private, just between you and them. Don't blab whatever they tell you to your boyfriend either, because if you do end up marrying him later, you don't want their words to impact his relationship with his in-laws or your close friends.

12. Watch his reactions to your requests. You might ask your boyfriend to read *Battle On, Battle Over* as a condition for dating you, for instance.

His reaction to this request will tell you plenty. If he loves God more than he loves himself, he'll agree to read this book without fuss, and you'll soon hear him saying, "Wow, *Battle On, Battle Over* taught me a lot about myself. Thank you so much for asking me to read it."

On the other hand, if he loves himself more than he loves God, he'll fight you on this, dawdling and dragging his feet. If he finally does read this book, he'll soon be crabbing, "*Battle On, Battle Over* is way too extreme and over-the-top. No one can live this way, and no one should even want to live this way. God wants us to be happy."

Another book that'll reveal the most about his commitment to God and your happiness is *Every Man's Marriage*. Mentioning this book may sound self-promoting, but I know it's content better than any other book I might recommend, and I know its impact upon relationships. I also know I'm practicing what I preach as I suggest it to you. I've told my own daughters, Laura and Rebecca, that they should not marry any guy until he's read *Every Man's Marriage*, and if he balks at the message, they should hightail it out of town and run for the hills.

I suggest you do the same.

Appendix 2

An Open Letter to Divorced Men from Fred Stoeker

D ivorce is as rough as it gets in our relationships with women. While I've never been divorced myself, Brenda and I have danced at its edge, so I've tasted its appalling anguish. Since my mom was divorced three times and my dad twice, I've witnessed up close and personal the crippling devastation when a dissolution of marriage wends its way through a lifetime of emotions.

As an author, I've also heard from countless men struggling desperately with their purity in the wake of a marital breakup. As your friend, I need to warn you about an insidious thought pattern that creeps into the minds of divorced men and poses a serious threat to sexual purity.

It goes something like this:

It's tough being single after being sexually intimate with someone for many years of marriage. I'm used to having sex. It's been a big part of my life, so if I'm honest, I feel entitled to an orgasm every now and then. The call to purity is so unfair, and avoiding sex is much more difficult for guys in my position.

Suppose you indulge in this line of reasoning. The clear implication is that a divorced man's plight in every man's battle is vastly worse than it is for a younger man who's never married. In that case, your woe-filled outlook will have your sexuality working against you because of the second major sexual vulnerability that I explored earlier in this book.

In short, your victim mentality eats away at your fresh wounds and raw emotions and keeps you feeling sorry for yourself. At the same time, a subtle, huffy sense of sexual entitlement takes you on a hasty dive into the warm, medicating streams of porn and masturbation. This course of action seems right, like the only fair and reasonable thing to do, given the cruel straits God has placed you in.

But it's all a fabrication of your mind. There's absolutely no difference whatsoever between the plight of the single man pre-marriage or post-marriage.

That's ridiculous, Fred! How can you possibly say that?

Look, I know you're used to the wondrous experience of having sex with a real, genuine woman, in the flesh and on a regular basis, and I know what that's like. It's divine, it's dazzling, and you undoubtedly miss the sensual experience passionately.

But as your mentor, I ask you to slow down for a moment and examine things together with me. When I was twenty-three, I had three girlfriends and was sleeping with all of them regularly, so I was having sex with a real, genuine woman at least as frequently as most husbands do—probably more. So when it comes to fighting for sexual purity, can you honestly say that your battle is any more difficult *post-marriage* than the battle would be for a young guy like I was, living *pre-marriage*? You can't.

Now let's consider that gangly, acne-faced, seventeen-year-old high school student who's been masturbating four days a week during sessions of internet porn. He's been going down that road on a smartphone since he was twelve because there wasn't a genuine girl on earth who ever looked at him twice. He's having more orgasms with his hand each week than you probably had with your wife, so don't try to tell me that's not the same thing.

Simply take a moment to recall what I've shared with you about the addictive chemistry of porn and masturbation in the pleasure centers of the human brain. Orgasm is orgasm, however it arrives, and I guarantee you that his sexuality is as wide awake as yours has ever been. Holding any other position would be unscientific, ludicrous, and just plain silly.

Let me make one additional point very clear to you. There are no varying degrees of your sexuality "being awake." The enemy wants you to believe that there *are* extremes and that you're right smack-dab on the edge of the outermost apex. Why is that? Because he wants you to feel overmatched in the battle and be overwhelmed by self-pity and petulance.

This is done for one apparent reason: the enemy is out to degrade your moral resistance, and he knows what he's doing. He definitely knows there are no degrees here, but he lies anyway because he understands how you are built. He knows your sexuality is tied to your emotions. If he can just get you feeling helpless and pathetic enough amidst this battle, you'll look away from your seemingly hard-hearted, treacherous, traitorous God and toward a soothing jar of Vaseline that will make the emotional pain go away.

Look, my friend. If the enemy knows what *he* is doing, you better understand what *you* are doing. Make no mistake about it: I'm telling you the truth, and you had better cling to this truth. There are no degrees of one's sexuality "being awake." Your sexuality is either awake or it's asleep. There are no degrees or half measures. You are simply living in one place or the other. Don't let the enemy dupe you, and above all, don't let your buddies in the adult singles group confuse you with their pity parties.

If your sexuality is awake, you're regularly washing your brain with the chemistry of orgasmic pleasure, either from sexual intercourse or porn and masturbation. If your sexuality is dormant, you're living above the fray, and that grinding, yearning desire to medicate is resting, and the tugging, urgent whispers of temptation are silent.

I understand that you are recently divorced, and your sexuality is awake. To win your battle, you simply need to put your sexuality to sleep again for a season. Putting your sexuality to sleep means living like my son Jasen did from his earliest, unsettling days of puberty to that grand, exultant moment on his wedding day when he shared his first kiss with his bride, Rose.

Jasen never touched a woman's body in dishonor. Jasen never left a girl worse off for having known him. He was deaf to the whispers of sexual temptation, and the jagged barbs of addictive masturbation never hooked his heart or emotions. He owned his sexuality completely, and his heart was at rest.

If there's anything consistent across this battlefield, it's that the single men who win this conflict—pre-marriage or post-marriage—are the guys who accept God's call to purity as fair and sensible and refuse to see their sexuality as a unique curse they're enduring. You're no worse off than anyone else in this conflict.

Stand up and fight as college-aged Zachary did, who describes his victory on the battlefield this way:

> I had all but given up hope of defeating sexual sin, and like so many others, I'd given up on getting free until I got married. But after reading your book, I suspected that was a lie, and I didn't think marriage would make the fight any easier. I had to just get up and get it done. I am getting better now and feel cleaner and closer to God than I have in a long time.

Zachary's sexuality was wide awake due to his porn and hooking up with girls, but he stopped seeing his sexuality as a curse unique to him and simply squared up, shouldered his weapons, and took the battle to his enemies. That's what real men do.

Will you choose to follow this path of righteousness, or will you sit around deceiving yourself into believing that Zachary had it easier than you?

If so, may I remind you that Zachary was living on a liberal state university campus in a warm climate overrun with lightly clad coeds. It would be more honest for you to simply admit that this nineteen-year-old's manhood is more developed than your own at the moment. He understood that he had a big battle to fight and a great adventure to live, so he refused to feel sorry for himself. He just engaged in the battle and got it done.

You are in a tough place, no question, but it's not an unfair or unusual place. Think about it: *every* man is called to be celibate for at least a season of his life. That's right, every last one of us. Living through a season of celibacy is just part of being male, and triumphing through a season of celibacy is a valuable ticket into manhood and excellent training for your next round of matrimony. The self-denial required to maintain purity flows from the humble, sacrificial, and forbearing attitudes that every man needs to build a successful marriage.

Let's shift gears and talk about manhood and marriage for a moment. No matter where I go, whether I'm being awestruck by the gracious, lovely marriage of an esteemed black pastor in Pretoria, South Africa, or being dumbstruck by the beastly, abominable marriage of a wealthy neurosurgeon in Jakarta, Indonesia, the truth is always the same: real men are living tremendous and joyous adventures in marriage, defending the hearts of the women they love. The others are generating very little oneness with their wives and will soon be divorced or continue to cruelly decimate those beautiful hearts lying near them each night.

I've never met a man who didn't *want* his marriage to be successful, and I'm sure that desire was in your heart too. But I have met countless men who didn't know *how* to lead a marriage into oneness, no matter how badly they wanted to do so. Perhaps you are one of these.

I sure was. Somewhere around the two-year mark of my marriage, I sat across the kitchen table from my wife, Brenda, and I could tell she was waiting until she had my undivided attention.

Once she had it, she looked intently into my eyes and changed my world. "I don't know how else to say this to you, so I'll say it straight," she began. "My feelings for you are dead."

Confusion overwhelmed me, but God was gracious. Over the next few months, the Lord opened my eyes to the truth about my leadership style. I hadn't picked the wrong girl. There were no irreconcilable differences. Brenda was not a witch or a brat.

My leadership was the problem. While I'd always been a natural leader elsewhere in my life, I simply didn't know how to lead in marriage. Leadership in a marriage is an entirely different kind of leadership, requiring an exceptionally sacrificial level of manhood that most of us have never practiced anywhere else. No wonder we can blow it so easily.

But that's all changed. Now that I *do* know how to lead in a marriage, I've laid out everything I've learned in *Every Man's Marriage*. These are not my truths. They're God's, and I've seen these truths turn marriages around on a dime, including my own. The transformation can be breathtaking. I'll let Heather explain:

> I'm not married, but I have been dating a pastor for about two-and-a-half years. I was ready to call it quits because something just wasn't right in our relationship. A friend suggested your book *Every Man's Marriage,* so I purchased it for my boyfriend. I read it first, though, and was so amazed by the content that I couldn't put it down.
>
> My boyfriend didn't read it right away, but he recently went through a situation that caused him a lot of pain, so he decided to leave town to get a break and pray for healing. He took your book with him and finally started reading it. This was two months after I gave it to him.
>
> I've been overwhelmed at *his* response to *Every Man's Marriage!* He has been so excited that sometimes he has even called me late at night to discuss the content. This book has completely changed our lives, and today was the best day I have ever had with him.
>
> After reading the book myself a while back, I told my sister that if my boyfriend would just read this book, our relationship might finally work out between us. I see now that I was unquestionably correct. He has apologized for everything and has even reflected with me on the things he'd done wrong in past relationships with others and what he would have done differently back then had he known what he knows now.
>
> It's funny. We had been studying forgiveness at church, and he had asked to be forgiven for some things, but *Every Man's Marriage* helped him really understand what he needed forgiveness *for,* which has allowed him to have a true breakthrough in his leadership of our relationship.
>
> We want to order more copies of *Every Man's Marriage* to have on hand because we know that this book will help a lot of couples in our congregation. Thank you for being open about your own marriage. Your book is truly amazing. I'm so happy right now that I don't know what to do!

Every man wants his woman gushing this way, but few of us know how to make that happen. I'm reminded of that every time I speak publicly on these truths because there's no end to the men who approach me afterward, lamenting through tears, "I finally understand where I went wrong in my marriage."

My friend, you are divorced. Maybe you didn't understand what male leadership in marriage was supposed to look like at the time, but now you can learn. I urge you to take time to understand your past so that you can prepare today for your happy future.

Appendix 3
An Open Letter to Single Young Men from Fred Stoeker

There's no one I've written to more extensively and exhaustively about sexual purity than young guys like you. Countless emails like this one have flooded my inbox:

> You and your book *Every Young Man's Battle* saved my life about three years ago. I was trapped in a prison of porn and masturbation addiction, but as soon as I read your book, that all came to an end. Today, I can say I've gone over a year without porn and masturbation by using the book's techniques of bouncing the eyes and starving the sumo sex drive . . .

But what if you're still struggling? Don't beat yourself up. You're not defective, you're not a pervert, and you're certainly not a rotten Christian. Your defenses are simply down. You haven't yet *learned* how to defend your sexual vulnerabilities.

It shouldn't surprise you that learning will be your key to victory because the Bible couldn't be clearer about it. God doesn't *give* sexual purity as a gift to a lucky few of His favorite sons. Purity must be *learned* by every last one of us. No exceptions. The Lord said so Himself in His Word:

> It is God's will that you should be sanctified; that you should avoid sexual immorality; that each of you should *learn to control* your own body in a way that is holy and honorable, not in passionate lust like the pagans, who do not know God . . . (1 Thessalonians 4:3–5, NIV; italics added for emphasis)

If you're still stumbling, don't hate yourself. Learn!

Some believe that when they become Christians, the Lord will simply "give them strength" to deal with their temptations, assuming He will do the rest since they've surrendered their lives to God. But if you've genuinely surrendered your life to God, you're actually starting a new school where you'll study, learn new class material, and go through difficult tests. Like any school, you need to pay attention to the teachers, do your homework, join study groups, and discuss the thorny aspects of these topics with your friends to understand more clearly what the teacher is saying. Learning will take time and effort from you.

When it comes to the topic of purity, you're called to avoid sexual immorality, which definitely requires reading, training, and teaming up with friends. Yes, go ahead and surrender your sexual desires to Him, as you should. But you should also take a *second* step: to make an effort to learn.

Everyone knows that learning implies a passage of time, and the Lord understands you won't have this down pat by next Thursday. He gets that, and He also understands that learning involves making mistakes, learning the triggers that make a guy stumble, and learning how to crucify the flesh. He's with you in this process, however long it takes. So commit to your training and learn to control your body. That's His will for you.

Above all, don't drown yourself in shame. Shame is pointless here. Simply recognize where your defenses are down, and then learn to control yourself in those areas. Build effective defenses that honor the Lord.

And don't forget to help those around you. If your brother or a friend is still struggling in his battle, team up with him. Make sure he gets the necessary knowledge to build a testimony like this one from Danny, who sent an email that hit my inbox on the very day I finished writing this open letter to you:

> I want to thank you personally for writing *Every Young Man's Battle* and the rest of the books in the series. Sixty-three days ago, I confessed to my girlfriend of over two-and-a-half years that I had been watching porn and lusting after other women. I had lied to her a lot.
>
> I was ashamed of what I did to her, myself, and my relationship with God. Sixty days ago, however, I picked up the copy of *Every Young Man's Battle* that had been sitting on my shelf forever. Someone had bought it for me years ago, but I'd let your book gather dust for far too long. After diving into your teaching, I'm now sixty-three days clean of masturbation and porn videos, and I stopped lying about everything and came clean to my girlfriend about everything.
>
> Our relationship was rocked when I told my girlfriend all that stuff, but now it's more solid than ever. A more important relationship has been transformed as well. I was raised in the church, brought up in a Christian

home, and attended a Christian college, but I was only going through the motions with God. Since that moment when I hit rock bottom and thought that my girlfriend would break up with me, I sought God like never before, and my life has changed tremendously.

It started when I finished *Every Young Man's Battle* thirty-seven days ago. That was just the start. Then, four days ago, I finished reading *Tactics.* Yesterday, I started reading *Hero*. Coming out of where I was, I'm grateful for you and Jasen. You have both inspired me greatly, and I'm not sure I would be where I am without the guidance provided by your books. Thank you again for being an answer to my prayers and for being the men of God that you are.

Good for Danny, who learned to control his body in the way God expects us all to do.

Now let's shift gears and talk about marriage for a moment since dating is supposed to lead you there eventually. I'll start by stating that marriage is clearly God's default position for us guys. If being single wasn't good for Adam, even when living in the perfection of Eden, then it is likely that it isn't good for you either (see Genesis 2:18). Marital companionship was God's answer to His sons' needs, so as a general rule, God's will is for a man to be married.

But you would be mistaken to believe that eliminating loneliness is the only thing God has in mind for you in marriage. He is after so much more for you, and His command to leave your father and mother and to cleave to your wife (see Genesis 2:24) provides a significant clue about His full plans for marriage.

So let's slow down and think more deeply about what God demands of you here. It's good to slow down because what He's desiring is quite shocking and unexpected. I say that because God placed you in a critical relationship with your dad, a vital interpersonal connection crucial for your development as a man. (I recognize that many of you may have grown up in homes *without* a father, which happened to be my situation during my school years. If you're in the same boat, stay with me anyway as I make this point.)

Before long, you became a young adult. Suddenly, without warning, God declares that your relationship with your dad is now entirely dispensable after all, and He rips away the centrality of that father-son bond while simultaneously directing you to cleave to a beautiful young woman whom you barely know, at least in comparison to how well you know your dad.

Why would He do that? Well, God needed your father to do the heavy lifting as your manhood evolved, but He also knew that a long-term, selfless, and sacrificial commitment in marriage would *complete* your development as a man. Without the imposition of a wife (and likely children) into your life, your growth into manhood wouldn't become complete. In other words, it isn't such a shocking reversal of God's position as it initially appears. God isn't so much *removing* the key relationship in your developing manhood but rather *replacing* it with an even more crucial one through matrimony.

God's position on marriage is clear, as Proverbs 18:22 tells us: "He who finds a wife finds a good thing, and obtains favor from the LORD" (ESV). That favor includes the completion of your move into adulthood. Marriage isn't a death sentence or some harness you slip into, much like a plow horse does. Marriage is a life source, a launchpad to finishing manhood.

But it's become alarmingly evident that your millennial and Gen Z colleagues seem quite satisfied to live in a sort of extended adolescence, unaware of how good a wife can be for them. If that statement applies to you, perhaps you aren't aware of how much marriage matters in developing your manhood. If you did, you wouldn't be slow to embrace the prospect and obtain the great favor from God that marriage uniquely brings to a man.

Listen, this hits close to home for me. I emailed my millennial son Michael one time to check up on his attitude toward marriage. His response: "I'm *really* enjoying being single and doing whatever I want. I don't feel interested in dating or marriage at all."

Hearing that stunned me—as if a coconut had been dropped on my head from twenty feet. *How in the world did that happen?* I wondered.

If you're a millennial like my son, it's quite unlikely you'll readily understand just how bizarre this mindset is to older guys like me. When I was Michael's age, I didn't personally know anyone who thought like this. Seriously.

Again, let's slow down and think this through for a moment. There has been a tremendous seismic shift in our culture. Somehow, in a single generation, your appetite and urgency for marriage have dropped so dramatically that a real man from a previous generation finds your thinking bizarre. That should trouble you.

There's also collateral damage from the quake's aftershocks, which has left hordes of single millennial and Gen Z girls shivering in the rubble, plaintively pleading, *Where are all the available men?*

This marriage-isn't-for-me attitude is epidemic among you guys everywhere I go around the world, and I don't think you understand just how much it's costing you as men and as Christians.

As I pondered Michael's words, I recalled a *Focus on the Family* radio broadcast

I'd heard years earlier. Perhaps these recollections can help you understand these costs more clearly. On the radio that day, the program host Dr. James Dobson claimed that it's quite tricky and challenging for young men to formulate their life's dreams outside of a marriage relationship. The reason? A loving and supportive wife delivers the aspiration, commitment, and clarity of purpose to her husband that most bachelors lack.

I was a young husband in my late twenties when I heard that broadcast. I'd been married for several years, so I could instantly relate to what Dr. Dobson said. I knew Brenda had an incredible and glorious impact on my life and developing manhood, but this broadcast helped me understand why. Since a young man needs a woman to help him formulate his dreams, I can't imagine why any sane young man would postpone such great favor from God for even a second.

I'm sure you're asking, *How does a woman do that for a guy? And why is a wife so indispensable on my journey into manhood, of all things?* Allow me to explain with a few stories.

When I turned to Christ at the age of twenty-three, I began attending a marriage class led by Cal Reynolds, the associate pastor of my new church, even though I was single and unattached. I was interested in what marriage would look like from a Christian perspective and how that knowledge could help me make sense of my poor relationships with women in my past.

Week by week, Pastor Cal rocked my world, laying out the wonders of women and explaining how God intended them to complement our nature as men. By the nine-month mark, I was so mesmerized by Pastor Cal's teaching that I was just dying to see what one of these godly women looked like in real life, so I prayed this simple prayer: "Lord, I've been in this class for almost a year and have learned a lot about women, but I haven't seen any of these godly ones up close, in real life. In fact, Lord, I've never personally known *any* Christian girls. Would You please show me a woman who embodies these godly characteristics so I can understand Your teaching better?"

Remember that I wasn't asking for a date, a girlfriend, or even a spouse. I just wanted to meet a godly young woman to see what she'd be like.

Well, God loves to answer prayer, right? But in my case, He did far more than show me a woman. He *gave* me one, introducing me to my future wife, Brenda, three weeks later. And you know what? Brenda embodied every one of the godly characteristics that Pastor Cal had taught me throughout that year.

The more I got to know Brenda, the more I wanted to be worthy of her. I had to be worthy of her. I was burning with a desire to be everything she'd dreamed of spiritually in a husband. That fire quickly sparked a conflagration of commitment and clarity of purpose in my business career as well. I ached to excel in everything because she was beyond awesome—a beauty worth defending and worthy of a great husband. As a man, I *had* to come through for her.

Her lovely, electric presence in my life focused my spirit, and now formulating my dreams for the future seemed effortless. According to Dr. Dobson, the promise of marriage for every man is the exponential acceleration of his developing manhood.

Dr. Dobson wasn't alone in making this case about men and marriage, and what he said back then about a man's need for marriage is just as true today as it has always been.

For a bit of perspective, let's look back at what was happening when I entered my twenties. First of all, I came of age at a unique time in history. Feminists were shelling our university landscapes, launching continuous and devastating ground offensives against men and marriage around the clock. As I stepped wide-eyed onto the cratered Stanford campus that first week of September, one of the first things the upperclassmen taught me was to never, ever hold open a door for a girl on campus, unless I liked being spat upon.

I regularly sat in on open-forum discussions, where feminists wondered openly—and with revolutionary zeal—whether matrimony was even necessary anymore. Their position seemed entirely plausible when marriage was discussed solely within the context of women's needs.

I noticed, however, that none of the feminists discussed marriage within the context of the needs of men, even though reasonable people understood exactly what we've always known about men: that marriage is critical in the development of full manhood. The sooner a man marries, the better off he is. This way of looking at things wasn't in the feminist worldview, however. They didn't want to hear it because that perspective cramped their cause.

They certainly didn't want to hear from folks like secular social scientist George Gilder who wrote that marriage changes everything for men. In his book *Naked Nomads*, Gilder laid out a case that marriage is *the* crucial institution for transfiguring a man and his sexuality, in that matrimony mobilizes his biology, economics, psychology, love, aggression, aspiration, and optimism for a common goal—building a life together with a woman. Gilder said that when a man gets married, he finds vital energy, often for the first time, and the focus and impetus to make durable changes in his developing manhood.

From where does this magic arise? "It is the consciousness that he has to struggle to be worthy of her which finally issues that spark," Gilder wrote.

Sound familiar? That's precisely the consciousness that Brenda sparked in me. She was that magical! I was fortunate to live out these words, thanks to her. Gilder claimed that without that marital magic and an urgent consciousness to "struggle to be worthy" of their women, men often have trouble establishing their manhood, focusing on their dreams, and launching their destinies. Gilder wrote this:

> The statistics are overwhelming. One can easily identify a bachelor pattern. It is marked by a lack of sustained commitment and a lack of orientation toward the future. The single man tends to move from one sexual partner to another, from job to job, city to city, rotating his life without growth or progress . . .
>
> Underlying all the superficial diversity of bachelor life is a syndrome of psychological instability. In a sense, the bachelor may never grow up. Thus the older unmarried man in many ways may resemble the young unmarried man unless he acquires direct dependents and responsibilities . . . All . . . may be naked nomads, lacking roots in the past and connections to the future.

Rotating his life without growth or progress . . .

Gilder might have been describing me when he wrote that single men, regardless of their intelligence and credentials, tend to be less stable and resolute workers than married men. As valedictorian of my large high school, I certainly had the intelligence to make something of my life. When I had a Stanford diploma rolled up neatly in my hand, I certainly had rock-solid credentials for success, or so it would seem.

So why can I list three different employers and three different cities of residence during my very first year out of Stanford? Was I less stable and resolute than a married man? Absolutely. As my millennial son Michael might say, I was "enjoying being single and doing whatever I wanted." But when it came to developing my manhood, I was my own worst enemy, ever rotating my life and relationships, never progressing forward anywhere in any meaningful way.

Now, let's use my story as a mirror. I want you to take a good long look at yourself. As a bachelor, you're likely your own worst enemy. The trouble is, it's easy to miss this about yourself. If you're out of college, got a good job, a hot car, and a nice place to live, I wouldn't blame you for thinking that you're living the dream! But that's a mirage. Without the imposition of a wife and responsibilities into your life, you can't easily even formulate your dream, let alone live it.

Sure, as a single man, you can change things up at a whim between girls and jobs and cities. Sure, you can race in any direction you like, but if you're honest with yourself, you're making little meaningful progress toward your destiny in God and toward living a full, complete life. If you continue in this direction, you'll eventually find a definite cap on your development as a man. You see, a man needs something in his life to live for and to love sacrificially. Without those aspects, he may rotate his life repeatedly, but he will rarely grow and mature as God designed him.

I never grew faster in the Lord and as a man than I did during my first three years of marriage. Brenda became a mirror that the Holy Spirit used to reveal countless character issues in my life. She helped me see all my facades once it was no longer possible to run or hide.

For instance, I discovered that I had a miserably bad temper that I never knew I had. I learned that it wasn't good enough to "not be as bad" as the next guy. Instead, I needed to rise above that low bar because it wasn't okay to be mediocre. She deserved far more, and I wanted to be worthy of her.

I learned that grace was no longer enough to whitewash that mess. I also learned that my leadership style was far more suffocating than I ever dreamed it would be. I had to man up. I had to change my style.

When I was single, my character faults and personality quirks hurt no one since it was all about me and me alone. But once I was married, I found out that those faults and quirks (and yes, sinful behavior) inflicted emotional scars on the heart of the one I treasured most. It wasn't enough to have the Lord's grace and be forgiven. I needed to stop trampling her heart in the first place. I needed character. I had to become righteous and strong.

The stories I've shared give you a good inspection of my life in my twenties. Let me make a further inspection of your life for a moment.

You are a man. God created you to fight big battles, live out great adventures, and defend the feminine beauty in your life.

So what great battles are *you* fighting today? Do you even have one? Or are you simply rotating your life, enjoying being single, and doing whatever you want? God declared that it isn't good for you to be alone, but it *is* good to have a wife, as she delivers His great favor to you. If that's true, then it can't be good to extend your adolescence for the sake of your freedom, ease, and enjoyment. Real men don't think that way. Real men think like God thinks, which, for most of us, means thinking about being married.

Is there a beauty waiting to rest in the shelter of your heroic protection? Can you set out on a grand adventure together? Or is your life in a holding pattern, your dreams unformulated, and your destiny still waiting to be launched?

You are a young adult man. End your adolescence and quit postponing marriage. You need a woman to love sacrificially and unleash you on destiny's way.

My oldest son, Jasen, is also a millennial. I remember well his angst over the decision to marry Rose, so worried that marriage would stunt his career growth and his pursuit of a graduate degree in computer security. He agonized over whether she would cramp his style and eliminate the freedoms of his downtime.

But I could also see he was struggling to formulate his rotating dreams, which shifted with every whim and breeze. He couldn't seem to find his future when his future was staring him right in his face.

As his feet turned cold again and again, I would return endlessly to the same line of questioning with Jasen when he was thinking about bailing on Rose and marriage.

"Does she love God more than she loves herself?" I asked one time.

"Yes, she does," he sincerely replied.

"Son, does she love marriage more than she loves herself?" I continued, knowing that she would make any sacrifice necessary to build a successful marriage at any personal cost if she needed to.

"Absolutely, Dad, no question."

"Does she make you laugh? Do you laugh away your evenings together?"

"Every time we're together, Dad."

"Son, she's a rare one. If what you say is true, and I believe it is, it will be at least ten years before you meet another girl like Rose. Are your other plans worth such a long wait? I don't think so. Marry her, now. Yes, some freedoms will be lost, but it'll all be for the better. You need her. She will grow you."

Emboldened, Jasen plunged ahead and tied the knot with Rose. Okay, he never got that graduate degree, but you should see him now. His manhood has moved off the charts. He's been a small group leader and a genuine pillar at his local church. The responsibilities of fatherhood have called him out onto a great adventure on the frontiers of intercession and prayer that he would have never explored outside of marriage.

In addition, he recently risked a gutsy and intimidating decision to leave a safe, secure job at a Fortune 100 company to take on an extremely ambitious and demanding position with a much smaller enterprise with no guarantees, but one that offered much higher pay for the sake of his family's resources. That took grit and daring.

I'm sure he would never have done that if he'd been single because he's a cautious person, but for Rose and his precious children, he took that heroic leap to protect them financially. In short, marriage helped to call the man out of the boy. He had a reason to fight big battles and live out a great adventure because he had a great woman standing with him. They united in one flesh to take on the world.

Jasen now has three beauties to protect heroically—Rose and daughters Halle and Linnea—and he's raising up another warrior named Johnny to carry the Stoeker name into battle and take on the mantle of manhood and marriage, just like his father.

Rose provided something big in Jasen's life to love sacrificially, and she blew the lid off his development as a man. Perhaps you have that same lid on your development and have been rotating your life but never quite advancing on destiny's way.

If so, get out from behind that elaborate facade you've created in that grandiose hall of mirrors called Facebook, Instagram, and WhatsApp. Get out there among real women. Find one for yourself, and soon.

Take on the biggest of all great battles—supporting a family. The struggle for your marriage and family is the struggle for life itself and for your destiny as a man. As Gilder said, without marriage, you'll become increasingly alienated from the patterns of family life, which offers the only widely available way to work out a full manhood of seventy years, or however long the Lord grants you to live.

It's time to step away from your game console and your *Call of Duty* screen. God's call of duty is to leave your father and mother and cleave to a beauty you can call your own. As you fight that greatest of battles to defend your children and raise them to love God amid a cultural cesspool, you'll experience genuine heroism on a far grander scale than you've ever known.

Here's the deal: unless you're the very rare exception that God is calling to greater service through remaining single, stretch out. Stop rotating your life. Take a risk.

In other words, marry.

Take on a wife and kids, and build something wonderful together. Read books and learn. Lead heroically. Unlock your destiny as a husband. Be a hero to your kids. Find genuine manhood.

In other words, live.

Download Your Free
Battle On, Battle Over
Workbook Today!

N ow that you've finished the book, you can go deeper with Brenda and Fred Stoeker by downloading a free pdf of the *Battle On, Battle Over Workbook*. All you need to do is go to www.BattleOnBattleOver.com, and you're good to go.

Resources
A Note from Fred Stoeker

In *Battle On, Battle Over*, Brenda and I mentioned several of our previous books, each with a different take on overcoming sexual sin. Here's a list of some of our earlier books, with guidance for whom they are targeted. You can order them through my website at FredStoeker.com at prices considerably better than those found online, and bulk orders are even cheaper. Shipping is free on orders over $90.

For those seeking eBook or audiobook versions, these resources can be found at the usual online shopping sources, such as Amazon, Christianbook.com, and Barnesandnoble.com.

Every Man's Battle: Revised and Updated 20th Anniversary Edition: Winning the War on Sexual Temptation One Victory at a Time **by Fred Stoeker and Steve Arterburn with Mike Yorkey**

With more than two million copies in print and translations into more than three dozen languages, *Every Man's Battle* brings to light the challenge that every man faces and the fight that every man can win.

The technological innovations of the digital age make pornography so easily accessible that nude pictures can be punched up on a smartphone twenty-four hours a day. This instant access to porn, along with the loose sexual morality in our culture and the tight—or skimpy—dress codes for women, means that any man seeking purity is standing on a slippery slope these days—truly miserable footing.

Considering these developments, it may seem impossible to avoid the temptation to look, linger, or lust, but *Every Man's Battle* provides a proven roadmap for overcoming these temptations and ultimately gaining permanent victory over them.

Recommended for: men dealing with "eye issues" that lead them to look at porn and to lust over women, and for women who want to understand how the male eye works so that they can help their husbands win their battle for sexual purity.

Every Man's Marriage: Every Man's Guide to Winning the Heart of a Woman by Fred Stoeker and Steve Arterburn with Mike Yorkey

Married men and women often have common misconceptions about the role of submission in a marital relationship. Fred Stoeker candidly reflects on how his misconceptions about male headship and leadership in marriage nearly cost him his marriage and how God corrected his approach through a more biblical understanding of Scripture.

Fred moved to a sacrificial, Christlike form of leadership and stopped trampling Brenda's heart, creating a home where she could genuinely blossom as a wife and daughter of God. In this best-selling, ECPA Silver Medallion-winning book, Fred reveals how men commonly trample their wives' hearts without knowing it and shares solid, time-tested biblical wisdom that can help men bless their wives and turn their marriages around on a dime.

Recommended for: married couples and engaged couples.

Every Heart Restored: A Wife's Guide to Healing for Wives Facing a Husband's Sexual Sin by Fred and Brenda Stoeker with Mike Yorkey

The title and subtitle say it all: when husbands are ensnared by sexual sin, wives suffer the most. In *Every Heart Restored*, an ECPA Silver Medallion winner, Fred and Brenda Stoeker declare unequivocally that a husband's sexual sin is not his wife's fault.

Then they help wives understand male sexuality and learn how to move from a place of rage and judgment to a place of mercy and reconciliation. God can enable you to survive your husband's betrayal and rebuild a solid, intimate, and joyful marriage. In fact, commit to reading this book as a couple. You won't be sorry if you do.

Recommended for: women (married or in a serious relationship) who discover that their men are entangled by pornography and sexual sin.

Preparing Your Son for Every Man's Battle by Fred Stoeker and Steve Arterburn with Mike Yorkey

Driving a stake into the ground and establishing sexual purity in your own life is only the first step in changing the destiny of your family. The second step is teaching your sons to arise and follow your example and to love God's pure ways.

The ten-chapter "Parent's Section" at the beginning of this ECPA Gold Medallion-winning book explains why starting early with this training is best and then teaches the how-to and the whys when it comes to training your boys to love sexual purity and to walk it out in practice. Going through this book with your sons will change your relationship forever. That's a promise.

Recommended for: dads and single moms of sons who desperately need the guidance of an adult in the sexual arena, perhaps more than any other.

Every Young Man's Battle: Strategies for Victory in the Real World of Sexual Temptation by Fred Stoeker and Steve Arterburn with Mike Yorkey

As a young man, you face incredible sexual temptations every day, but *Every Young Man's Battle* shows you how to rise above today's highly sexualized, self-seeking culture by examining God's standards, training your eyes and mind to obey God's standards of purity, and cleaning up your thought life. This best-selling, ECPA Gold Medallion-winning book will help you develop a plan to see things through with strategies that have worked for millions of other young men.

Recommended for: single men between the ages of sixteen and twenty-four and for women in a serious dating relationship.

Hero: Becoming the Man She Desires by Fred and Jasen Stoeker with Mike Yorkey

Heroic men will always seek to take personal purity to its logical conclusion, which is to never leave a woman worse off for having known them. *Hero* shows you what it takes to be an ultimate hero to women by teaching you to control your sexuality and to protect your girlfriend from illicit sexual play before marriage.

Jasen Stoeker never left a girl worse off for having known him, and now he shares the mindset and practices necessary to defend your relationship and protect your convictions and promises to God.

Can you have an electric dating relationship without moving into the sexual arena? Yes, you can. Are you up for the challenge?

Recommended for: young men and women who are dating or marriage minded.

About the Authors

Brenda Stoeker is a registered nurse and seasoned marriage teacher with life experience in rebuilding broken marriages. She and Fred have been married for more than forty years.

Fred Stoeker is the founder of Living True Ministries and co-author of the *Every Man's* series, which has impacted millions of readers worldwide.

After stumbling upon his father's *Playboy* magazine under his father's bed in first grade, Fred struggled with pornographic materials for the next twenty years. He found that his marriage to Brenda did not eliminate the problem, and the negative effects of his sexual sin upon his intimacy with God and his wife grew with each passing year.

Embarking on a study of Christian literature on his issues with porn, Fred searched for answers to his problems with his whole heart yet found little help there. However, the Holy Spirit responded to his search with great zeal and passion, conveying the practical knowledge that Fred needed to transform his mind and change his behaviors permanently. Before long, God broke the stranglehold that sexual sin had over his life.

That struggle—and victory—led Fred to write *Every Man's Battle* in the late 1990s. His first book, co-authored with Steve Arterburn, hit a cultural nerve, and word-of-mouth resulted in more than 2 million copies being sold and his work being translated into dozens of languages.

Since the release of *Every Man's Battle*, Fred has written more than a dozen other books that challenge men and women to be sexually pure and connect in genuine intimate relationships. Today, he is a popular conference speaker and has counseled hundreds of married couples.

He and his wife, Brenda, are the parents of four adult children and make their home near Des Moines, Iowa.

His website is FredStoeker.com.

Mike Yorkey is an experienced author and co-author who has collaborated with Fred and Brenda Stoeker in all their books for the *Every Man's* series and has written more than 110 books. His most recent efforts include *Out of the Wilderness* with Elishaba Doerksen, who survived horrible sexual and physical abuse from her father in Alaska, and *At First Light* with Walt Larimore, who shares the heroic story of his father fighting in World War II.

Mike and his wife, Nicole, are the parents of two adult children and live in Encinitas, California. His website is mikeyorkey.com.

Ask Fred Stoeker to Speak at Your Community Event or Church Conference

F red Stoeker, a well-known conference speaker who has spoken in or been televised into fifty-nine nations, is bent upon challenging people to become sexually pure and to connect in true intimate relationships with their Father in heaven and with their spouses and children on earth. His mission is to encourage and equip men and women to rise up and *be* Christian rather than simply *seem* Christian, and he's available to speak at community events or church conferences.

If you would like to contact Fred, you can reach him through his contact page on his website at FredStoeker.com.